"Lost Techno

TOOL MAKING 1905

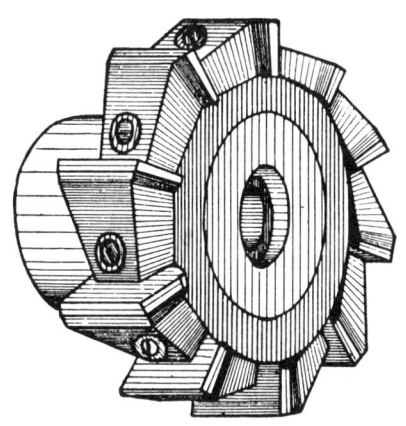

reprinted by Lindsay Publications

TOOL MAKING 1905

American School Correspondence
Frank W. Gunsaulus, Editor-in-chief

Copyright©1982 by Lindsay Publications, Manteno IL

All rights reserved. No part of this book may be reproduced in any form or by any means without written permission from the publisher.

Printed in the United States of America.

ISBN 0-917914-04-X

Reprinted from "Modern Engineering Practice" originally published and copyrighted in 1902, 1903, and 1905 by American School of Correspondence

1 2 3 4 5 6 7 8 9 0

INTRODUCTION

Technology gets more and more complicated in an effort to provide more and better goods at a lower cost. New technology provides impressive levels of productivity but requires very high investments. New technology is usually very expensive and very complicated — particularly for the home experimenter.

The backyard mechanic on the other hand is not interested in productivity. If in operating his backyard foundry, he makes one casting an afternoon and enjoys what he's doing, then he does not need the new high-priced technology. Old methods will do.

The purpose of this book is to preserve old methods before they become lost forever.

In effect, *Tool Making 1905*, is a textbook revealing the skills of the tools and die trade. At first it might seem ridiculous to consider such old technology, but remember back then the high grade alloys and tool steels did not exist. Sophisticated electro-machining and space-age technology did not exist. The tool and die man had to rely on skill to produce precise long-wearing tools. Back then the poorer grade of materials could be offset by craftsmanship.

Here is a book on lost technology and lost craftsmanship.

While some of the tools you may not wish to fabricate because they're low cost and easier to buy, just mastering the fabrication techniques will make you a much better machinist and metalworker overall. You'll be improving yourself. You'll be much more of a craftsman.

WARNING!

Remember that the materials and methods described here are from another era. Workers were less safety conscious then, and some methods may be downright dangerous. Be careful! Use good solid judgement in your work. Lindsay Publications has not tested these methods and materials and does not endorse them. Our job is merely to pass along to you information from another era. Safety is your responsibiliity.

Write for a catalog of other unusual books available from:

> Lindsay Publications
> PO Box 12
> Bradley IL 60915-0012

TOOL MAKING.

PART I.

As generally understood, a tool maker is a machinist who has a greater knowledge of the trade than is simply sufficient to enable him to make such machines or parts of machines, as may be the regular product of the shop in which he may be employed.

The business of the tool maker is to make the tools for producing the different parts of the machine, implement or apparatus, and relates not only to cutting tools, but to jigs and fixtures for holding the work while the various operations are being done, and making the necessary gauges to determine when the different parts are of the correct size and shape. Also the making of the models for the different fixtures and gauges. In some shops where there is work enough of the two latter described classes, the tool makers regularly employed on this work are termed gauge makers and model makers respectively. Yet in the average shop the models and gauges and such special machinery as may be required are made by the tool maker.

In order to acquire any degree of success, the tool maker must not only be able to work accurately and within reasonable time, but he must have a knowledge of drafting to enable him to read quickly and accurately any ordinary drawings. Unless he can read decimal fractions readily and accurately, he will experience much difficulty when working to measurements that require accuracy within one ten thousandth part of an inch. As most of the measuring instruments used by the tool maker read to one thousandth part of an inch, and some of them to the ten thousandth part of an inch, or even closer, it will be readily seen that in laying off measurements for gauges, models, drill-jigs and similar work, a thorough knowledge of Arithmetic is essential.

A tool maker should be familiar with the accurate reading of the micrometer and of the vernier as applied to the vernier caliper, vernier depth gauge and vernier height guage. He must bear in mind when using the vernier caliper for inside measurements that it is necessary to add the amount of space occupied by the caliper points A A Fig. 1 to the apparent reading on the vernier side.

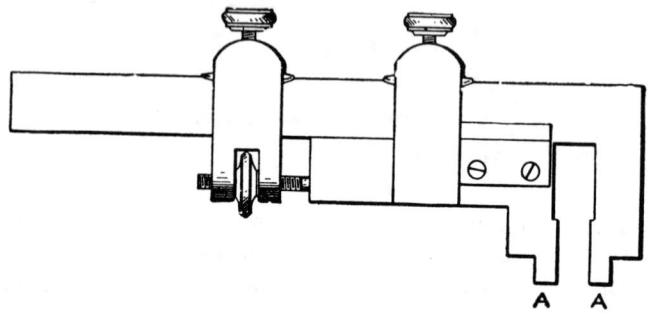

Fig. 1.

When measuring the distance between the centers of two holes as in Fig. 2, the vernier may be set so that the portions of the jaw marked A A Fig. 1 will exactly caliper the distance from B to B' in Fig. 2. To the apparent reading of the vernier add the space occupied by the caliper points, and from this subtract one-half the diameter of each of the holes. It is necessary to

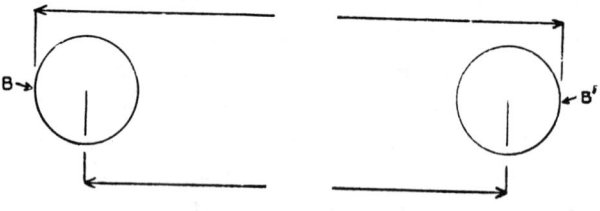

Fig. 2.

caliper the size of *each hole*. Do not take anything for granted when accurate measurements are necessary. A reamer *should always* cut an exact size, but experience proves that it does not always do so. If the size of the hole is taken for granted, a variation of .002 inch means an error of .001 inch in a measurement.

TOOL MAKING.

While extreme care should be exercised where accuracy is essential, there are parts of a tool where *approximate* measurements will do. If within $\frac{1}{16}$ inch is sufficiently accurate, it is folly to spend time to get a dimension within a limit of one ten thousandth part of an inch.

Approximate measurements are those made with the aid of calipers, dividers, surface guage, etc., set to an ordinary steel rule. Precise measurements are obtained by the aid of the various measuring instruments graduated to read to very small fractions of an inch. Also by the use of standard reference discs, and standard test bars, accurate within a limit of variation of $\frac{1}{50000}$ part of an inch. In using the micrometer, vernier or any of the measuring

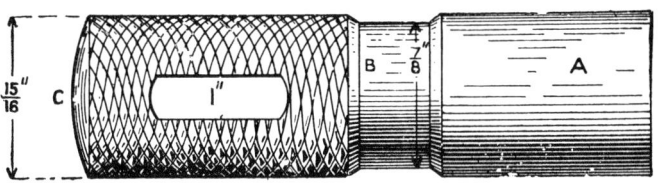

Fig. 3.

instruments supposed to give accurate readings, it is necessary to exercise great care in setting the tools. In setting the vernier it is well to use a powerful eye-glass in order that any error in setting may be so magnified as to be readily apparent.

The difference between the two characters of measurements described — approximate and precise — may be readily seen in the plug gauge shown in Fig. 3. The gauge end A must be, when ground and lapped, *exactly* 1 inch in diameter, as shown by the stamped size on the handle C. The handle should be $1\frac{5}{16}$ inch in diameter and knurled, and the neck $\frac{7}{8}$ inch. While the end marked A is necessarily a *precise* measurement, B and C are approximate, and an error of $\frac{1}{64}$ inch or more on either diameter would not interfere with the accuracy of the gauge. This does not mean that so great an amount of variation from given sizes should ever occur, but the illustration is given to show that the practical workman will never spend an unnecessary amount of time to produce accurate measurements when approximate measurements will do. On the other hand, all care possible should be taken when lapping the gauge end A to size.

Points to be Observed. Keep the working parts of any machine you may be running as clean as possible. Do not allow chips to collect on the shears (Vs) of your lathe. If these become roughed or worn, accurate turning cannot be done. Keep the machine thoroughly oiled, clean the oil holes out occasionally with a piece of wire, in order that the oil may get to the bearings.

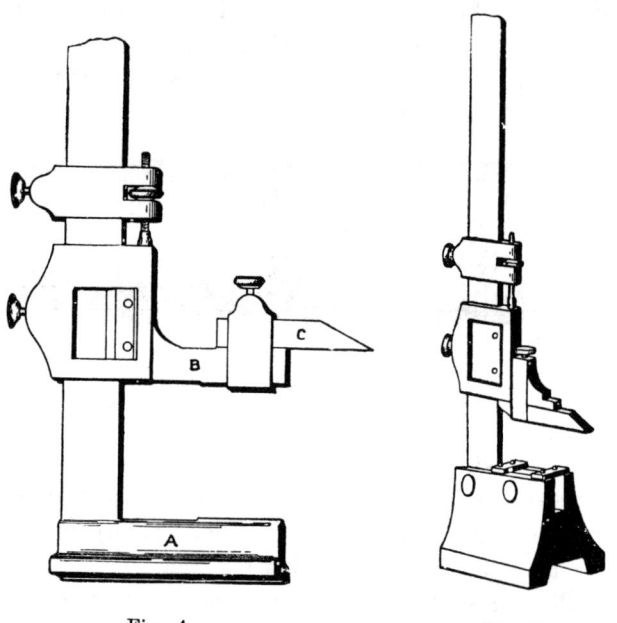

Fig. 4.   Fig. 5.

Keep the centers of your lathe in good condition, have them to gauge, and be sure the live center runs *true* before taking any finishing cuts. Try the center gauge on your countersink occasionally to see that it maintains its correct shape. Keep your center punch ground to a good point. It is advisable to grind the prick punch used in locating working points in some form of grinder having a chuck or collet to hold the punch while revolving it against the emery wheel; if the point is not perfectly round it will be impossible to indicate a piece of work perfectly on the faceplate of the lathe by means of the center indicator.

Special Tools. A vernier height gauge (Fig. 4) is a very handy tool for making drill jigs, templets and other tools requiring very accurate measurements, and for locating working points, holes or drill bushings. It is used for obtaining the height of projections from a plane surface, or the location of bushings in drill jigs, etc. The fixed jaw A is of sufficient thickness to allow the gauge to stand upright. An extension C attached to the movable jaw B can be used for scribing lines when laying off measurements. In the absence of a height gauge the regular vernier caliper may be made to answer the same purpose by making a base, which may be attached to the fixed jaw as shown in Fig. 5.

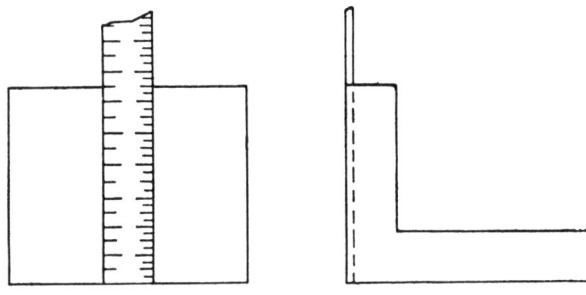

Fig. 6.

A small angle iron having a slot in the upright face to receive a scale for use in connection with a surface gauge when laying off measurements is shown in Fig. 6. The slot should be planed perfectly square with the base of the angle iron.

A pair of accurately machined V blocks is a necessary part of every tool maker's kit. If made of machinery or tool steel they will not need truing as often as if made of cast iron. After roughing out the V's, every surface should be planed square. They should be then clamped against the rail on the planer table by means of finger pieces, having previously trued the edge of the rail. The head of the planer should then be set to the proper angle, usually 45°, and one of the angles finished; the head may now be set over the opposite way and the other angle face planed. The tool used should be ground to give a smooth cut, as it is not advisable to do any finishing with a file or scraper.

8   TOOL MAKING.

A few small gauges of the most common angles will be found very convenient, as they can be used in places not accessible with the ordinary bevel protractor; the angles most commonly used are 60°, 65°, 70° and 80°. The form of gauge is shown in Fig. 7.

If the tool maker should be called on to make punch-press dies, one or more angle gauges, as shown in Fig. 8, will be found very useful. Many die makers use an adjustable square having a narrow blade which passes through the aperture in the die. The amount of clearance given is determined by the judgment of the workman; while this method does very well when practiced by an experienced man, it is rather uncertain when attempted by the novice. To get the proper clearance, the beginner should use the gauge shown in Fig. 8, called (improperly) a die maker's square.

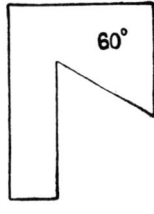
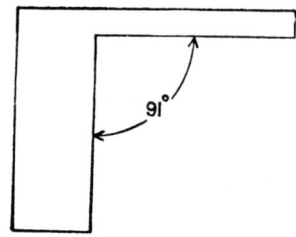

Fig. 7.   Fig. 8.

The angle depends on the nature of the stock, and the custom in the individual shop; but a set of three gauges, one 91°, one $91\frac{1}{2}$°, and one 92° will meet the requirements, as the clearance is seldom less than 1° or more than 2°. The angle should be stamped on the wide part of the gauge, as shown in Fig. 7. To avoid springing out of shape the stamping should be done before the gauge is finish-filed at any point.

The tool maker should always have at hand a solution of blue vitriol for coloring the surface on which he is to draw lines. To make the solution, dissolve in a two-ounce bottle of water all the blue vitriol crystals the water will take up; to this add one-half teaspoonful of sulphuric acid. This produces a copper-colored surface when put on polished steel free from grease and dirt.

STEEL.

Tool steel is used for tools intended for cutting, pressing, or working metals or other hard materials to shape. In order to successfully work tool steel a knowledge of some of its peculiarities is necessary.

Carbon is the element in tool steel that makes it possible to harden it by heating to a red heat and plunging into a cooling bath. A bar of steel from the rolling mill or forge shop is decarbonized on its outer surface to a considerable depth; consequently this portion will not harden, or if it does the results will be far from satisfactory. For this reason if a tool is to be made having cutting teeth on its outer surface, it is necessary to select stock of somewhat greater diameter than the finish size, so that this decarbonized portion may be removed. About $\frac{1}{16}$ inch for sizes up to $\frac{1}{2}$ inch, $\frac{1}{8}$ inch for sizes up to $1\frac{1}{2}$ inches, $\frac{3}{16}$ inch for sizes up to 2 inches, and $\frac{1}{4}$ inch for sizes above 2 inches will usually be sufficient.

Tool steel may be procured in almost any form or quality. It is ordinarily furnished in round, octagonal, square or flat bars. Many tool makers prefer octagonal steel for tools which are to be circular in shape, but experience shows that steel of various shapes of the same make does not differ materially provided the quality and temper are the same.

Cutting tools should be made of high carbon steel if it is to be forged or hardened by skillful operators. If the steel is to be heated by an inexperienced man, it is not safe to select a steel having a high percentage of carbon.

For non-cutting tools, such as mandrels, it is well to select a low carbon steel (one per cent carbon or less), because with this steel there is not as great a tendency to spring when hardening.

Hammered steel is prized more highly than rolled steel by fine tool makers, but authorities do not agree on this point. It is generally conceded, however, that the best tools can be made from forgings if the heating and hammering have been correctly done. The steel should be heated uniformly throughout, and hammered carefully with heavy blows at first. Lighter blows should follow, and, when the piece passes from low red to black, great care is needed to prevent crushing the grain. Steel properly heated and hammered will have a close, fine grain.

Cutting from Bar. It is advisable when cutting a piece of stock from the bar to use a *cutting tool* of some description, such as a saw or cutting-off tool. It is decidedly poor practice to weaken the bar with a cold chisel and then break by a sudden blow or yank. This process so disarranges the particles of steel that they do not assume their proper relations with one another when hardened. If it is necessary to cut the steel with a chisel heat the bar to a *red heat*, as it may then be cut off without injury.

Centering. When centering, care should be taken that the center punch mark is exactly in the center of the piece on each end, so that an equal amount of the decarbonized material will be turned from all parts of the piece (see Fig. 9.) If centered as shown in Fig. 10 the decarbonized portion will be entirely removed

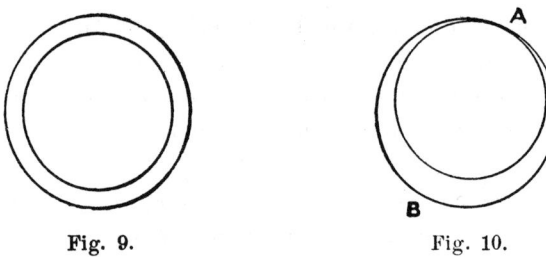

Fig. 9.   Fig. 10.

at side marked B, and will not be on the side marked A, consequently when the piece is hardened the side marked B will be hard, while the opposite side A will be soft, or at least not as hard as B.

Straightening. A piece of tool steel that is to be hardened should *never* be straightened when cold. If it is bent too much to remove all the decarbonized steel when turning to size, it is best (generally speaking) to use a straighter piece of stock. But if the bent piece must be used, heat it to a red heat and straighten. A piece of steel straightened when cold is almost sure to spring when hardened.

ANNEALING.

In order that it may be soft enough to work easily, tool steel must be annealed. It can generally be bought in this condition cheaper than it can be annealed when needed in the factory. Annealing also removes the strains, or the tendency of the steel to crack and spring when hardened. Strains are caused by rolling and hammering in the steel mill or forge shop. In order to remove this tendency to spring, the piece of steel should be machined somewhere near to size, yet leaving sufficient stock to machine all over after the annealing. If it is a piece with a hole in it, such as a milling machine cutter blank, the hole should be drilled somewhat smaller than finish size ($\frac{1}{16}$ inch is the amount generally allowed) and the piece turned in a lathe to remove all the outer surface which contains the marks of the hammer or rolls. The piece is now ready for annealing. To anneal a piece of steel it should be heated to a uniform red heat and allowed to cool slowly. Steel may be annealed by any one of several methods.

Box Annealing. For this method it is necessary to have a furnace large enough to hold an iron box of sufficient size to take the piece to be annealed. To do this work cheaply, enough pieces should be annealed at a time to fill one or more boxes, according to the capacity of the furnace.

The material used in packing the box is wood charcoal, which should be ground or pounded until the particles are about the size of a pea. A layer of charcoal covering the bottom to a depth of one inch is first placed in the box, then a layer of steel. The different pieces should not come within 1 inch of each other nor within 1 inch of the box at any point. The spaces between the pieces are filled with the charcoal, and they are covered to a depth of 1 inch. Another layer of steel may be put in if the box is of sufficient size. When within $1\frac{1}{2}$ inches of the top fill with charcoal, tamp down, put on the cover, and lute around the edges with fireclay, to prevent the direct heat of the fire entering the box.

Test Wires. There should be several $\frac{1}{4}$-inch holes drilled through the cover near the center, and through each of these a piece of $\frac{3}{16}$ inch wire should be placed. The wires should extend to the bottom of the box and project about 1 inch above the top of the cover in order to be readily grasped by the tongs. These wires are intended to be drawn from the box in order to determine when the contents are red hot. The box should be placed in the furnace. After the box has become thoroughly heated, one of the wires may be drawn out by means of a pair of long tongs. If no such tongs are available the legs of ordinary tongs may be lengthened by pieces of gas pipe. Note the time when the wire is red hot the entire length. If not red hot draw another in ten or fifteen minutes, and continue doing so until a wire is drawn that is red the entire length. The work should be timed from the time the box is heated through; this is shown by the wire.

The heat should be maintained a sufficient length of time to insure a uniform heat, which should not be allowed to go above a full red. The length of time the pieces remain in the fire depends somewhat on the size; for steel 2 inches and under, one hour after the box is heated through will do; larger pieces require a longer time. After running for the necessary length of time the heat should be shut off and the boxes allowed to cool slowly; the pieces should be left in the box until cold.

When there are no facilities for annealing by the method described, the piece may be heated to a uniform red and placed on a piece of board in an iron box, having one or two inches of ashes under the board. A second piece of board should be placed on the steel and the box filled with ashes. The pieces of wood will smoulder and keep the steel hot for a long time.

Another common method of annealing tool steel is to heat the piece to a red heat and bury it in ashes or lime. This is likely to give unsatisfactory results unless the ashes or lime are also heated. This can be accomplished by first heating a large piece of iron and burying in the contents of the annealing box. When the steel to be annealed is sufficiently heated the piece of iron may be removed and the piece to be annealed put in its place and thoroughly buried in order that it may take a long time in cooling; it should be allowed to remain in the ashes or lime until cold.

There is another method of annealing practiced in some shops, which answers in an emergency, but it is not to be recommended for general use. This is known as the *water anneal*. The piece of steel should be heated to a *low red*, making sure that the heat is uniform throughout. It should be removed from the fire and held in the air where no draft can strike it until no trace of red can be seen, even if the piece is held in a dark place; it should then be plunged in water, and allowed to remain until cold. Better results may be obtained if plunged in soapy water or oil.

Long pieces which spring when annealed should not be straightened when cold, if they are to be hardened.

HARDENING.

Tool steel may be hardened by heating to a low red heat and plunging in some cooling medium, as water, brine or oil.

Heating. A piece of steel should never be heated any hotter than is necessary to give the desired result. The heat necessary varies with the make of the steel, the amount of carbon it contains, the size and shape of the piece, and the purpose for which it is to be used. Much depends on heating uniformly; a piece of steel should be given a *uniform heat throughout*, the edges and corners should be no hotter than the center, and the interior should be of the same temperature as the surface. If not, the piece is likely to crack in the cooling bath, on account of the uneven changes which take place in the molecular structure. While it is highly important that the steel is heated no hotter than is necessary, yet it is of *much more* importance that it be heated uniformly.

If the piece is heated in an ordinary forge, be sure that the air from the blast does not strike it. For a large piece build a large high fire; have it well heated through before putting in the steel. Use the blast only enough to keep a lively fire; have the steel well buried in the fire in order that the air may not strike it.

Cooling. When the piece is uniformly heated it should be plunged into a suitable bath to give it the proper hardness. It must be worked rapidly up and down, or around in the bath in order to get it away from the steam generated by the red hot steel coming in contact with the liquid, and also that it may constantly come in contact with the cooler parts of the bath. If the piece is long and slender it must be worked up and down; if it is short with teeth on the outer edge, as a milling machine cutter, it should be worked around rapidly in order that all the teeth may be cooled uniformly. If it is flat and has a hole through it whose inner walls must be hard, it should be swung back and forth in order that the bath may pass through the aperture and at the same time strike both faces.

If the tool is not to be hardened all over, and it is necessary to heat it higher than the point where the hardening is to stop, it may be dipped in the bath to a point a trifle higher than we wish it to harden, and then worked up and down a little. If this is not done there will be a line where the piece is expanded at one side and contracted on the other; it is likely to crack at this line, which is called a "water line."

Delicate articles, or those tools having long projections or teeth, should not be dipped in a bath of very cold water or brine; for such work a tepid bath gives better results.

Steel should always be hardened at a heat that leaves the grain *fine* when the piece is broken. This can be determined by hardening and breaking a small piece from the same bar from which the tool to be is made. A *coarse grain* denotes a heat higher than the steel should receive.

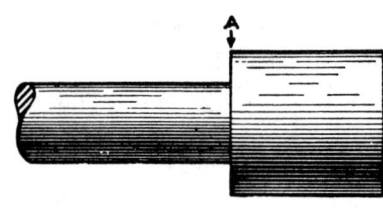

Fig. 11.

It will be found necessary when heating some kinds of steel to put the articles in an iron tube so that air cannot come in contact with them; this is especially true when hardening such tools as taps or formed mills whose outer surfaces cannot be ground, because the oxygen in the air acting on the carbon at the surface of the piece of steel *burns* it, leaving the surface decarbonized. Better results can be obtained with any tool if it is kept from the action of the fire when heating for hardening.

When hardening a piece having a shoulder A, on the outside, as shown in Fig. 11, or inside, as shown in Fig. 12, hardening should not stop at the shoulder, as the unequal strains occasioned by the contraction of the hardened part at the shoulder are likely to cause it to crack at that point. The piece should not be hardened as high as the shoulder, but should it be necessary to do so, it is well to harden a little beyond.

Citric Acid Bath. An excellent bath for hardening small pieces may be made by dissolving one pound of citric acid crystals in one gallon of water. It should be kept tightly closed when not in use or it will evaporate. Small tools heated to a low red heat and dipped in this solution harden more uniformly than when immersed in clear water.

Pack Hardening gives excellent results with pieces that cannot be hardened by the methods ordinarily employed without risk of springing or cracking. The article is packed in an iron box with some carbonaceous material, and subjected to the action of heat to allow it to absorb enough carbon to harden in oil. While this method is not generally used, it is very valuable when hardening such pieces as milling machine cutters, blanking dies for punching presses, gauges, and taps where it is necessary that the diameter and pitch are not altered. The carbonaceous material is charred leather, which should be ground or pounded very fine (usually about one-half the size of a pea), and mixed with an equal quantity (volume) of wood charcoal whose granules are of about the same size. These should be thoroughly mixed. An iron box somewhat larger each way than the piece to be hardened should be selected. A layer of the packing material one inch deep should be placed in the bottom of the box and the piece laid on this; the box should then be filled with the packing material and tamped down. Fill the space between the cover and the box with fire clay, thus sealing it so that the gases in the box cannot escape and the direct heat of the fire cannot get into the box.

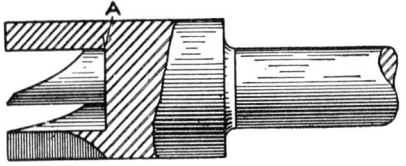

Fig. 12.

It is much more economical to pack a number of pieces at a time, as several may be hardened at the cost of one, and at a saving in packing material. The pieces should be wired with ordinary iron binding wire of a sufficient size to sustain the weight when the wire is red hot. One end of the wire should project over the outside edge of the box, and should be covered with the luting of fire clay. Several holes should be drilled near the center of the cover for test wires, as when annealing. The wires should extend to the bottom of the box. The box may now be heated sufficiently to charge the pieces with carbon. As steel does not commence to absorb carbon until it is red hot, the time is determined by means of the test wires as described under "Annealing." For ordinary tools $\frac{1}{2}$ inch diameter and under, run 1 hour to $1\frac{1}{2}$ hours after it is red hot; pieces from $\frac{1}{2}$ inch to 1 inch diameter, 2 to $2\frac{1}{2}$ hours; pieces from 2 to 3 inches diameter, $2\frac{1}{2}$ to 4 hours. The above must be varied according to the nature of the work.

After remaining in the furnace, the box should be taken out, the cover removed, and the piece taken out by means of the wire attached to it. It should then be immersed in a bath of *raw linseed oil*. The piece should be worked around in the bath until the red has disappeared; it may be then lowered to the bottom of the bath and allowed to remain until cold.

When a piece of steel one inch in diameter or larger is hardened, it should be reheated over the fire immediately on taking out of the bath, in order to avoid cracking, from the strains caused by molecular changes which take place after the outside surface is hardened and unable to yield to the internal strains. Reheating the surface to a temperature of about 212° will accomplish the desired result without materially softening the steel.

TEMPERING.

The hardening of a cutting tool makes it too brittle to stand up well when in use, and consequently it is necessary to soften it somewhat. This is known as "drawing the temper," and is accomplished by reheating to the proper temperature, which is ordinarily determined by the color of the surface of the tool, which must be brightened previous to this operation. As the piece of steel is heated, a light, delicate straw color will appear; then, in order, a deep straw, light brown, darker brown, light purple, dark purple, dark blue, pale blue, blue tinged with green, black. When black, the temper is gone. These colors furnish a guide to the condition of hardened steel.

The following list gives the color denoting the tempers generally used for tools:

Light straw	For lathe and planer tools, scrapers for brass, etc.
Deep straw	For milling cutters, reamers, large taps, etc.
Brown	For twist drills, drifts, flat drills for brass, etc.
Light purple	For augurs, screw slotting saws, etc.
Dark purple	For saws for wood, cold chisels, screwdrivers, etc.

The following table gives the degree of heat corresponding to the different colors mentioned in the previous table.

Light straw	430 degrees F.
Deep straw	460 degrees F.
Brown	500 degrees F.
Light purple	530 degrees F.
Dark purple	550 degrees F.
Dark blue	570 degrees F.
Pale blue	610 degrees F.
Blue tinged with green	630 degrees F.

When work is tempered in large quantities the above method is expensive. Also it is not as reliable as when the articles are heated in a kettle of oil, using a thermometer for indicating the temperature. A piece of perforated sheet metal or wire cloth should be used to keep the articles two or three inches from the bottom of the kettle. A perforated sheet iron pail two inches smaller in diameter than the kettle, resting on a piece of iron, or a frame placed in the bottom will keep the pieces from the sides and bottom of the kettle.

The thermometer should be placed in the kettle outside the pail in order that the bulb may be at the same depth as the lower pieces.

Case Hardening. When an article of wrought iron or machinery steel is to have a hard surface it is treated while red hot with some material which forms a coating or case of steel, which hardens if dipped in water while red hot. Small articles such as nuts, screws, etc., may be case hardened by heating red hot and covering with a thin layer of powdered cyanide of potassium; when the cyanide of potassium melts, the article may be heated red hot again; it is then plunged into water. Care should be exercised when using this substance, as it is *extremely poisonous*.

The above method may be used for hardening a few pieces quickly, but it is not recommended for large quantities of work. When many pieces are to be case hardened at a time, the following method will be found less expensive and much more satisfactory:

Granulated raw bone and granulated charcoal should be mixed in equal quantities, and a layer of this mixture placed in an iron hardening-box to the depth of 1 or $1\frac{1}{2}$ inches. A layer of articles is then placed on this; the pieces should not come within $\frac{1}{2}$ inch of each other, nor within 1 inch of the walls of the box at any point; they should be covered with a layer of the mixture of bone and charcoal to the depth of $\frac{1}{2}$ inch. Successive layers may be placed in the box until it is filled to within 1 inch of the top, when the cover may be put in place and the edges luted with fire clay. The test wires should be used as described for annealing. The heating should be timed from the time the contents of the box are red hot, which can be determined by the test wires. The length of time the work is allowed to run while red hot depends upon the desired depth of the hardened surface; generally carbon will penetrate wrought iron $\frac{1}{8}$ inch in twenty-four hours, but as it is rarely necessary to harden deeper than $\frac{1}{32}$ inch, the work may be kept red hot three to four hours. With small pieces, the contents of the hardening-box may be dumped into a tank of running water; if the pieces are large, it is necessary to dip them one at a time in a bath, the same as for tool steel. For extreme toughness, the pieces, if small, may be dumped into a perforated sheet-metal pan and the *packing material sifted out*, after which they may be placed in a bath of oil; if not sifted out, the packing material will stay at the top of the oil and set fire to it. If the pieces are large, they may be dipped one at a time.

Spring Tempering. A piece of steel may be spring tempered by first hardening and then drawing the temper to a degree to which the piece, when bent, will return to its normal shape, when the pressure is removed. This may be accomplished by covering the surface with tallow or some animal oil, and then heating until the oil catches fire from the heat in the piece.

DRILLS.

The forms of drills commonly used in the machine shop are the flat drill, single-lip drill and twist drill.

Flat Drills, intended for use in the engine lathe for chucking, are usually forged to shape in the forge shop. After centering the end, which rests on the tail center of the lathe, the lips are ground to shape and the drill is ready for use. A drill of this description is shown in Fig. 13.

If it is necessary to have the drill cut nearly exact to size, it should be forged somewhat wider than finish size, and the edges turned in the lathe as in Fig. 14. The projection A must be left on the cutting end to provide a center for turning. If the drill is to be ground to size after hardening, the projection must be left on until the grinding has been done, but, ordinarily, this class of drill is not intended to cut exact enough to require grinding.

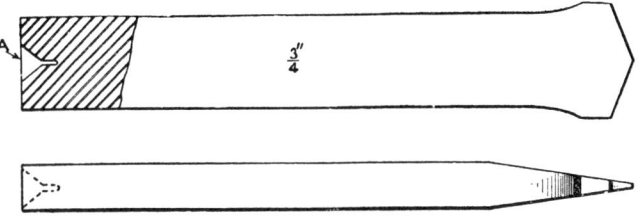

Fig. 13.

If the edges of the drill are not to be ground to size, they should be draw-filed a small amount to avoid binding. The filing should not come within $\frac{1}{64}$ inch of the edge, and should be only a small amount (.003 or .004 inch will be found sufficient); if given too much relief the drill will jump and chatter. The shank should be somewhat smaller ($\frac{1}{32}$ to $\frac{1}{16}$ inch) than the cutting end

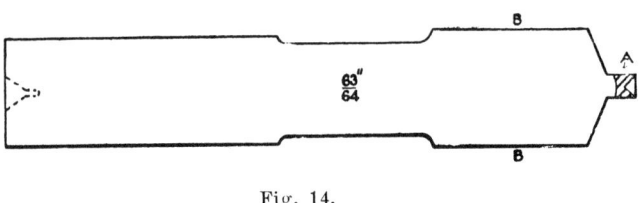

Fig. 14.

in order not to touch the sides of a hole drilled deep enough for the shank to enter. The center in the shank end should be large, to insure a good bearing on the tail center of the lathe, as shown at A, Fig. 13.

When hardening, the drill should be heated a *low red* to a point above the cutting end, preferably about one-half the length of the portion turned smaller than the ends. When dipped in the bath it should be plunged about one inch above the cutting end. To insure good results it should be worked up and down and around in the bath, which may be either water or brine. The temper should be drawn to a brown color.

When a flat drill is intended for use in a drill press, the shank is left round, in order that it may be held in a chuck or collet.

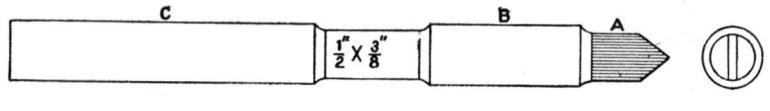

Fig. 15.

Transfer Drill. Another form of flat drill termed a transfer drill, is very useful when a small hole is to be transferred from a larger. The shank C, Fig. 15, may be made of any convenient size; the portion B is of the size of the larger hole, while A is of the size of the hole to be transferred, and is a short *flat* drill.

When making this drill, if a lathe is used having draw-in split chucks, the drill may be made from drill rod, which should be enough larger than finish size to allow B to be turned, to insure its running true with A; the cutting part A may be milled or

Fig. 16.

filed to thickness. The cutting lips are then backed off, and the drill hardened. It should be hardened high enough so that A and B are hard, as the portion A does the cutting, while B, being a running fit in a hole, is likely to rough if it is soft.

To harden it should be heated in a tube and dipped in water or brine, and worked up and down, to avoid soft spots caused by steam keeping the water from the metal, as sometimes happens when a piece has different sizes close together. The cutting portion A should be drawn to a deep straw color; B should be left as hard as possible, to resist wear.

Straightway, or straight fluted drills, have the flutes cut parallel to a plane passing through the axis of the drill, as shown in Fig. 16. They are used in drilling brass, and in drilling iron and steel when the holes break into one another, as shown in Fig. 17.

The smaller sizes may be made of drill rod. After cutting to length, the blank may be put in a chuck in the lathe and the end pointed to the proper cutting angle. When milling the flute, the shank may be held in the chuck on the end of the spiral head spindle. The head should be set at an angle that makes the flute deeper at the cutting end of the drill than at the shank end; this causes an increase of thickness at the shank, thus making the drill stronger than if the flute were of uniform depth throughout. The

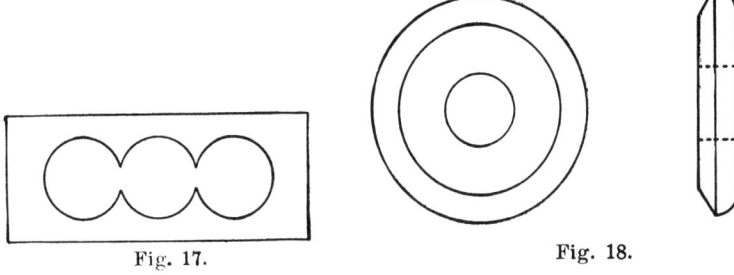

Fig. 17.   Fig. 18.

milling cutter should be of a shape that will make the cutting face of the drill a straight line when the drill is ground to the proper cutting angle. The corner should be somewhat rounded. The general shape of the cutter is shown in Fig. 18.

Single Lip Drill. For certain classes of work the single lip drill is very useful. Having but one cutting edge its action is similar to that of a boring tool used for inside turning in the engine lathe. The body of the drill being the size of the hole drilled insures its cutting a straight hole, even when used in drilling work partly cut away, or castings having blow-holes or similar imperfections. It does not cut as rapidly as the other forms, consequently is not used where a twist drill would do satisfactory work. Fig. 19 shows a form of single lip drill to be used with a bushing. The steel for this drill should be somewhat larger than finish size, in order that the decarbonized surface may be removed;

the cutting end A and the shank B should be turned .014 to .020 inch larger than finish diameter to allow for grinding after the drill is hardened. The portion C should be turned to finish size and stamped. In order that the drill may be ground to size after it is hardened it will be found necessary to face the end back,

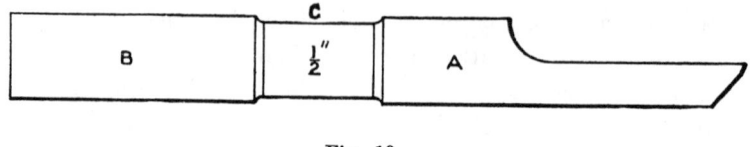

Fig. 19.

leaving the projection containing the center as shown at A in Fig. 20. The cutting end should be milled to exactly one-half the diameter of B. After milling, the face C should be draw-filed until it is flat and smooth. When hardening, the drill should be

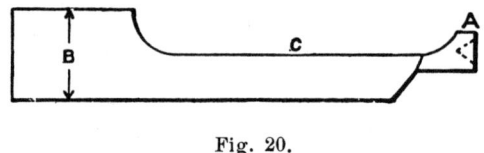

Fig. 20.

slowly heated to a low red, a trifle higher than the portion that is to be cutting size; it should be plunged in a bath of warm water or warm brine in order to avoid as far as possible any tendency to

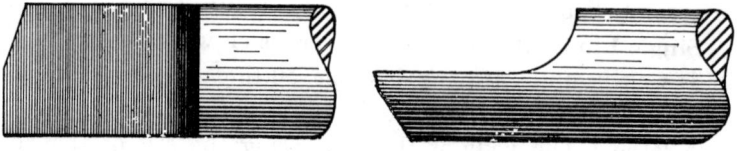

Fig. 21.

springing or cracking in the projection A. The tendency to crack is due to its peculiar shape and the difference in its size and that of the drill. After hardening it may be drawn to a straw color.

When grinding it is advisable to grind the shank first, in order that the grinding machine may be adjusted to grind straight;

after grinding the shank and cutting end to size, the projection A may be ground off, and the cutting end given the required shape, as shown in Fig. 21.

When a single-lip drill is to be used on iron and steel and not upon brass, it may be made to cut more freely by giving the cutting-face rake, as shown in Fig. 22. This may be done by mill-

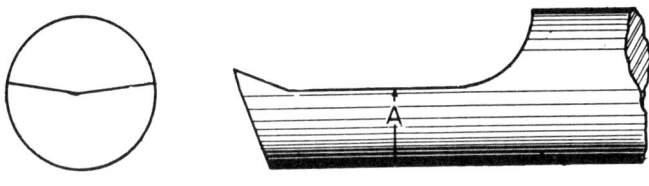

Fig. 22.

ing the portion A to the proper dimensions, which should be one-half the diameter of the blank. The end and sides of the drill may now be coated with the blue vitriol solution and the desired shape marked out, after which it may be placed in the milling machine vise at the proper angle, and the required

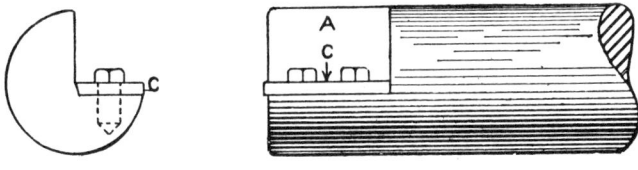

Fig. 23.

amount of rake given by means of small end cutters. After giving the necessary end clearance as shown in the two views of Fig. 22, the drill is ready for hardening.

In order to adjust a drill of this kind to compensate for wear, it may be made as shown in Fig. 23, in which one-quarter of the circumference is cut away at A and a blade or cutter fastened in position; the top face of the cutter should be radial. To compensate for wear, pieces of paper or thin sheet metal may be inserted under the blade.

When cutting away the portion A, three holes may be drilled, as shown in Fig. 24. If square corners are desired, care should be taken that the holes are located so that they will machine out when milling to the proper dimensions. After drilling, the body of the drill may be placed in a vise in the shaper, and by the use of a cutting-off tool (parting tool) the portion may be removed, but as it would be impossible to cut to finish dimensions it will be necessary to finish with small end milling cutters, holding the tool in the chuck on the spindle of the spiral head. After machining one surface, the spindle may be revolved one quarter turn and the other surface machined; this insures square corners, and two surfaces at right angles to each other. The surface on which the cutter is to rest should be cut below the line of center, so that the top edge of cutter may be radial; that is, it should be cut the thickness of the cutter below a line passing through the center. See Fig. 23.

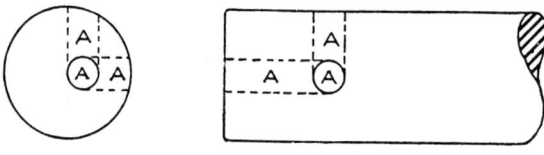

Fig. 24.

The cutter should be made of tool steel; two holes should be drilled for the fastening screws. After fastening the cutter in position it may be turned to the proper diameter by running the body of the tool in the steady rest of the lathe. Care should be used not to cut into the body or holder. After turning to size and facing the end square, the cutter may be removed from the holder, and necessary clearance given the end by filing; the outer edge may be draw-filed in order to smooth it, and a slight clearance given to prevent binding; this may be done by removing a trifle more stock at the bottom than at the top edge. To harden it should be heated to a low red heat and dipped in luke-warm water; the temper may be drawn to a straw color.

Twist Drills. In general it is cheaper and more satisfactory to buy twist drills than to attempt their manufacture in the ordinary machine shop; but at times a *special* size or length of drill is needed, or, for some cause, it is necessary to make them.

For the smaller sizes it is best to use commercial drill rod. For drills larger than ½ inch diameter select larger stock and turn it to the desired size. If true holes of the size of the drill are required, it is advisable in the case of drills larger than ½ inch diameter, to turn them .010 to .015 inch larger than finish size, and grind to the required size after hardening. A projection (Fig. 25) containing the center should be left on the cutting end of the

Fig. 25.

drill until after the grinding has been accomplished. After cutting the flutes and grinding the drill, the projection may be ground off and the cutting lips ground to the proper shape, as shown in Fig. 26.

When making drills of the smaller sizes from drill rod, the blanks may be cut and pointed to the proper angle on the cutting end; this may be done in the lathe holding the blank in a chuck.

Fig. 26.

The proper angle is 59° from one side of the blank. When milling the flutes of a **tw**ist drill on a universal milling machine, the shank of the drill, if straight, may be held in a chuck or collet of the right size, and if very long may be allowed to pass through the spiral head.

The following explanation and table are taken from Brown & Sharpe Co.'s book, entitled "Construction and Use of Milling Machines," and are intended for use with the cutters manufactured by them when cutting the flutes in twist drills.

The cutter is placed on the arbor directly over the center of the drill, and the bed is set at the angle of spiral, as given in the following table:

Diameter of Drill.	Thickness of Cutter.	Pitch in Inches.	Gear on Worm.	First Gear on Stud.	Second Gear on Stud.	Gear on Screw.	Angle of Spiral.
$\frac{1}{16}$	.06	.67	24	86	24	100	16° 20′
$\frac{1}{8}$	.08	1.12	24	86	40	100	19° 20′
$\frac{3}{16}$	.11	1.67	24	64	32	72	19° 25′
$\frac{1}{4}$	.15	1.94	32	64	28	72	21°
$\frac{5}{16}$	.19	2.92	24	64	56	72	20°
$\frac{3}{8}$	.23	3.24	40	48	28	72	21°
$\frac{7}{16}$	.27	3.89	56	48	24	72	20° 10′
$\frac{1}{2}$	.31	4.17	40	72	48	64	20° 30′
$\frac{9}{16}$	.35	4.86	40	64	56	72	20°
$\frac{5}{8}$	.39	5.33	48	40	32	72	20° 12′
$1\frac{1}{16}$	.44	6.12	56	40	28	64	19° 30′
$\frac{3}{4}$	.50	6.48	56	48	40	72	20°
$1\frac{3}{16}$	.56	7.29	56	48	40	64	19° 20′
$\frac{7}{8}$	.62	7.62	64	48	32	56	19° 50′
$1\frac{5}{16}$	.70	8.33	48	32	40	72	19° 30′
1	.77	8.95	86	48	28	56	19° 20′

The depth of groove in a twist drill diminishes as it approaches the shank, in order to obtain increased strength at the place where the drill is otherwise generally broken. The variation in depth depends on the desired strength or the use of the drill. To obtain the necessary variation of depth, the spindle of the spiral head is elevated somewhat, depending on the length of the flute to be cut; when less than 2 inches in length the angle should be $\frac{1}{2}$ degree: 5 inches and over in length, 1 degree. Usually this will be found satisfactory, but for extremely long drills the elevation must exceed these amounts. The outer end of the drill must be supported, as shown in Fig. 27, and when small should be pressed down firmly until the cutter has passed over the end.

It is somewhat better to use left-handed cutters, so that the cut may begin at the shank end, in order to lessen the tendency of lifting the drill blank from the rest. When large drills are held by the centers the head should be depressed in order to decrease the depth of the groove as it approaches the shank.

TOOL MAKING.

Another very important operation on the twist drill is that of "backing off" the rear of the lip, to give it the necessary clearance. In Fig. 28 the bed is turned to about ½ degree, as for cutting a right-hand spiral, but as the angle depends on several conditions it will be necessary to determine what the effect will be under different circumstances. A study of Fig. 28 will be sufficient for this by assuming the effect of different angles, mills, and the pitches of spirals. The object of placing the bed at an

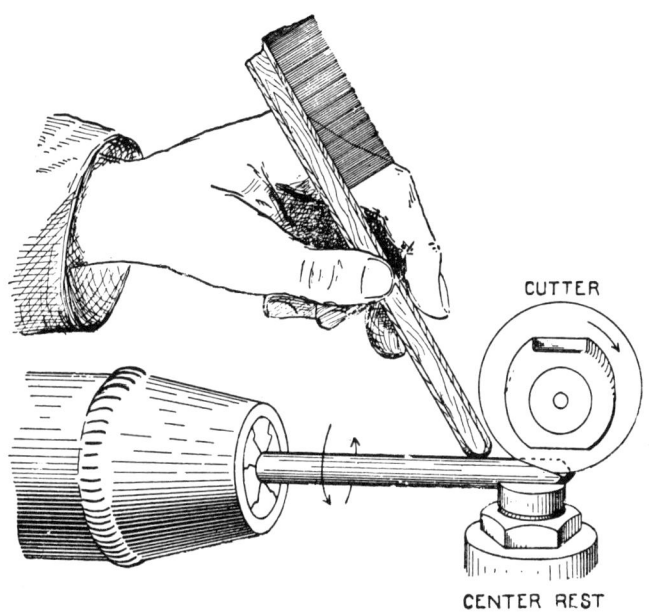

Fig. 27.

angle is to cause the mill E to cut into the lip at C and have it just touch the surface at C. The line R being parallel with the face of the mill, the angular deviation of the bed is clearly shown at A in comparison with the side of the drill.

While the drill has a positive traversing and relative movement, the edge of the mill at C must always touch the lip a given distance from the front edge, this being the vanishing point; the other surface forming the real diameter of the drill is beyond the reach of the cutter, and is left to guide and steady it while in use.

The point C as shown in the enlarged view, Fig. 28, shows where the cutting commences and its increase until it reached a maximum depth at C, where it may be increased or diminished according to the angle employed in the operation; the line of cutter action being represented by I I.

Before backing off, the surface of the smaller drills in particular should be oxidized by heating until it assumes some distinct color to clearly show the action of the mill on the lip of the drill, for, when satisfactory, a uniform streak of oxidized surface, from the front edge of the lip back, is left untouched by the mill, as represented in the cut at E.

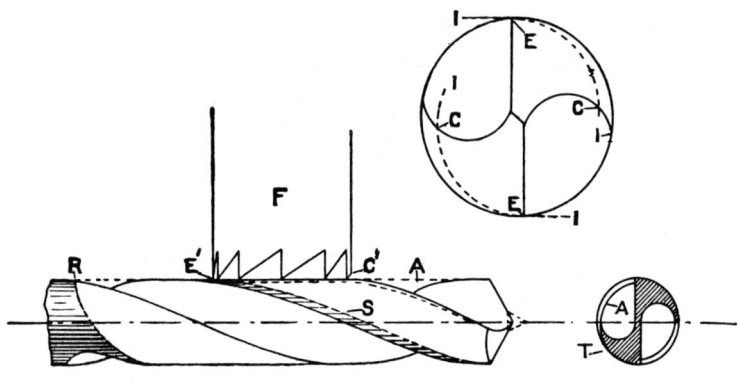

Fig. 28.

If the drills are to be ground without being centered, pointed projections (60°) may be made on the ends as shown in Fig. 28; these projections may be run in female centers in the grinding machine. If tapered back about .003 inch in 6 inches it will be found that the clearance thus obtained will cause them to run much better.

Hardening Twist Drills. Twist drills are hardened by special processes which, generally speaking, are not understood outside the shop where the drills are made. Very good results, however, may be obtained if the drills are heated somewhat and dipped into a solution of the following:

Pulverized charred leather	1 pound
Fine Family Flour	1½ pounds
Fine Table Salt	2 pounds

TOOL MAKING.

The charred leather should be ground or pounded until fine enough to pass through a number 45 sieve. The three ingredients are thoroughly mixed while in the dry state, and water is then added *slowly*, to prevent lumps, until the mixture formed has the consistency of ordinary varnish.

After the drill has been dipped in the mixture it should be laid in a warm place to dry; when thoroughly dried the drill may

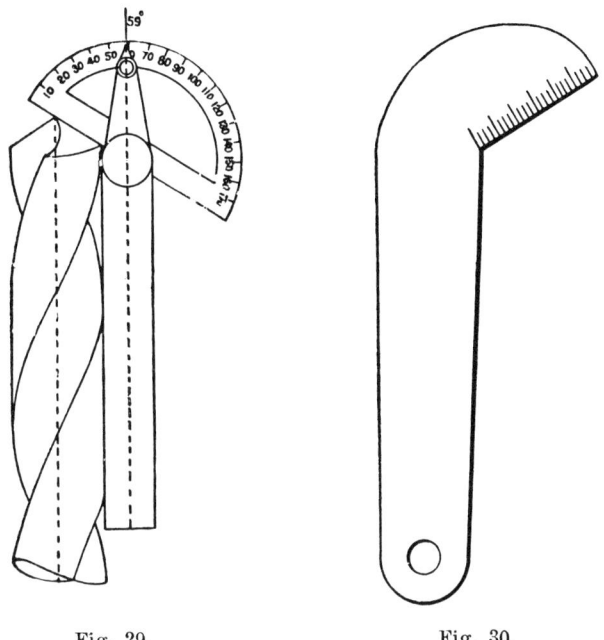

Fig. 29.   Fig. 30.

be heated in a tube, or preferably in a crucible of red-hot lead until it is a low red, when it may be plunged in a bath of lukewarm water, or brine; small drills may be dipped in a bath of oil. The drill must not be put in red-hot lead until the coating is thoroughly dried, as the moisture may cause minute particles of lead to fly in all directions, endangering the eyes of the operator. After hardening, the temper may be drawn to a full straw color. If several drills are hardened at a time the temper may be drawn by placing them in a kettle of oil over a fire gauging the amount of heat by a thermometer, as explained under heading of "Drawing Temper."

TOOL MAKING.

Grinding Twist Drills. The cutting edges must make a proper and uniform angle with the longitudinal axis of the drill; they must be equal in length, and the lips of the drill sufficiently backed off for clearance, otherwise they will not cut easily, or they will make a hole *larger* than the size of the drill.

Drills properly made have their cutting edges straight when ground to a *proper* angle, which is 59 degrees, as in Fig. 29. Grinding to an angle less than 59 degrees leaves the lip hooking, which is likely to produce a crooked and irregular hole.

A very satisfactory form of angle gauge for this work is shown in Fig. 30; the graduations on the upper part of gauge show when the lips are ground to an equal length, which is essential in order that the drill shall cut the proper size. As the operator becomes experienced he can gauge the angle and length of lips very accurately by the eye, but until he has the necessary experience it is advisable to use some form of gauge.

REAMERS.

A reamer is a tool that makes a smooth, accurate hole; however, in many cases reamers are used to enlarge a cored hole, or a hole already drilled, without particular reference to the exact size or condition of the hole. Reamers may be classified according to

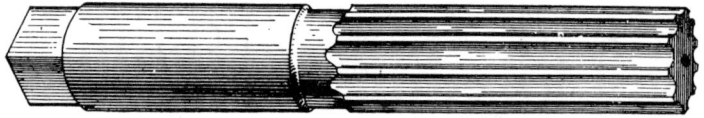

Fig. 31.

shape as follows: straight reamers, taper reamers, and formed reamers. Reamers are made solid, adjustable, and with inserted blades.

Solid reamers (Fig. 31) are so called because the cutting teeth and head are made from one piece; they have no means of adjustment as to size. The cutting teeth of inserted blade reamers are made from separate pieces of steel, and inserted in the head as shown in Fig. 32. The adjustable reamer may be made with inserted teeth, or with cutting teeth solid with the head; but in either case having some means of adjusting the size.

TOOL MAKING.

STRAIGHT REAMERS.

Under this heading the following kinds of reamers are to be found: fluted hand reamers, fluted chucking reamers, rose reamers, single lip reamers, and three and four lipped roughing reamers.

The Fluted Hand Reamer is made straight on the cutting lips, with the exception of a short distance at the end (A Fig. 33) which is slightly tapered in order that the reamer may enter the hole. In making such reamers, use steel from $\frac{3}{32}$ inch to $\frac{1}{8}$ inch above finish size. Turn a chip off the outside surface to a depth

Fig. 32.

of $\frac{1}{32}$ inch and anneal, then turn A and B Fig. 33 to sizes .010 to .015 inch larger than finish size; turn C to finish size, mill the end D square for a wrench. The reamer is now ready to have the flutes cut.

Number of Cuttting Edges. Fluted reamers designed to remove but a small amount of stock, and intended to cut holes to an accurate size are rarely given less than six flutes.

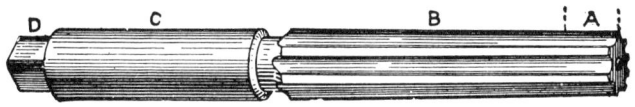

Fig. 33.

The following table gives the number of cutting edges that give satisfaction for solid reamers whose flutes are milled by cutters made to give the proper shape.

TABLE OF CUTTING EDGES FOR REAMERS.

$\frac{1}{8}''$ to $\frac{7}{16}''$ diameter	6 teeth
$\frac{1}{2}''$ to $\frac{11}{16}''$ "	6 to 8 "
$\frac{3}{4}''$ to $1''$ "	8 "
$1\frac{1}{16}''$ to $1\frac{1}{2}''$ "	10 "
$1\frac{9}{16}''$ to $2\frac{1}{8}''$ "	12 "
$2\frac{1}{4}''$ to $3''$ "	14 "

Formerly it was considered necessary to have an odd number of cutting edges; but an even number if unevenly spaced will be as satisfactory. The chief objections to an odd number are the difficulty experienced in calipering unless a ring gauge is used, and the great cost of grinding.

Fig. 34 shows a form of cutter that makes a strong reamer tooth and allows the chips to be removed very readily. These cut the tooth ahead of the center, and should be given a negative rake of about 5°. In general, a reamer will cut more smoothly if the tooth has a slight negative rake, as it then takes a scraping cut.

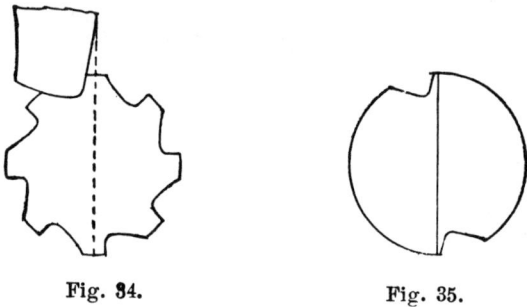

Fig. 34. Fig. 35.

With this form of flute, the depth of cut must be so gauged that the land will be about $\frac{1}{5}$ the average distance from one cutting edge to the other; if cut deeper, the teeth will be weak and have a tendency to spring, if not as deep, there will not be room for the removal of the chips. The following table shows the number of cutter (shown in Fig. 34) for any size of reamer.

NUMBERS OF CUTTERS FOR REAMERS.

No. 1 Cutter cuts reamers from $\frac{1}{8}''$ to $\frac{3}{16}''$ diameter.
No. 2 " " " " $\frac{1}{4}''$ to $\frac{5}{16}''$ "
No. 3 " " " " $\frac{3}{8}''$ to $\frac{7}{16}''$ "
No. 4 " " " " $\frac{1}{2}''$ to $\frac{11}{16}''$ "
No. 5 " " " " $\frac{3}{4}''$ to $1''$ "
No. 6 " " " " $1\frac{1}{16}''$ to $1\frac{1}{2}''$ "
No. 7 " " " " $1\frac{9}{16}''$ to $2\frac{1}{8}''$ "
No. 8 " " " " $2\frac{1}{4}''$ to $3''$ "

In order that reamers may be calipered readily when grinding — if the teeth have been unevenly spaced — the teeth must be diametrically opposite each other; the unevenness in spacing must

TOOL MAKING.

be between adjoining teeth. This is done by cutting one tooth, then turning the spiral head of the milling machine half-way round (by giving the index pin twenty revolutions) and then cutting the opposite tooth. When cutting the flutes in pairs, the number of times the cutter must be set for depth of cut is reduced one half. Fig. 35 shows an end view of reamer having the first pair of flutes cut as described.

The irregularity of spacing is obtained by moving the index pin a different number of holes for each adjoining pair of flutes.

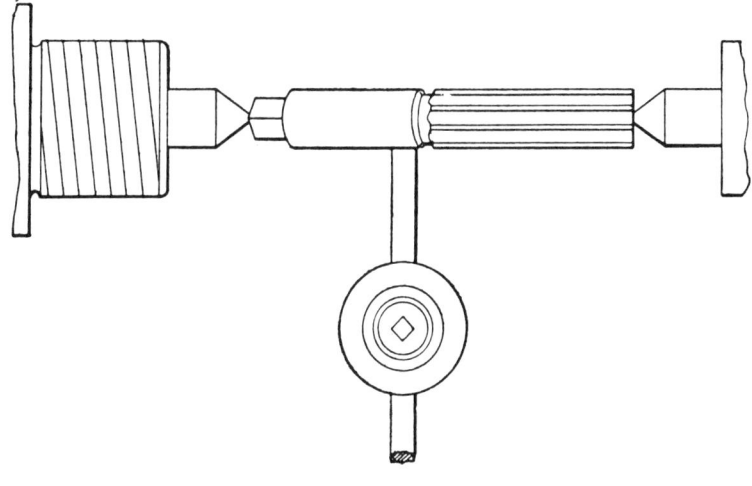

Fig. 36.

This irregularity need not be great; a variation of a few degrees, 2°, 3° or 4° from an angle corresponding to regular spacing is generally considered good practice.

Hardening Reamers. In order that a reamer may not spring when hardened, great care should be exercised in heating. If a muffler furnace is at hand, a uniform heat may be obtained. If heated in a blacksmith's forge the reamer should be placed in a tube to prevent the fire from coming in contact with the steel; it should be turned frequently to insure uniform results. While cooling, the reamer should be held vertically to avoid springing, and should be worked up and down in the bath.

If the reamer is one inch diameter, or larger, it should be

removed from the hardening bath when it stops *singing*, and plunged into oil, and allowed to remain until cold. The temper may be drawn to a light straw color.

If reamers are hardened by the "Pack Hardening" process, the danger of springing is greatly reduced.

Straightening Reamers. If a reamer springs while hardening and tempering, it may be straightened by the following method: Place the reamer between the centers of the lathe; fasten a tool, or piece of iron or steel having a square end in the tool

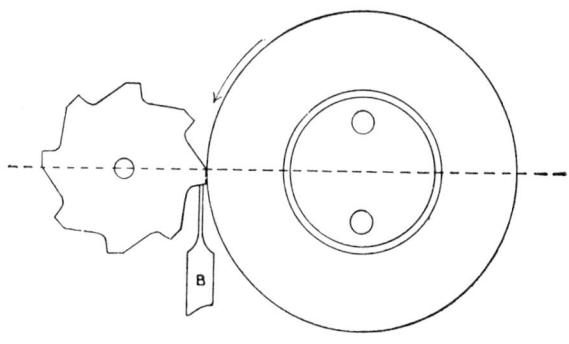

Fig. 37.

post (Fig. 36), placing the square end against the reamer at the point of greatest curvature. The surface of the reamer should be covered with a thin coating of sperm, or lard oil. With a spirit lamp, a plumber's hand torch, or a Bunsen burner, heat the reamer evenly until the oil commences to smoke; pressure may now be applied by means of the cross-feed screw, slowly forcing the reamer over until it is bent a trifle the other way. It should be cooled evenly while in this position. After it is cool the pressure may be relieved and the reamer tested for truth. If it does not run true the operation may be repeated. This method of straightening is equally effective when applied to other classes of work.

The straightening should be done before drawing the temper. When drawing the temper the heat should be applied evenly or the piece will spring from uneven heating.

Before *grinding a reamer* be sure that the centers of the grinding machine are in good shape, then clean the centers of the reamer. The reamer should first be ground to run true. It may be ground to within .001 or .002 inch of finish size; large reamers having the greater amount. In backing off a reamer tooth for clearance use an emery wheel of as large diameter as possible without striking the cutting edge of the next tooth. The correct clearance is given by a finger which can be adjusted. Fig. 37 shows an end view of reamer being ground for clearance together with the finger and emery wheel. The emery wheel should run in the direction indicated by the arrow, in order that the pressure of the wheel will tend to force the reamer tooth down on the finger B. To give clearance, the finger is adjusted so that the cutting edge is below the line of centers as shown. The lower the finger the greater the amount of clearance. Unless a free cutting wheel, free from glaze is used the temper will be drawn, thus rendering the reamer worthless. To avoid softening the teeth, the stock must be removed by a succession of light cuts going way around the reamer each time the adjustment is changed.

A reamer will soon lose its size if the clearance is ground to the edge of the teeth; consequently it is best to grind to within from .01 to .015 inch of the edge, according to the size of the reamer. The reamer is then brought to an edge and to the desired size by oilstoning. To do satisfactory work the stone should be free cutting. Select a stone of medium grade for removing the stock, and use a " fine " stone for finishing the cutting edge. An oilstone should *not* be used dry; keep the face free from glaze. If there are deep depressions or marks in the stone, face it off on a wet grinding machine.

Fluted Chucking Reamers. The same general instructions given for making fluted-hand reamers, can be applied to this form; except that the shank may be finished to size before the reamer is hardened, unless the shank is to fit a collet or be held in a chuck.

The regular jobbing reamer used in the lathe is shown in Fig. 38; the form for the chucking lathe or drill press, where the shank is held in a collet or chuck is shown Fig. 39. When making this style of reamer, B may be left .010 to .015 inch above size to allow for grinding. The portion C may be finished to size and the dimension of the cutting part of the reamer stamped on it as shown; if the reamer is made for special work and is to be used on no other, the name of the piece, or operation it is intended for should also be stamped.

On account of the uncertainty of a reamer cutting exactly to size when used in a lathe, chucking reamers are frequently made somewhat under size. Standard *hand* reamers are used for finishing. The amount of stock left for the hand reamer varies: some tool makers consider .005 inch the proper amount for all reamers up to 3 inches in diameter; while others think that for 1 inch or less diameter .004 inch is right; and for sizes from $1\frac{1}{16}$ inches to 2 inches, .007 inch should be allowed. For reamers larger than

Fig. 39.

2-inch diameter an allowance of .010 inch should be made. The exact amount necessary for finishing with hand reamers depends on the nature of the work and the stock operated on. Fluted chucking reamers are made with either straight or spiral flutes.

When a reamer is used in a screw machine or turret lathe, on work where accuracy and straightness of hole is essential, it should be held in some form of special holder, which allows it to properly

Fig. 39.

locate itself as to alignment. Such holders will be described later under the heading " Reamer Holders."

Rose Reamers. This form of reamer has its cutting edges only on the end as shown in Fig. 40, the grooves being cut the entire length of body to reduce the amount of frictional-bearing surface and to furnish a channel to conduct the lubricant to the cutting lips. In case there are blow holes or other imperfections in the material being operated on, this reamer will cut a more nearly parallel hole than the fluted chucking reamer.

Fig. 40 shows the ordinary form of rose chucking reamer. The shank B is turned to finish size; in case it is to fit a holder it is left slightly larger and turned or ground to size after hardening. The body A is turned .015 to .020 inch above finish size, the flutes cut, the size stamped as shown, and the reamer hardened

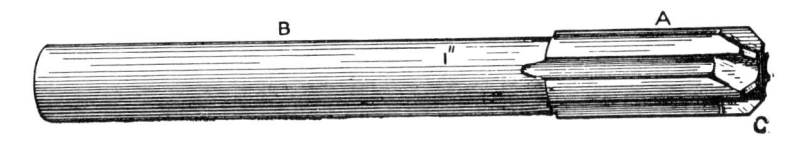

Fig. 40.

a little above the body. It is customary when grinding a rose reamer to make it a trifle smaller on the end of body next to the shank; a taper of $\frac{1}{4000}$ inch in the length of the cutting part gives good results.

Small rose reamers can be made of drill rod, which runs very true to size, if ordered by the decimal equivalent rather than by the drill gauge number, or in terms of common fractions. For

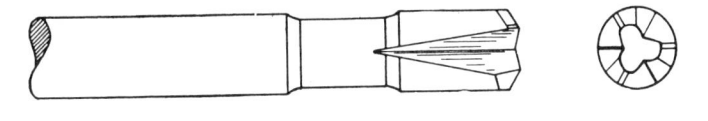

Fig 41.

instance, if drill rod is wanted of a size corresponding to No. 1 Browne & Sharpe drill gauge, the wire will come much more accurate if ordered .228 inch diameter rather than by the gauge.

The wire may be sawed to length, put in lathe chuck, and cornered for the cutting lips. When making small reamers that are not to be ground to size after hardening, it is advisable to neck them down back of the cutting edge, as shown in Fig. 41. The drill rod often swells or expands at a point where the hardening ends, and by necking down and hardening into the necking this difficulty is overcome.

Small rose reamers may be given three cutting edges. The flutes may be filed with a three-square or a round-edge file. If a three-square file is used, a groove of the form shown in Fig. 41 may be made. This has a tendency to push the chips ahead when cutting, while a groove filed with a round-edge file, if it be of a spiral form, will draw the chips back into the flute, provided it is a right-hand helix, as shown in Fig. 42.

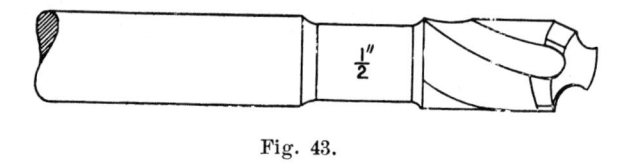

Fig. 43.

Rose reamers intended for reaming holes of exact size must be ground to correct dimensions after hardening, but small reamers intended for reaming holes where *exactness* of size is not essential may be made to size before hardening, and the cutting edges backed off with a file for clearance. If reamers are ground on the circumference for size, the lips or cutting edges should be

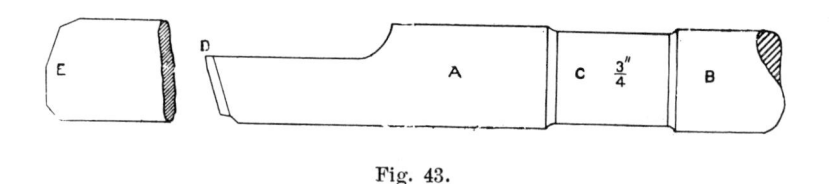

Fig. 43.

given clearance by grinding. After grinding, the corners of the cutting edges next to the body of the reamer, as shown at C, Fig. 40, should be rounded by oilstoning.

A Single Lip Reamer is very useful for reaming a *straight* hole. When the nature of the hole or the condition of the stock would cause the ordinary forms to *run*, the single lip reamer will cut a straight hole if started right. Having but one cutting lip, its action is similar to a boring tool used for internal turning in the lathe, and as a large proportion of the body of the reamer acts as a guide, it must cut a straight hole. Fig. 43 shows two views of this form of reamer.

Steel for this reamer should be sufficiently large to allow the decarbonized surface to be entirely removed. After a roughing chip has been taken,— leaving the piece about $\frac{1}{16}$ inch above finish size,— the stock should be annealed, after which the portions A and B should be turned to a size that allows for grinding. C may be finished to dimensions given, and the size of the reamer stamped as shown.

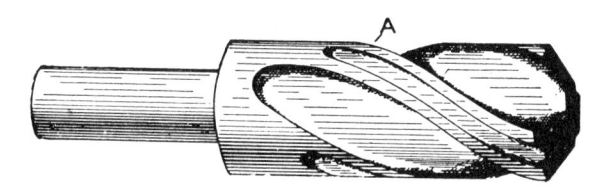

Fig. 44.

The reamer is now ready for milling. This should be done with the reamer in the centers in the milling machine, using a shank mill or a small milling cutter on an arbor. The depth of the cut should be about one-third the diameter of the reamer; for large reamers it may be somewhat deeper. After milling, the face may be smoothed with a fine file, and the end and cutting lip backed off for clearance, as shown in Fig. 43 at D and E.

When hardening, the end A should be heated to a low red and dipped in the bath about one-half an inch on the necked portion C. The temper may be drawn to a light straw. A and B are now ready for grinding. If the grinder has no provision for water to run on the work, care should be used not to heat the reamer, as it is likely to spring.

Three and Four Lipped Roughing Reamers are used to advantage in chucking machines for enlarging cored holes, or holes that have been drilled smaller than the required size. This is often done in making large holes in solid stock, as most manufacturers consider it more economical to use a smaller drill and a roughing reamer in order to bring them to proper size for the final reamer. Fig. 44 shows a reamer of this description.

The instructions already given for making the various reamers may be followed for this form, with the exception of cutting the grooves, which should be of a sufficient size to hold the chips. The small groove cut in the center of the lands is to feed oil to the cutting edges when cutting steel. When cast iron is the material to be operated on, the grooves are cut straight and the oil groove omitted. If a finish reamer is to be used in sizing the

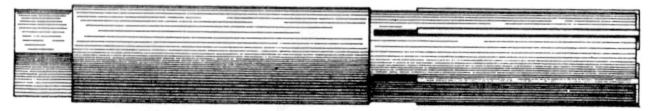

Fig. 45.

holes, it is customary to make the roughing reamer $\frac{1}{64}$ inch smaller than finish size. On account of the rough usage, great care should be exercised in hardening. While satisfactory results may be obtained by heating to a *low* red, plunging in a bath of brine, and drawing the temper to a light straw, the tools will do a great deal more if they are pack hardened by the process already described.

Inserted Blade Reamers. The particular advantage of solid reamers with inserted teeth is that when worn, new blades may be put in at a cost much less than that of a new solid reamer. Inserted blade reamers are usually made in such a manner that the size may be altered; in such cases they are termed expanding reamers. A simple form is shown in Fig. 45. The slots for the blades are milled somewhat deeper at the front end than at the end toward the shank; they are also somewhat wider at the bottom than at the top. The first is accomplished by depressing the spiral head a trifle, while the latter is done by first milling the slots with a cutter a little narrower than the top of the slot wanted, then turning the spiral head enough to produce the desired angle on one side of slot as shown at A in Fig. 46. The object in making

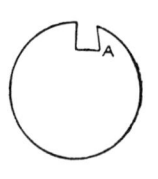

Fig. 46.

the slot deeper at the front end is that the blades, as they become dulled (and consequently cut small), may be driven farther into the body. As the slot is shallower, the blade is forced out as it advances, thus increasing its diameter; it may then be sharpened by grinding to size. The side of the slot is cut at an angle to hold the blade solidly and prevent any tendency it might have to draw away from its seating when the reamer is cutting. The body of the reamer is not hardened; the blades are machined to size, hardened, driven into place and ground to size. If the

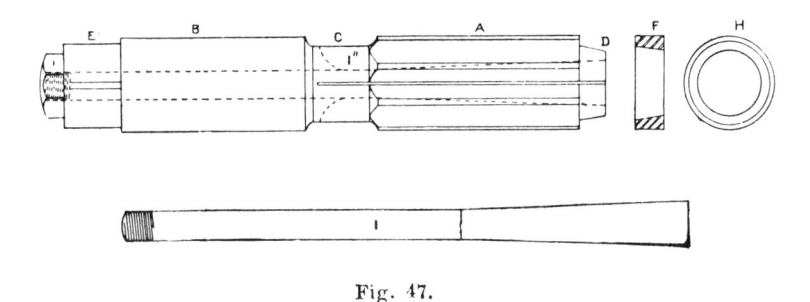

Fig. 47.

reamer is of the form known as *fluted reamer*, the teeth may be backed off for clearance as already described.

Adjustable Reamers are made of a form that allows them to be adjusted to a varying size of parts of machines where interchangeability is not essential. Fig. 47 shows the cheapest form of adjustable reamer; this form is sometimes objected to because it does not expand or contract uniformly its entire length; for ordinary work, however, it is very satisfactory, if used for a limited range of sizes.

Stock should be selected at least $\frac{3}{32}$ inch larger than finish size. After carefully centering and squaring the ends, a chip should be turned the entire length of the piece. It should then be drilled, and the taper hole reamed for the expansion plug. When drilling the outer end, the blank should run in the steady rest; the hole in the *shank* end should be drilled to the proper depth with a drill $\frac{1}{32}$ inch *larger* than the straight stem of the expansion plug. The end should be chamfered to a 60° angle to run on the lathe center when turning and grinding. The piece may be reversed and the opposite end drilled and reamed with a taper reamer; this end should be chamfered also to a 60° angle. Fig. 48 shows a sectional view of the blank drilled and reamed, and the ends of the hole beveled.

The reamer may now be turned .020 to .025 inch above finish sizes on A and B, while C and D may be turned to finish sizes, and the size stamped at C. The end E may be milled square for a wrench, the grooves milled and the reamer split, in order that the size may be altered with the expansion plug.

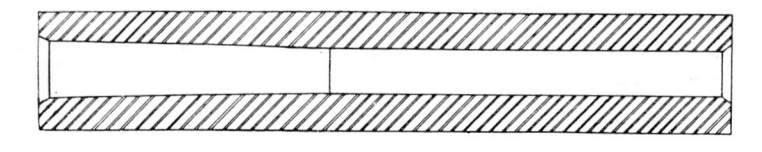

Fig. 48.

When splitting the reamer, a metal slitting saw of the required thickness (usually $\frac{1}{16}$ inch) should be used. The saw cut should not extend to the end of the reamer, but a small portion should be left solid to prevent the reamer from springing when hardening. The circular saw leaves a cut at the end of the shape shown in Fig. 49, which would be extremely difficult to part after hardening. In order that the thin partition of stock may be easily severed with an emery wheel, the slot may be finished, as shown in Fig. 50, with a hand hack saw.

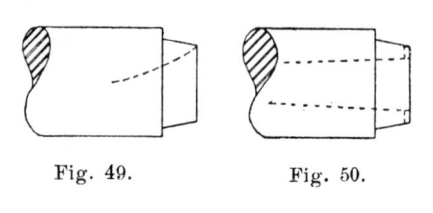

Fig. 49.

Fig. 50.

The expansion rod I, Fig. 47, should be turned to fit the taper in the reamer, the straight end should be $\frac{1}{32}$ inch smaller than the hole running through the reamer, and should be threaded on the end for a nut to be used in drawing the rod into the reamer. The collar shown at F and H should have a taper hole fitted to the tapered end of the reamer. The outside diameter of collar should be a trifle smaller than the hole to be reamed; this collar, when forced onto the end of the reamer, holds it in place. In order to increase the size of the reamer, the collar may be driven back a trifle and the rod drawn in by means of the nut.

After the reamer is hardened and tempered, the thin partitions left at the ends of the slots may be ground away with a beveled emery wheel, the rod inserted, the collar forced on the end, the reamer ground to size, and the teeth backed off for clearance.

TAPER REAMERS.

If a taper reamer is intended for finishing a hole, the same general instructions may be followed as for *fluted hand reamers*, except that instead of being straight, the body, or cutting part, is tapered.

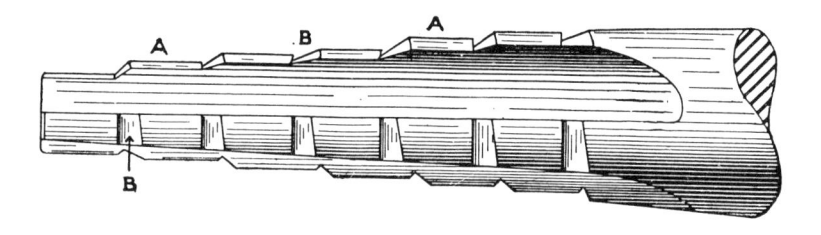

Fig. 51.

Roughing taper reamers are frequently made in the form of a stepped reamer, or it might be called a multiple counterbore, since each step acts as a pilot for the next larger step, as shown in Fig. 51. The steps A are turned straight, each one correspondingly larger than the preceding. The cutting is done at the end of the step B, which must be given clearance; this is ordinarily done with a file. The reamer may be given four cutting edges; these should be cut with a milling cutter intended for milling the flutes of reamers. The number of the cutter selected will depend on the form and amount of taper of the reamers. It is advisable to neck down into the reamer $\frac{1}{32}$ inch at the end of each step; this may be done with a round nose tool, or a cutting-off tool having its corners slightly rounded. The necking facilitates the filing of the cutting edges, and also allows the emery wheel to traverse the entire length of each step when grinding to size after hardening.

Roughing reamers are sometimes made of the form shown in Fig. 52. The left-hand thread cut the entire length of the cutting portion breaks the chips into short lengths, and greatly increases the cutting qualities. After turning the tapered part to a size that allows for grinding, the lathe may be geared to cut a four-pitch thread. The threading tool should be about $\frac{1}{16}$ inch thick at the cutting point, and have sufficient clearance to prevent the heel dragging when the tool is cutting. The corners should be slightly rounded in order to reduce the tendency of cracking when the reamer is hardened. The thread should be cut to a

Fig. 52.

depth of from $\frac{1}{64}$ to $\frac{1}{32}$ inch. After threading, the flutes may be cut, the reamer hardened, and the temper drawn to a light straw.

When grinding a *taper reamer* the proper clearance is given to the tooth back for a distance of $\frac{3}{64}$ inch from the cutting edge, the balance of the tooth is given a greater amount of clearance, as shown in Fig. 53.

Shell Reamers. As a matter of economy, the larger sizes of reamers are sometimes made in the form of shell reamers, as shown in Figs. 54 and 55. As several reamers may be used on the same arbor, there is quite a saving in cost of material.

The following table gives the size and length of shell reamers from one inch to three inch diameter, together with the size of holes, and width and depth of tongue slot.

			Tongue Slot.	
Diameter.	Length.	Size of Hole.	Width.	Depth.
$1''$ to $1\frac{1}{4}''$	$2\frac{3}{4}''$	$\frac{5}{8}''$	$\frac{1}{4}''$	$\frac{1}{4}''$
$1\frac{5}{16}''$ to $1\frac{5}{8}''$	$3''$	$\frac{3}{4}''$	$\frac{5}{16}''$	$\frac{5}{16}''$
$1\frac{11}{16}''$ to $2''$	$3\frac{1}{2}''$	$1''$	$\frac{3}{8}''$	$\frac{5}{16}''$
$2\frac{1}{16}''$ to $2\frac{1}{2}''$	$3\frac{3}{4}''$	$1\frac{1}{4}''$	$\frac{1}{2}''$	$\frac{3}{8}''$

After drilling a hole $\frac{1}{16}$ inch smaller than finish size, the blank should be placed on a mandrel and a heavy chip taken to remove all the original surface. It should then be annealed.

After annealing it may be placed in a chuck on the lathe and the hole bored .005 inch smaller than finish size. After putting on a mandrel, the ends should be faced to length and the outside diameter turned, leaving .010 to .015 inch on the cutting part for grinding. The balance of reamer should be turned to size. If it is to be a *rose reamer* the edge should be chamferred the proper amount.

The reamer should be held in a chuck on the spiral head spindle in the milling machine, and the tongue slot cut. In order

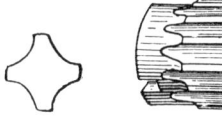

Fig. 53.   Fig. 54.   Fig. 55.

to get the slot central with the outside of the reamer, a cutter somewhat narrower than the desired slot should be used, which should be set as centrally as possible by measurement, a cut taken, the spiral head turned one-half way round and another cut taken; the width of the slot should be measured, and the saddle of the machine moved by means of the graduated adjusting screw one-half the amount necessary to make the slot of the right width. The reamer may now be placed on a mandrel between centers on the milling machine, and the grooves cut.

The reamer should be heated for hardening in some receptacle in order that the fire may not come in direct contact with it; when it reaches a *low uniform* red heat it may be placed on a wire bent in the form of a hook, and plunged in the bath; it should be worked up and down rapidly until all trace of red has disappeared. When cold it may be heated to prevent cracking from internal strains; if it is to be a rose reamer it may be left *dead* hard, if a fluted reamer the temper should be drawn to a straw color. The hole should be ground to fit the shank on which it is to be used, or a plug gauge, if there is one for the purpose. The reamer may then be placed on a mandrel and ground according to directions given for grinding reamers.

The holes in *shell reamers* are sometimes made tapering — the end of the arbor being made of a corresponding taper — to avoid the necessity of grinding the holes, as any slight change in the size resulting from hardening would be compensated for by the taper hole.

Arbors for Shell Reamers are made as shown in Fig. 56. The shank B and end A to receive the reamer, are made in one piece. The collar C having two tongues to engage in the slots in the reamer, is made of tool steel; the hole is made of a size that allows it to slide over A. When in position a hole is drilled through both collar and arbor and the pin D driven in. When making the collar the hole is drilled and reamed; it is placed on a mandrel, the ends faced to length, and the collar turned to proper

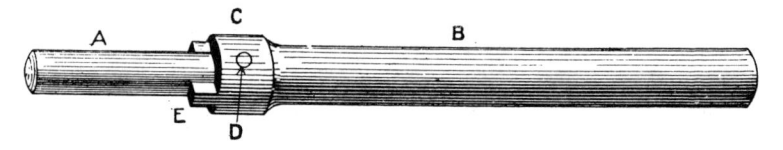

Fig. 56.

diameter. It is then removed from the mandrel and the tongues milled. While doing this the collar is held in the chuck on the spindle of the spiral head and a side milling cutter is used. One side is milled, the spiral head spindle turned one-half revolution, and the opposite side milled; the thickness is measured and the saddle moved enough to bring the tongues to the required thickness when the finish cut is taken on each side. After putting on an arbor and drilling the pin hole, the collar may be removed and spring tempered. It may now be placed on the arbor and the pin driven in place.

When the hollow mill is made with a taper hole, the arbor is made with the end A of a corresponding taper. Otherwise the construction would be the same as for hollow mills having straight holes.

Formed Reamers are used for holes of an irregular shape, or rather of a shape neither straight nor tapering. They are used

TOOL MAKING.   47

chiefly by gun makers in reaming the end of the gun barrel for the shell, and are termed, when used for this class of work, *chambering reamers*.

It is essential when making this class of reamer, that the stock be rough turned a little above finish size and then annealed. Reamers of this form are accurate as to size and shape, consequently it is customary to use a gauge. This is generally a piece of steel having a hole of the proper form reamed in it, after which the stock is cut away on one side, leaving a trifle more than one-half of the hole as shown in Fig. 57.

To make the reamer blank fit the gauge the operator must understand the use of hand turning tools, as most shapes must be made with these tools. The teeth must be cut with a milling cutter of small diameter following the different shapes of the

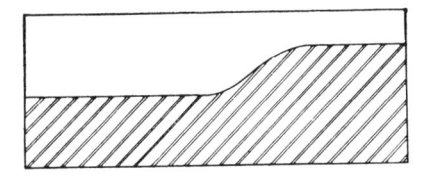

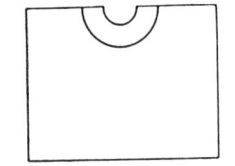

Fig. 57.

reamer in order to have the top of the land of as uniform a width as possible. After cutting, the teeth may be backed off for clearance with a file, taking care not to remove any stock at the cutting edge.

When hardening, heat very carefully in a tube until the reamer is of a *low* uniform red heat; it should then be plunged in a bath of lukewarm brine. It may be brightened and the temper drawn to a light straw. After hardening it should be tried in the gauge, and any high spots removed by oilstoning.

If a large number of reamers of one form are to be made, the grinding machine may be rigged with a form which makes it possible to grind many of the shapes in common use, but some shapes will be found quite impracticable to grind, consequently the above method of fitting before hardening must be adopted. Excellent results are obtained by hardening by the "Pack Hardening" process.

Reamer Holders. On account of the uncertainty of exact alignment of every part of a screw machine or turret lathe, it is desirable to use a holder for the reamer that allows it to properly align itself. The form of holder shown in Fig. 58 is in common use and gives excellent results. It consists of the body A which has a hole drilled and reamed its entire length; the hole must be somewhat larger than the shank of the reamer, $\frac{1}{16}$ inch being considered sufficient. The center B of tool steel should be (after hardening) .010 to .015 inch larger than the hole in the holder; the point should be ground to a 60° angle, and the straight part ground to a forcing fit in the holder. After being forced to position a hole may be drilled through the holder and center, and the

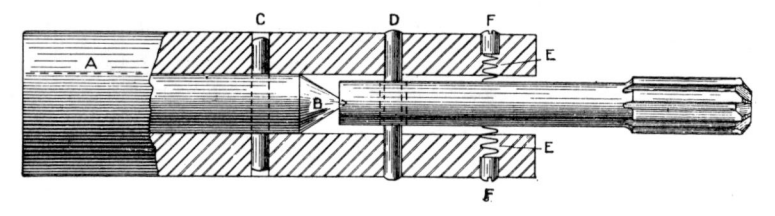

Fig. 58.

pin C driven in to keep the center from being pressed back by the reamer when in operation. A pin should be put through the holder at D; a hole $\frac{1}{16}$ inch larger than the pin should be put through the reamer shank at this point. This pin is simply to prevent the reamer from turning when it comes in contact with the work. The coil springs E E hold the reamer in position to enter the hole, and the proper tension is given by means of the screws F F.

ARBORS.

Mandrels. The ordinary taper arbor, known as the mandrel, is in common use in most machine shops. Up to and including $1\frac{1}{2}$ inches diameter, mandrels are made of tool steel, hardened all over and ground to size. Some tool makers advocate making all mandrels up to 4 inches diameter in this way; others prefer hardening the ends B B (Fig. 59), leaving the center A soft, while others maintain that for mandrels above $1\frac{1}{2}$ inches diameter, machinery steel is most satisfactory if thoroughly case hardened.

TOOL MAKING.

When making mandrels of tool steel that are to be hardened the entire length, it is not necessary to use the best quality of steel, as a lower grade may be used if it will harden well. Select stock somewhat larger than finish diameter, say $\frac{1}{16}$ inch for sizes up to $\frac{1}{2}$ inch; $\frac{1}{8}$ inch for sizes up to 1 inch; $\frac{3}{16}$ inch for sizes up to $1\frac{1}{2}$ inches, and $\frac{1}{4}$ inch for sizes above. Take a chip off the out-

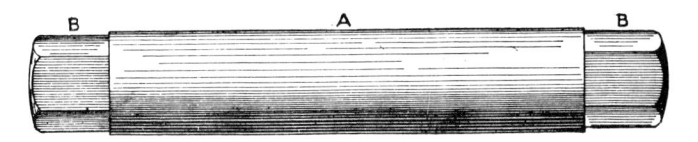

Fig. 59.

side sufficiently heavy to remove all scale, yet leaving $\frac{1}{32}$ inch for a finish cut on sizes up to $\frac{1}{2}$ inch and correspondingly more for the larger sizes. It should now be annealed, preferably in the annealing box. The ends should be countersunk deeper in mandrels than in tools where the centers are not used after they are completed, in order that the centers may not be mutilated when driven

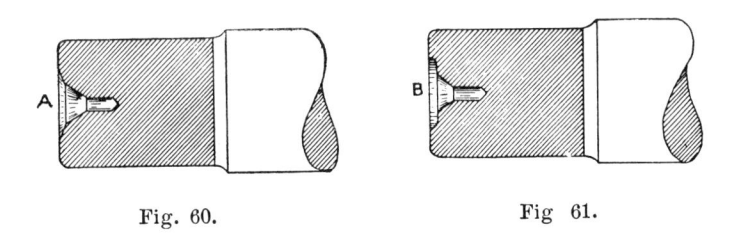

Fig. 60.   Fig 61.

in or out of the work. The centers should either have an extra countersink, as at A in Fig. 60, or else the cut should be recessed as at B in Fig. 61.

The ends B B, Fig. 59, should be turned to size, the corners slightly rounded, and the flat spots for the dog screw milled or planed. The body of the mandrel should be turned somewhat larger than finish size; those smaller than $\frac{1}{2}$ inch should have an allowance of .015 inch; from $\frac{1}{2}$ to 1 inch an allowance of .020 to .025 inch; over 1 inch an allowance of .025 to .030. As the length of mandrels larger than 2 inches diameter does not increase in proportion with the diameter, the amount given will generally be sufficient if proper care is used when hardening. The size should be stamped on the end next to the large end of body.

Before hardening, the centers should be re-countersunk to true them; for this operation it is best to use a special countersink having an angle of 59° instead of the regular 60° tool, as it facilitates the lapping of the centers to a 60° angle after hardening, due to the unequal amount of grinding caused by the shape of the countersinking.

If a blacksmith's forge must be used when heating the mandrel for hardening, the fire should be large enough to heat the piece evenly; it is advisable to heat it in a tube. More uniform results can be obtained from a muffler furnace than in the open fire. In either case the piece should be turned frequently, to

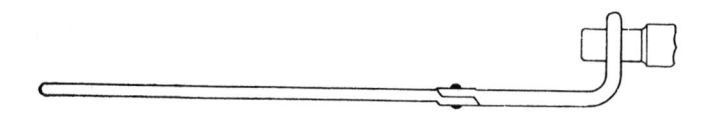

Fig. 52.

insure an even heat. To dip in the bath, a pair of tongs of the shape shown in Fig. 62 should be used, so that the bath may come in contact with both centers. The tongs should grapple the mandrel at the large end, in order that the small end may be harder; it should be worked up and down rapidly in the bath to insure uniform results. A bath of brine will be found very satisfactory for this work.

A mandrel larger than 1 inch diameter should be removed from the bath as soon as it ceases *singing*, and held in a tank of oil until cold. The ends should be brightened and drawn to a deep straw color, in order to toughen them so that they will not break or chip off when driven. Mandrels smaller than $\frac{3}{4}$ inch should have the temper drawn to a light straw color the entire length of body.

After hardening, the body of the mandrel should be cleaned with a coarse emery cloth, to remove the scale or grease which would glaze the emery wheel. It should then be tested between centers to see if it has sprung more than will grind out before it reaches the proper size.

The centers should now be lapped, to insure proper shape and alignment. The lap may be a piece of copper of the proper shape (60°) charged with diamond dust or emery. After lapping, the centers should be thoroughly cleaned with benzine. (When using benzine do not allow it to get near a flame of any kind.)

Examine very carefully the condition of the centers of the grinder, as the truth of the mandrel depends in a great measure on their condition. A mandrel may be ground in a lathe having a grinding attachment or in any universal grinder. Better results can be obtained, however, if ground in some form of grinder having a stream of water to keep the work from heating, as heat is likely to spring the piece, especially if it does not run true, thus making the grinding heavier on one side than the other. If a dry grinder must be used, do not force the grinding fast enough to heat the piece. The mandrel should be ground to within about .005 inch of size with a coarse wheel free from glaze, and then finished with a fine wheel.

The amount of taper varies: some manufacturers prefer .0005 inch taper per inch, while others make them of .001 inch taper for every inch of length, claiming that if a piece having a long hole is to be held on *any* taper mandrel it will not fit at the end nearest the small end of mandrel, consequently the turned surface will not be true with the hole; also that for such work a mandrel should be made for the job having a body nearly or quite straight. They claim that the mandrel should be made to taper .001 inch for every inch of length, in order that it may be adapted to a greater range of work.

Mandrels with Hardened Ends. When making a mandrel whose ends are to be hard and body soft, follow the instructions given for hardened mandrels, except that a larger amount of stock should be left on the body. The ends should be hardened for a distance that insures the *centers* being hard; this can be accomplished by heating one end at a time to a red heat, and inverting under a faucet of running water. As the center is uppermost, the water can readily enter it, forcing the steam away. After drawing the temper of the ends and lapping the centers, the body may be turned to size. The centers of the lathe should be carefully trued before starting this operation. If the body of the mandrel is left .008 inch to .010 inch larger after turning, and then ground to size, the results will be surer; but with *extreme care* a very satisfactory job may be done by the method described.

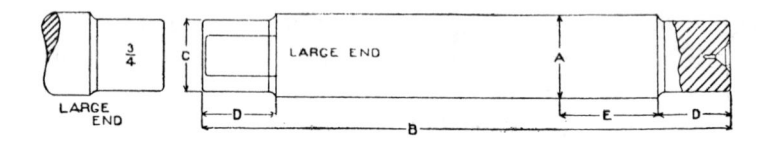

Table of Dimensions of Mandrels to 1 Inch.

A	B	C	D	E	F
$\frac{1}{4}$	$3\frac{3}{4}$	$\frac{7}{32}$	$\frac{1}{2}$	$\frac{1}{2}$	$\frac{1}{8}$
$\frac{5}{16}$	4	$\frac{9}{32}$	$\frac{1}{2}$	$\frac{9}{16}$	$\frac{5}{32}$
$\frac{3}{8}$	$4\frac{1}{4}$	$\frac{11}{32}$	$\frac{1}{2}$	$\frac{5}{8}$	$\frac{3}{16}$
$\frac{7}{16}$	$4\frac{1}{2}$	$\frac{13}{32}$	$\frac{9}{16}$	$\frac{11}{16}$	$\frac{7}{32}$
$\frac{1}{2}$	5	$\frac{7}{16}$	$\frac{5}{8}$	$\frac{3}{4}$	$\frac{1}{4}$
$\frac{9}{16}$	$5\frac{1}{4}$	$\frac{1}{2}$	$\frac{11}{16}$	$\frac{13}{16}$	$\frac{9}{32}$
$\frac{5}{8}$	$5\frac{1}{2}$	$\frac{9}{16}$	$\frac{3}{4}$	$\frac{7}{8}$	$\frac{5}{16}$
$\frac{11}{16}$	$5\frac{3}{4}$	$\frac{5}{8}$	$\frac{13}{16}$	$\frac{15}{16}$	$\frac{11}{32}$
$\frac{3}{4}$	6	$\frac{11}{16}$	$\frac{7}{8}$	1	$\frac{3}{8}$
$\frac{13}{16}$	$6\frac{1}{4}$	$\frac{3}{4}$	$\frac{7}{8}$	$1\frac{1}{16}$	$\frac{13}{32}$
$\frac{7}{8}$	$6\frac{1}{2}$	$\frac{13}{16}$	$\frac{15}{16}$	$1\frac{1}{8}$	$\frac{7}{16}$
$\frac{15}{16}$	$6\frac{3}{4}$	$\frac{7}{8}$	$\frac{15}{16}$	$1\frac{3}{16}$	$\frac{15}{32}$
1	7	$\frac{15}{16}$	1	$1\frac{1}{4}$	$\frac{1}{2}$

Machinery Steel Mandrels. With the exception of hardening, the instructions given for making mandrels of tool steel apply to those made of machinery steel. It is necessary to *case harden* mandrels made of machinery steel, using the method already described. The work should be run in the fire from seven to ten hours after the box is red hot throughout; dip in a

TOOL MAKING.

a bath having a jet of water coming up from the bottom to force the steam away from the work, to avoid soft spots. It is not necessary to draw the temper, as the hardening does not extend far below the surface.

Expanding Mandrels. There are several forms of expanding mandrels in common use. One form has a sleeve with a taper hole fitting on a mandrel that has a corresponding taper; the sleeve is split to allow it to expand as it is forced on the mandrel.

It is not advisable to give the mandrel very much taper, because a heavy cut with the pressure toward the small end would crowd the sleeve toward that end, thereby releasing the work. Ordinarily a taper of $\frac{1}{2}$ inch to the foot will give good results.

Fig. 63.

It is obvious that the range of adjustment for a sleeve as described is small, but sleeves of different diameters may be fitted to the same mandrel, the thickness of wall being increased to give the desired size. The diameter of the sleeve should be such that the work may enter without forcing, the tightening being accomplished by forcing or driving the sleeve toward the large end of the mandrel.

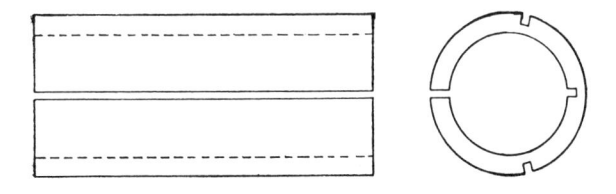

Fig. 64.

If a sleeve is required for a special sized hole, and is to be used but a few times, and through a limited range as to size, it may be made of cast iron. A hole is bored in it corresponding in size and taper to its mandrel; the hole should be made to allow the small end of the mandrel to go through and be flush with the end of the sleeve. The sleeve should be forced on the mandrel and turned to size; the outside diameter should fit the hole in the piece to be machined when the sleeve is at the small end.

In order that the sleeve may be expanded it is split as shown in Fig. 64. This should be done in the milling machine, the sleeve being held by the ends in the vise and the cut made with a metal slitting saw. When the sleeves are intended for permanent

Fig. 65.

equipment it is good practice to make them of either machinery steel or tool steel,— if made of the former they may be case hardened, if of the latter they may be hardened and spring tempered. In either case the hole should be .010 inch small, and the outside diameter .020 to .025 inch large, and ground to size after hard-

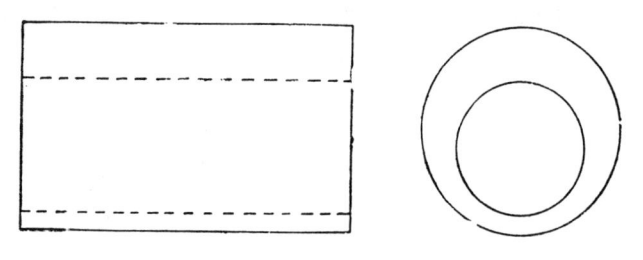

Fig. 66.

ening. A method of splitting the sleeve for a more uniform expansion is shown in Fig. 65; small sizes have four cuts for adjustment, while the larger sizes have six or eight.

On account of the peculiar construction of the sleeve shown in Fig. 65 it must be held while grinding the hole, so that it will not spring. To do this the sleeve may be placed in a hole in a collar and held by several drops of solder so placed as to hold it rigidly in position. In order that the solder may stick, the outside of the sleeve must be brightened. When soldered securely the collar may be placed in the chuck on the grinding machine and the hole ground to the desired size, after which it may be heated to melt the solder, and the sleeve removed from the collar. It can then be placed on the mandrel and the outside diameter ground to the proper size.

Eccentric Arbors. Arbors are made eccentric in order that the outside of a piece of work may be made eccentric to the hole running through it, as shown in Fig. 66.

When making an eccentric arbor the general directions given for making mandrels may be followed, except that the centers should be quite small. The mandrel should be placed in a V block or in a pair of centers, and by means of a surface gauge, the needle of which has been set at the exact height of the center, a line may be drawn, as shown in Fig. 67, across each end of the mandrel. The mandrel may now be turned so that the line will be vertical; the point of the surface gauge may be raised to give the required amount of eccentricity, and a line, as shown in Fig. 68, scribed on each end. The ends should be prick punched where the lines intersect, and drilled and countersunk at this point.

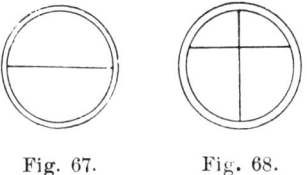

Fig. 67. Fig. 68.

Fig. 69.

After hardening, both pairs of centers should be lapped to shape. The centers marked A A (Fig. 69) must be used when grinding the mandrel to size or in turning work which is to be concentric with the hole, while the centers B B are used when turning the eccentric parts. This method of laying off and drilling the eccentric center may not give the necessary accuracy; in such case a jig must be used in drilling the center holes. A suitable jig is shown in Fig. 70. The ends of the arbor must be turned to fit the hole A, Fig. 70, in the jig, which is a collar having a straight hole through it. A piece of steel, which is a forcing fit in this hole, has a hole the size of the centering drill laid off with the proper amount of eccentricity. This piece of steel is forced to the center of the collar, as shown at B. A straight line should be drawn across the collar and down the beveled edges, as shown at C. A line should now be scribed the entire length of the mandrel, which should be set to match the line on the jig, which may be secured in its proper position by means of the set screws.

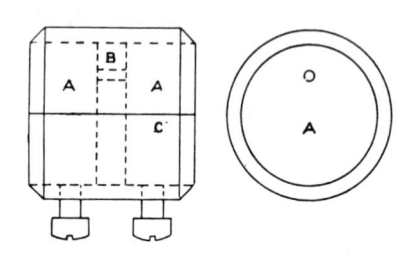

Fig. 70.

For machining a cylindrical piece having a hole through it to receive an arbor, and the faces of the piece not parallel, as shown in Fig. 71, it is well to use a mandrel having two sets of centers, as shown in Fig. 72, one of which, A A, are the regular centers, while the eccentric centers, B B, should be equidistant from the regular centers, but on opposite sides.

Milling Machine Arbors. Arbors for milling machines should be made from steel strong enough to resist (without twisting or springing) the strain caused by tightening the nut. When a limited number of arbors is made, tool steel is generally used; but for many milling machines, necessitating a great many arbors, a lower priced steel having the necessary stiffness is selected.

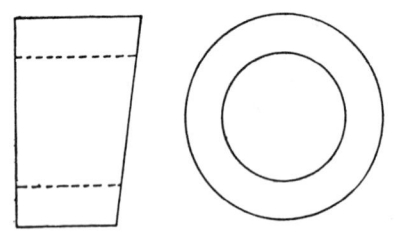

Fig. 71.

After centering and squaring the ends, a chip is turned the entire length of the piece, to remove all the outer surface. The ends D and C, Fig. 73, are next turned to size, and the tenon milled to the desired dimensions; when milling for the tenon, the arbor should be held between centers, and the cutting done with an end mill of the form shown in Fig. 74; the circumference of the cutter, leaving the proper shape at end of tenon. The centers should be hardened, and the temper drawn to a straw color. If the projection on the end of the arbor at C, Fig. 73, is to be run in a socket in the tail block of a milling machine, it must be hardened the entire length, in which case the thread for the

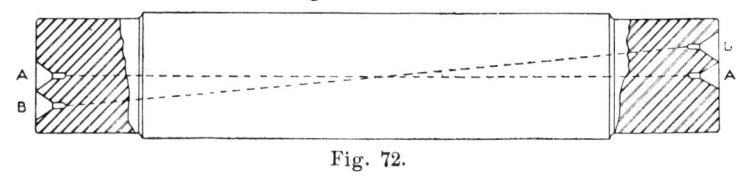

Fig. 72.

nut should be cut before hardening the end. If a lathe having a taper attachment is used, there is no particular method of procedure other than that the arbor should be roughed nearly to size before either the taper or straight end is finished. It will save time, however, if the straight end A, Fig. 73, is roughed first, then the taper B roughed and finished, after which the shoulder E and the straight part A may be turned to size and finished. If the projection C is to run in a socket, it should be turned .010 or .015 inch above finish size, and ground to the proper dimensions.

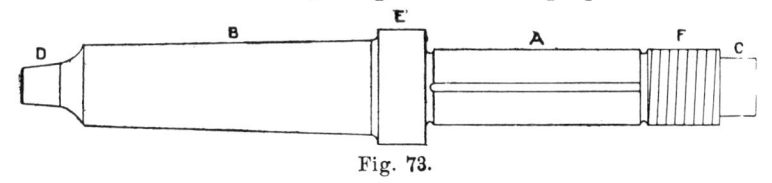

Fig. 73.

If it is necessary to use a lathe having no taper attachment, the necessary taper must be obtained by setting over the tail block. In this case it is better to turn and fit the taper first. If the taper were turned to finish size after finishing the straight part, the centers would become changed to a degree that would throw the arbor out of true. These instructions should be followed wherever a straight and taper surface are to be turned on the same piece of work, in a lathe having no other means of turning tapers except by setting over the tail block.

Milling machine arbors should have a spline slot cut the entire length of the part that is to receive the cutters; this can best be done in a shaper. Before putting the arbor in the shaper vise a hole should be drilled close to the shoulder for the tool to run into; the drill used should be about $\frac{1}{32}$ inch larger in diameter than the thickness of the splining tool, and the hole drilled a trifle deeper than the slot to be cut. When the arbor is placed in the vise a piece of sheet brass or copper should be placed between the

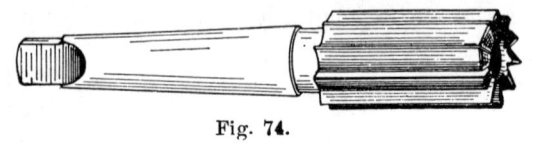

Fig. 74.

arbor and the vise jaws to prevent bruising the arbor.

Where *extreme* accuracy is required, it is advisable to leave the straight and taper parts a few thousandths of an inch above size and grind to size all over after the spline cut is taken.

The nut is usually made of machinery steel, case hardened. A bar of steel $\frac{1}{16}$ inch larger than finish size of nut is selected, and a piece $\frac{1}{16}$ inch larger than finish length is cut; it is then put in a chuck on the lathe, the hole drilled, and the thread cut; if no tap of the desired size is at hand the thread may be chased. If a tap can be obtained, the thread should be chased nearly to size and finished with the tap; before taking from the chuck the end of nut should be faced and the hole recessed to the depth of the thread for a distance of two threads. After taking from the chuck it should be placed on an arbor having a screw which fits the thread in the nut. The nut should be turned to size and length, and the two opposite sides milled to receive the wrench used in tightening. Fig. 75 gives two views of the nut. It should be made and case hardened before the thread is cut on the arbor, in order that the thread on the arbor may be made to fit the nut. Milling machine arbor nuts should fit the thread on the arbor in such a manner that they may be turned the entire length of the thread without the aid of a wrench, yet not be loose.

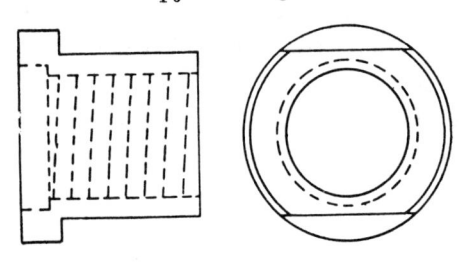

Fig. 75.

TAPS.

When making taps ¼ inch diameter and smaller, the threads are often cut with screw dies, of which there are two styles. The form of screw plate shown in Fig. 76 is termed a *jam die plate*. With this form the die is opened to allow the wire to pass through until it is even with the outside edge of the die, which is now forced into the wire by means of the adjusting screw A; the screw plate is revolved until a thread the desired length is cut. This operation is continued, the die being closed a trifle each

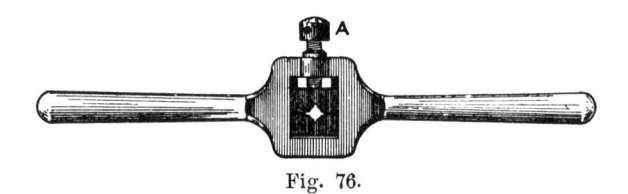

Fig. 76.

time until the desired size is obtained. The method taken of gauging the correct size varies in different shops; if only one is made, the tops of the threads are measured with a micrometer caliper; but for many taps of the same size, such as for sewing machines, guns and bicycles, a sizing die is used to give the threads an exact size. The threads are cut to within a few thousandths of an inch with the die plate, and finished with the sizing die. One form of sizing die is shown in Fig. 77.

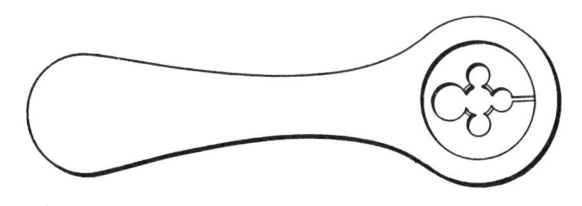

Fig. 77.

Where a great many taps of a size are cut, it is customary to use several dies of different sizes, one of which (the finishing die) is always made adjustable. The roughing dies may be made solid or adjustable, but the finishing must be adjustable for wear, or when it is found desirable to change the size of the taps. These dies are sometimes held in separate holders of the form shown in

TOOL MAKING.

Fig. 77, but a very convenient form of holder is shown in Fig. 78. If all the dies are in one holder they do not become scattered around the shop. When making many taps at a time, the work can be done better and cheaper if the wire is held in a chuck in a lathe. The die plate should be placed against a drill pad held in the tail spindle of the lathe, in order to insure starting the threads

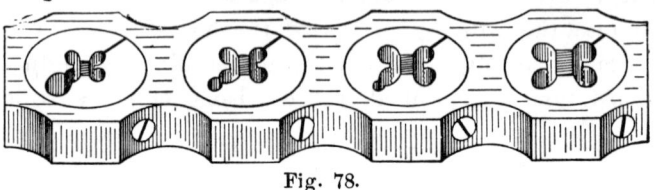

Fig. 78.

true. The largest die should of course be run on first, the second largest next and so on to the finish die.

For taps up to and including $\frac{1}{4}$ inch diameter, it is customary to use drill rod. The taps should be chamferred for a distance of three or four threads, as shown at A, Fig. 79, in order that the point may enter the drilled hole.

Taps for general use around the shop are often made in sets of three; the first tap to enter the hole is called the taper tap,

Fig. 79.

because of tne long chamferring or taper. The second is known as the plug tap; this tap has the first two or three end threads chamferred, and is used when the screw is to go nearly to the bottom of the tapped hole. The bottoming tap is used when the thread is to go to the bottom of the hole being tapped; the end of this tap is not chamferred. See Fig. 80.

Taps larger than $\frac{1}{4}$ inch are made from tool steel. Taps $\frac{1}{4}$ to $\frac{1}{2}$ inch diameter should be made of stock at least $\frac{1}{16}$ inch large; it should be centered quite accurately with a small drill, because a large center hole weakens the tap and increases the liability of its cracking when hardened. After taking a chip sufficiently deep to remove all the outer coating, it should be "box annealed" if possible.

HAND TAPS.

Hand taps are intended for tapping holes by hand and are usually made in sets of three, as previously explained. After annealing, the shank should be turned to size and the square end milled for a wrench. The body should now be turned to size, and the thread cut. Before turning any of the parts to size or starting to cut the thread, be sure that the centers of the lathe are in good condition; the live center should run true, the dead center should fit the center gauge, and be in good shape.

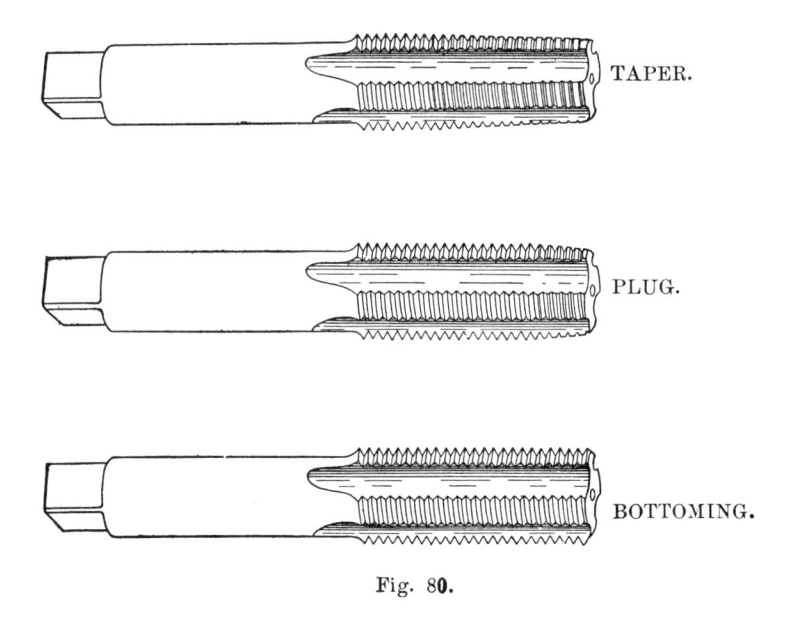

TAPER.

PLUG.

BOTTOMING.

Fig. 80.

It is advisable to cut the tap slightly tapering, the thread being from .0005 to .001 inch smaller at the end toward the shank. This prevents the tap binding when slightly worn, yet it is not tapering enough to affect the accuracy of the thread. The thread tool should be an exact fit to the gauge, and placed in the tool post so that the top of the shank stands about level. The top of blade shown at A, Fig. 81, should be ground parallel with the top of the shank; the cutting point should be set at the exact height of the point of the head center. Many tool makers consider it advisable to rough the thread nearly to size with a single point tool, finishing it with a chaser which may be held in the same holder. A chaser blade is shown in Fig. 82. After the thread is cut to size and the end chamferred, the tap is ready to be grooved in the milling machine. The tap is held between centers and the grooves cut with a cutter especially adapted to the size and style of tap. While the grooves should be cut with a milling machine cutter, it is possible to cut them in a planer or shaper, using a tool of the proper shape. Great care must be used not to stretch the tap by heavy chips, or by using a dull tool.

The grooves cut in taps are ordinarily termed flutes. When making taps for the market it is usual to cut four flutes in all taps

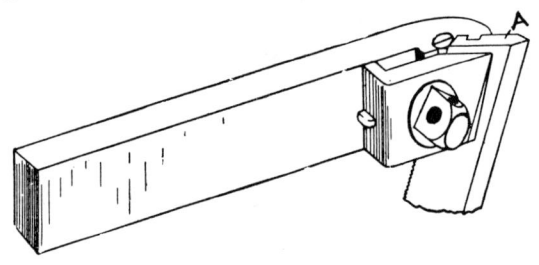

Fig. 81.

up to and including $2\frac{1}{2}$ inches diameter. But when taps are made in the shop where they are to be used, the number and shape of the grooves depend on the nature of the intended work. A tap that is to run through the work without any backing out, can have a different shaped flute from one that is to tap a deep hole in a piece of steel, where it is necessary to reverse the motion of the tap every two or three revolutions to break the chip, and also to allow the lubricant to reach the cutting lips.

While all taps up to and $2\frac{1}{2}$ inches diameter are usually given four straight flutes, spiral flutes are sometimes desirable, especially with small taps for some classes of work. With spiral flutes, it is generally necessary to cut a less number, and as taps are not ground after hardening, there is no objection to giving an odd number of teeth, as in case of a reamer. Three spiral flutes are often cut.

If a tap 1 inch in diameter, having four flutes of the regulation width, were used to tap tubing having thin walls, the tubing between the lands would have a tendency to close into the flutes of the tap, which might break the tubing. In such a case there should be double the number of flutes, in order to provide enough lands to hold the tubing in shape. If the hole to be tapped has part of its circumference cut away as shown in Fig. 83, more than four lands are necessary.

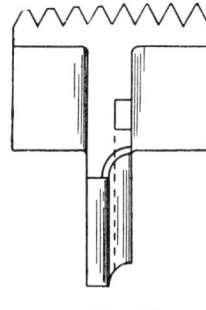

Fig. 82.

Fig. 83.

However, for general machine shop work four flutes work well in hand taps up to and including $2\frac{1}{2}$ inches diameter. For larger sizes, some tool makers advocate six flutes; others claim best results from taps having four flutes regardless of size. The class of work and the stock used in the individual shop must determine this.

Forms of Flutes. The most commonly used form of flute is that cut with a convex milling cutter (Fig. 84) for milling half circles. The advantages claimed for this form are: the flutes are of sufficient depth to provide for the chips, and yet leave the lands strong enough; and the form of the back of the land is such that the chips cannot be wedged between the land and the work when the motion of the tap is reversed. The form of groove made with this cutter is shown in Fig. 85. In order to support the tap when starting to cut, and to prevent cutting the hole large at the outer end, hand taps have their lands left wider (as shown at A, Fig. 85) than is the case with machine taps. If the forms

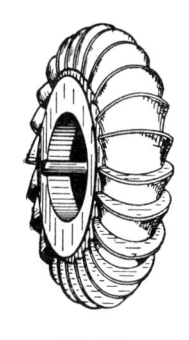

Fig. 84.

of cutter shown in Fig. 85 or Fig. 86 are used, the width of lands as shown at A may be one fourth the diameter of the tap. A Brown & Sharpe Tap and Reamer Cutter is shown in Fig. 86.

Fig. 87 shows a special form of cutter made by Brown and Sharpe. It does not make as deep a groove (Fig. 88) in proportion to the width as a Tap and Reamer Cutter.

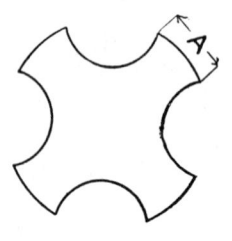

Fig. 85. 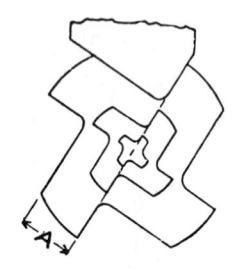   Fig. 86.

After cutting the grooves, the lands should be backed off to give the tap cutting edges; this is usually done with a file. Commence at the heel of the land, A Fig. 89, file the top of the land, and gradually approach the cutting edge, making sure that no stock is removed at that portion; simply bring it to a sharp edge. Enough should be filed off the heel A to make it cut readily, yet not enough to cause it to chatter. The size and number of threads per inch should be stamped on the shank of the tap. If it has a thread differing from that in general use in the shop, that should also be stamped on the shank, as U. S. S., if it is a United States Standard thread.

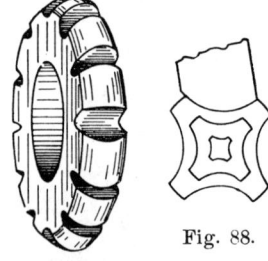

Fig. 87.   Fig. 88.

The following table gives the number of cutter for different diameters of taps when the form shown in Fig. 87 is used.

No. 1 Cutter Cuts Taps   to $\frac{1}{8}$ inch diameter.
"   2   "   "   "   from $\frac{5}{32}$ inches " $\frac{1}{4}$ "   "
"   3   "   "   "   " $\frac{9}{32}$ "   " $\frac{3}{8}$ "   "
"   4   "   "   "   " $\frac{7}{16}$ "   " $\frac{5}{8}$ "   "
"   5   "   "   "   " $\frac{11}{16}$ "   " $\frac{7}{8}$ "   "
"   6   "   "   "   " $\frac{15}{16}$ "   " $1\frac{1}{4}$ "   "
"   7   "   "   "   " $1\frac{5}{16}$ "   " $1\frac{5}{8}$ "   "
"   8   "   "   "   " $1\frac{11}{16}$ "   " 2 "   "

TOOL MAKING.

Hardening. If but a few taps are to be hardened at a time, it is customary to heat them in a gas jet or an open fire of charcoal or hard coal. It is advisable, however, to heat the taps gradually in a tube. They may be plunged one at a time into the bath a little above the threads. The tap should be worked up and down and around in the bath to prevent soft spots. Taps

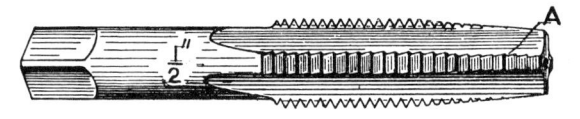

Fig. 89.

1 inch diameter and smaller should be left in the bath until cold; if larger they may be removed from the bath as soon as the singing noise ceases, and immediately plunged in oil and left until cold. For taps less than $\frac{1}{4}$ inch diameter, the citric acid bath will be found satisfactory; for larger taps use strong brine.

To have the tap retain as nearly as possible its size and correctness of pitch, use the "pack hardening" process. Run taps

Fig. 90.

$\frac{1}{8}$ inch diameter and smaller, $\frac{1}{2}$ hour after they are red hot; taps $\frac{1}{8}$ to $\frac{1}{4}$ inch diameter, 1 hour; taps $\frac{1}{4}$ to $\frac{1}{2}$ inch diameter, $1\frac{1}{4}$ hours; taps larger than one inch diameter, 2 hours. Harden in a bath of raw linseed oil.

It is advisable to grind the flutes of the taps with an emery wheel of the proper shape in order to brighten the surface, so that the color may be readily seen when drawing the temper. It also sharpens the cutting edges and breaks the burrs that have been thrown between the teeth when cutting the flutes. The temper should be drawn to a full straw color. Much more satisfactory results may be obtained by heating the taps in a kettle of oil, drawing the temper to a point from 460° to 500°, according to the size of the tap and the nature of the stock to be cut.

MACHINE TAPS.

As the name implies, machine taps are intended for screw machines, tapping machines, and lathes. They are held in chucks or collets by their shanks, and are supported firmly. Consequently the lands may be made narrower than those of hand taps to make them offer less surface to the work, thereby reducing the amount of frictional resistance. Also, they may be relieved between the teeth, by filing with a sharp cornered three square file, commencing at the heel of the tooth and filing nearly to the cutting edge.

Fig. 91.

It is not good practice to relieve the teeth very much because chips may be drawn between the work and the lands when backing out of the work. When taps are to be used in an automatic tapping machine without reverse motion the shanks are left long as shown in Fig. 90 in order that the nuts may pass over the thread and on to the shank. When this is full the tap is taken from the machine and the nuts removed; this can be readily done as they will pass over the end of the shank.

If a tap is to be used on nuts whose holes are punched to size, much better results are obtained by using a tap having five flutes, as shown in Fig. 91, instead of four. The uneven number of cutting edges reduce the liability of an imperfectly tapped hole, while the extra land furnishes additional support.

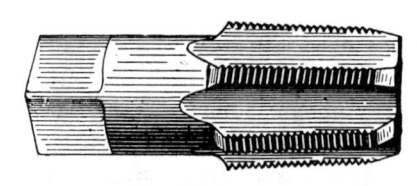

Fig. 92.

Taper Taps. When cutting the threads of a taper tap, Fig. 92, it is necessary to use a lathe having a taper attachment, as the pitch of the threads is not correct if the taper is obtained by setting over the tail stock. Like machine taps, the teeth of a taper must be relieved back of the cutting edge.

In setting the threading tool for cutting taper taps, care

should be taken that it is square with the axis of the tap, rather than square with the taper sides.

Screw Die Hobs. Die hobs are finish taps for sizing the thread in screw cutting dies. The several flutes are narrower than those of an ordinary tap and the lands are correspondingly wider. The tap shown in Fig. 93 has eight flutes. The increased number and broader lands support the tap while running through dies whose clearance holes are drilled, in order to remove burrs thrown in the threads when drilling. It is customary to give screw die hobs six to ten flutes.

When hobs are used for solid dies they must be of exact size. When intended for tapping adjustable dies, such as are ordinarily used for cutting threads in screw machine work, the hobs are made

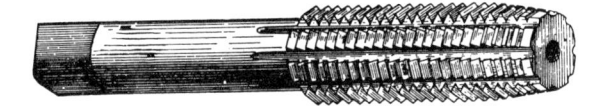

Fig. 93.

from .003 to .005 inch above the size of the screw to be cut. The extra size gives relief to the threads of the die.

While it is generally considered advisable to run one or more taps through a die before the hob, some tool makers consider it better to make a hob that will do all the cutting, claiming that

Fig. 94.

no two taps can be made and hardened so that the pitch will be exactly the same. In such cases a hob (Fig. 94) is made that will cut a full thread by passing through the die.

Some manufacturers cut the thread tapering for about three-quarters of the entire length of the thread, leaving the balance straight for use in sizing the die. Others cut the thread straight and taper the outside of the thread for three-quarters its entire length. If the threads are cut tapering, they must be relieved back of the cutting edges, as already described.

ADJUSTABLE TAPS.

A solid tap made to cut to exact size, having no leeway for wear, soon becomes too small. This is overcome by making a tap that may be adjusted from time to time. Another reason for making taps adjustable is that the holes may be tapped to fit hardened screws which vary in size on account of having been hardened.

Probably the most common form of adjustable tap is the one shown in Fig. 95. This tap is made in one piece, and then split. It has some means of adjustment whereby the tap may be expanded or contracted through a limited range. This may be accomplished by using a taper bodied screw. The hole to receive the screw should be drilled, tapped and taper reamed, before the

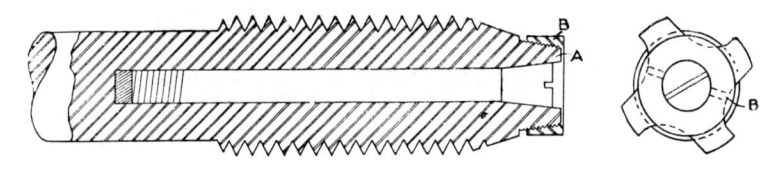

Fig. 95.

tap is turned to size. The thread should then be cut and the taper thread cut on the end at A. There is less tendency to spring when the tap is hardened if the projection shown in Fig. 96 is provided; this may be ground off after the tap is hardened and tempered. After cutting the flutes, the tap may be split in the milling machine using a metal slitting saw; the tap should be held between centers. It is split on two opposite sides, as shown at B, Fig. 95. The splitting should not go to the end of the projection.

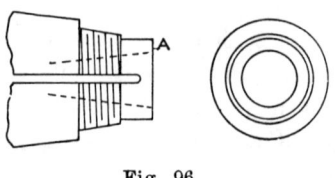

Fig. 96.

For hardening taps "Pack Hardening" is the best method. But, if it is impossible to use this method, heat the tap very carefully in a muffler furnace, or in a tube, having previously plugged the hole for the adjusting screw with fire-clay mixed with water to the consistency of dough. When the tap is heated to the proper degree it should be dipped in a bath of luke-warm brine, and worked up and down rapidly. After hardening, it should be ground in the flutes, and the temper drawn to a full straw color. The projection on the end may be ground off, the taper screw inserted, and the locking nut B, Fig. 95, screwed to place. This nut has a taper thread cut inside to correspond with the thread on the tap at A, Fig. 95. It will be found necessary to cut the taper thread on the tap and in the nut by means of the taper attachment.

Inserted Blade Taps. The first cost of an inserted blade

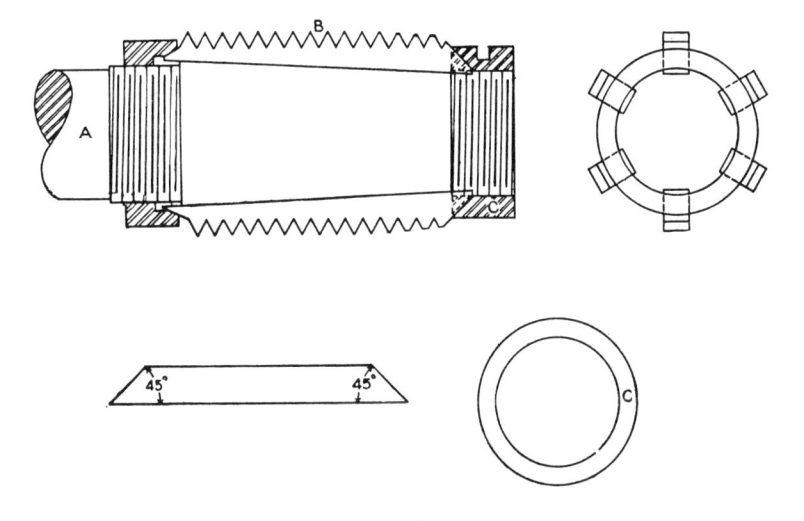

Fig. 97.

tap may not be much less than that of a solid tap of the same size, yet on account of the comparatively small cost of new blades which can be inserted in the same body, or holder, when the first set becomes worn, this form is very valuable for taps larger than $1\frac{1}{2}$ inches diameter. The tap shown in Fig. 97 may also be used as an adjustable tap. The shank or holder A is made of machinery steel, and the adjusting collars C C are beveled on the inside at one end at an angle corresponding to the angle on the ends of the blades. An angle of 45° will be found satisfactory.

After turning the body, or holder to size, and cutting the threads to receive the nuts, the slots for the blades may be milled;

these should be cut deeper at the cutting end in order that any change in the location of the blades may alter the size of the tap. A taper of $\frac{1}{16}$ inch in three inches is ample. If the slots are milled on the universal milling machine, and the tap held in the universal centers the spiral head may be depressed sufficiently to give the desired angle. If a pair of centers of the form shown in Fig. 98 are used they may be held in the milling machine vise at

Fig. 98.

the desired angle. The milling cutter should be set about $\frac{1}{32}$ inch ahead of the center in order that the face of the blade may be milled enough to take any inequality in the teeth at the cutting face of the blade occasioned by the thread tool striking the face

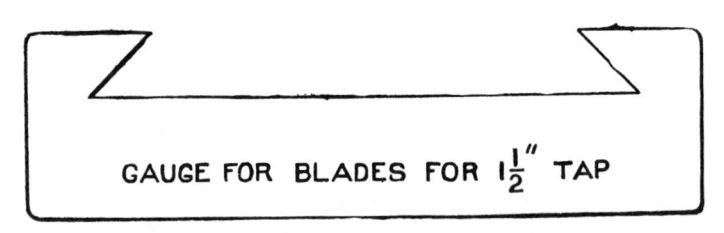

Fig. 99.

when it starts to cut. The amount milled from the face should be just enough to leave the cutting face radial. The blades should be of an exact length and should fit accurately in the slots. A gauge of the form shown in Fig. 99 will insure uniform length. After the blades have been carefully fitted to the slots and to the gauge, they may be inserted in the holder and secured by the nuts as shown in Fig. 97. The outside diameter is then turned about

.005 inch smaller than the size the tap is to cut and the threads very carefully cut; after which the face of the blades may be milled as explained, the cutting end chamferred, and the necessary amount of clearance given the cutting edges by filing. The blades are now ready for hardening.

When hardening, the blades should be subjected to a slow heat in a muffler furnace, or a tube. When a blade reaches a low uniform red heat, it should be immersed in a bath of luke-warm water or brine, and worked up and down to insure uniform results. After hardening it may be brightened and drawn to a deep straw color. It is well to place all the blades in a pan having a long handle, as shown in Fig. 100. Coarse sand to a depth of about $1\frac{1}{2}$

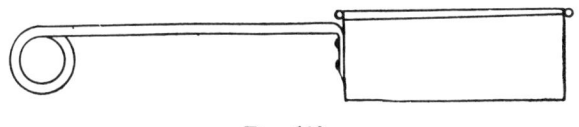

Fig. 100.

inches may be placed in the bottom of the pan with the blades. The pan should be placed over a bright fire and shaken carefully so that the teeth will not be dulled by striking the other hardened blades, while the sand and the blades are heating. The motion causes it to heat uniformly and the sand keeps the surface of the work bright so that the temper colors may be readily seen. This method of drawing temper will be found very satisfactory on many classes of work. It is also used extensively when coloring pieces by heat where a great many pieces are to be colored uniformly.

Square Thread Taps. Although the square thread is not as extensively used as formerly, having given place in many shops to the "Acme Standard," yet it is sometimes necessary to make taps for this form.

Steel should be selected sufficiently large and the decarbonized portion removed; the shank should be turned to size. The square should be milled for a wrench and the size and number of threads per inch stamped on the shank. The cutting end of the tap should be turned to size, the necessary amount of taper given the tap and then the threads cut

72 TOOL MAKING.

The tool used for cutting square threads is similar in form to a cutting-off (parting) tool except for its angle of side rake; it should be made of the proper thickness at the point but should be somewhat narrower back of the cutting end, as shown in Fig. 101, in order that it may clear when cutting.

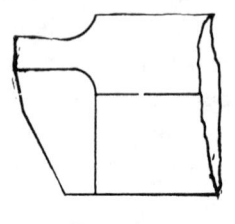

Fig. 101.

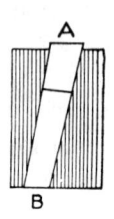

Fig. 102.

The thickness of the cutting end should be one half the distance from the edge of one thread to the corresponding edge of the next thread. For a square thread of 2 pitch, the land and space together would be $\frac{1}{2}$ inch, while the land and space would each be $\frac{1}{4}$ inch wide. The point of the tool would be $\frac{1}{4}$ inch thick.

The sides of the tools from A to B, Fig. 102, must be inclined to the body as shown, the amount of the inclination depending upon the pitch of the thread and diameter of the tap to be cut. It may be determined, however, by the method shown in Fig. 103. Draw the line A B, and at right angles to it draw C D, whose length must be equal to the circumference of the thread to be cut, measured at the bottom or root of the thread. On A B lay off from the point C a distance E C equal to the pitch of the thread to be cut. Then draw the line D E, which will represent the angle of the side of the thread; the angle of the side of the cutting tool must be sufficiently greater to give the

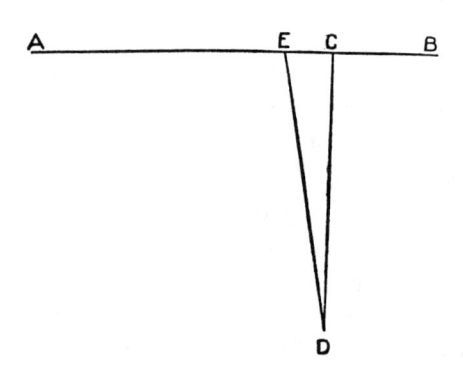

Fig. 103.

necessary clearance. It is advisable to cut the thread with a tool somewhat narrower than the required width at first, and finish with a tool of the proper thickness.

Square thread taps may be fluted according to directions given for V thread taps. If a tap is intended to cut a full thread, it must be well backed off, in order to avoid the necessity of using so much force that the tap would be broken. When a tap is to

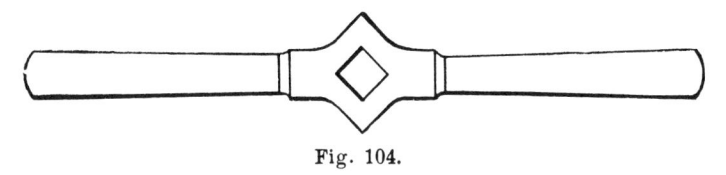

Fig. 104.

be used to size a hole whose thread has been cut by a smaller tap, very little clearance is necessary.

Tap Wrenches. When taps are used whose squares are all of a size, a solid tap wrench may be made, as shown in Fig. 104. This wrench is forged nearly to shape, the handles turned to size

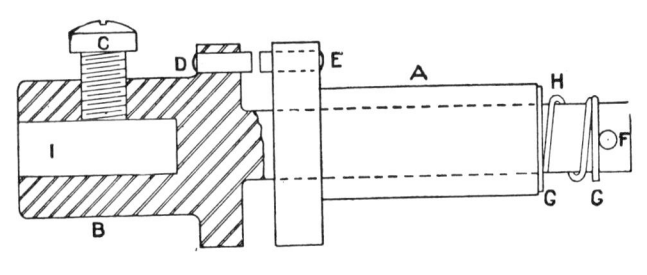

Fig. 105.

in the lathe, and the square hole in the center drilled and filed.

Releasing Tap Holders. When holes are to be tapped to a uniform depth in a screw machine or turret lathe, a tap holder is used which automatically releases the tap when it reaches the required depth. A very common form which gives excellent results when properly made and adjusted is shown in Fig. 105. It consists essentially of a sleeve A, which fits the tool holes in the turret of the screw machine, and the tap holder B, which fits the hole in the sleeve in such a manner as to slide longitudinally. The sleeve A should be made of tool steel if of a diameter that makes the wall around the hole thin; the hole should be drilled and reamed to size, and the outside turned to size. The portion of the sleeve which enters the hole in the turret should be a snug fit. The tap holder B should be made of tool steel, or of a grade of machinery steel possessing great stiffness and good wearing qualities. After roughing out to sizes somewhat larger than finish, the end which is to hold the tap may be turned to size and the (stem) end which is to run in the sleeve may be fitted, after which the hole I, to receive the tap may be made of a convenient size. In order that the hole may be perfectly concentric with the holder it will be necessary to run the large end of the holder in the steady rest of the lathe; the opposite end should be fastened against the head center of the lathe in such a manner that the stem runs perfectly true. With work of this nature, the head center of the lathe must be in good condition and run true.

After the hole has been drilled somewhat smaller than finish size, it is necessary to true the hole with a boring tool; the hole should be bored to within .010 inch of finish size, after which it may be reamed with a rose reamer. Before reaming, however, the outside edge of the hole should be chamferred to the shape of the point or cutting end of reamer, to avoid any possibility of the reamer running. Some tool makers never ream a hole of this nature if it can be avoided, always boring to size with a tool that makes a smooth cut; but if extreme care is used, results good enough for a tool of this character may be obtained if the holes are finished to size with a reamer.

TOOL MAKING.
PART II.

THREAD CUTTING DIES.

The size of a die is always denoted by the diameter of screw it will cut; a die that will cut a ½ inch screw is called a ½ inch die, irrespective of the outside diameter of the die itself.

Thread cutting dies are made solid or adjustable. Solid dies are used when extreme accuracy is not required. They are comparatively inexpensive, and may be used to advantage as a roughing die when an adjustable die is used for finishing. Owing to the tendency of dies to change their sizes when hardened, and to the fact that there is no provision for wear, they cannot be used

Fig. 106. 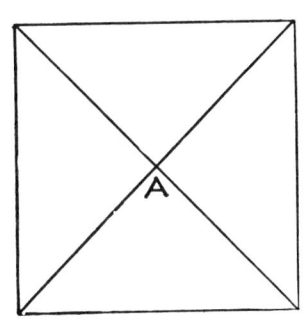   Fig. 107.

where work must be made to gauge. They are extensively used in cutting threads on bolts, and for this class of work are made square, as shown in Fig. 106.

In making a square die the blank may be machined to thickness and to size on the square edges. One of the flat surfaces should be coated with blue vitriol, or the blank may be heated until it shows a distinct brown or blue color. The center may be found by scribing lines across corners, as shown in Fig. 107. It should be prick punched at A where the lines intersect. The die blank may be clamped to the face plate of a lathe and made to run true by means of the center indicator. If there is no tap of the proper size, and only one die is to be made, the thread may be cut with an inside threading tool, provided the hole is of sufficient size; if not, a tap must be made. If the thread is cut with a threading tool, the size must be determined by means of a male gauge, which may be a screw of the proper size. After threading, the hole should be chamferred to a depth of three to four threads, the amount depending on the pitch of the thread; a fine pitch not requiring as many threads chamferred as a coarse pitch. The chamferring should not be much larger on the face of the die than the diameter of the screw to be cut. Figs. 108 and 109 show two views of a die chamferred and relieved on the cutting edges. The chamferring may be done with a countersink or taper reamer of the proper angle. In the absence of such a cutter, a tool held in the tool post of the lathe may be used.

Fig. 108. 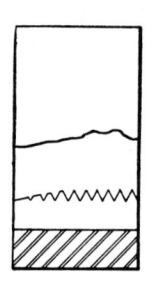   Fig. 109.

Most manufacturers making dies for the market give four cutting edges to all sizes up to and including four inches. When dies are made in the shop where they are to be used, custom varies. Some tool makers advocate three cutting edges for all dies smaller than $\frac{1}{4}$ inch, and five or more cutting edges for dies above two inches. The objection to more cutting edges than are absolutely needed on large dies is the increase in the cost of making.

When making dies for threading tubing, or for work where part of the circumference is cut away, it is better to give them a greater number of cutting edges than would otherwise be the case.

Rake of Cutting Edges. For general shop work, where the dies are to be used for all kinds of stock, it is advisable to make the cutting edges radial as shown in Fig. 110, the cutting edges

TOOL MAKING.

A A A A all pointing to the center. For cutting brass castings, the cutting edges should have a slight negative rake as shown in Fig. 111, the cutting edges A A A A all pointing back of the center.

Clearance Holes. After threading and countersinking (chamferring), screw in a piece of steel threaded to fit the die, and face it off flush. Lay out the centers of the clearance holes

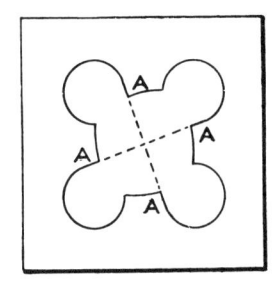

Fig. 110.

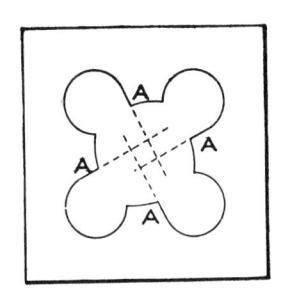

Fig. 111.

on the back of the die, and drill with a small drill the size of the pilot of a counterbore whose body will cut the right size for the clearance hole. The centers of these holes for dies having four cutting edges, and from $\frac{3}{8}$ to $\frac{3}{4}$ inch may be the intersections of a circle having a diameter equal to the diameter of the screw to be cut, and lines drawn across the corners as shown in Fig. 112. Prick punch these points. For a die having four clearance holes whose centers are laid out as shown in Fig. 112, it is customary to make the clearance holes one half the size of the die; that is the size of clearance holes in a $\frac{1}{2}$ inch die would be $\frac{1}{4}$ inch. The width A, Fig. 113, of the top of the lands should be about $\frac{1}{16}$ of the circumference of the screw to be cut. The

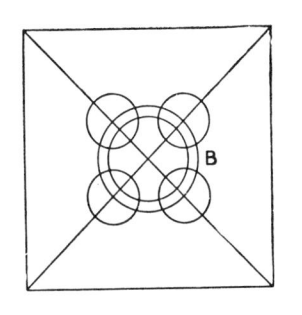

Fig. 112.

diameter of clearance holes given does not apply to dies smaller or larger than sizes given ($\frac{3}{8}$ to $\frac{3}{4}$ inch), especially if the dies are to be used in the screw machine, as the clearance hole not only provides a cutting edge, but also makes a convenient place for the chips; if these are so small that the oil cannot wash the chips out, the chips clog the holes and tear the thread.

For small dies the clearance holes are of a size that allows the chips to collect in the holes without tearing the threads, and are located a greater distance from the center of the die, in order to give sufficient strength to the lands. The desired shape and thickness may be given the sides of the lands by filing. When it is considered advisable to give screw dies above $\frac{3}{4}$ inch larger clearance holes than the size mentioned, they may be located at a distance from the center of the die that will give the desired thickness to the land.

Fig. 113.

For screw machine and turret lathe work, dies are generally made circular, and as holders for dies are part of the equipment of every shop having screw machines, the dies should be made to fit these holders; but it is not considered good practice to make the diameter of dies less than $2\frac{1}{2}$ times the diameter of the screw to be cut, and the thickness of the die may be $1\frac{1}{4}$ times the diameter of the screw.

ADJUSTABLE DIES.

While round dies for screw machine work may be made solid for roughing out a thread that is to be finished by another die, the finish die should be made adjustable in order that the desired size may be obtained. When making adjustable dies the same general instructions may be followed that are given for making solid dies, except that some provision must be made for adjustment. This is done by splitting the dies at one side as shown at A in Fig. 114. In order that the die may not spring out of shape in hardening, it is advisable to cut the slot from the center of the die, leaving a thin margin as shown at A, Fig. 115; after the die is hardened this may be cut away with a beveled emery wheel. If the thickness at B is too great to allow the die to close readily when ad-

TOOL MAKING. 79

justed to size, the hole shown may be drilled and connected with the clearance hole by means of a saw cut.

If many round dies of the same diameter are to be made it is economical to have a holder with a shank which fits the hole in the spindle of the lathe; the opposite end should be made to

Fig. 114.

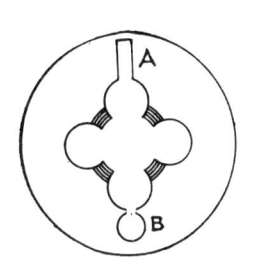

Fig. 115.

receive the die blanks which should be turned to fit the die holder in the screw machine. Fig. 116 shows the holder to be used in the lathe. A represents a die blank in the holder; B is the shank which fits in the spindle of the lathe; C is a recess in the holder to provide for the projection left on the blank when it is cut from

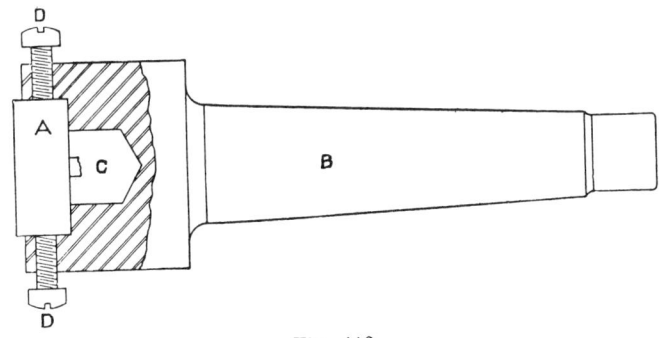

Fig. 116.

the bar and also provide an opening to receive the drill and tap after they run through the die. After the blank is placed in the holder and secured in position by the screw D, the outer surface may be faced smooth and true with the circumference, after which it may be reversed and the opposite side finished to the proper thickness. The die may now be drilled and tapped. Before drilling, the die should be carefully centered in the lathe; to insure a full thread in the die, a drill a few thousandths of an inch smaller than tap size should be used in drilling, after which a reamer of the proper size may be run through. When tapping the thread, it is advisable to use two or three taps of different sizes; the finish tap should be the size of the desired hole in the die, and should be of the form known as screw die hob. Where several taps are used in tapping a die, there should be some difference in the diameter so that any inequality in the shape or pitch of the thread may be removed by the larger tap, otherwise imperfect threads will result. For instance if three taps are to be used for a $\frac{1}{4}$ inch die, the first tap may be .230 inch diameter; the second .240 inch diameter, and the finish tap .250 inch diameter if the die is to be solid. If it is to be an adjustable die, the

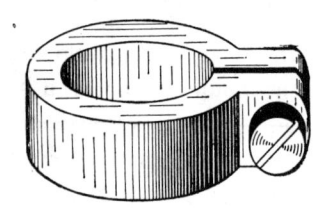

Fig. 117. 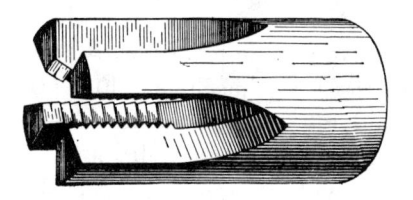   Fig. 118.

finish tap should be .253 inch diameter in order to furnish clearance to the lands when it is closed to .250 inch.

Dies should be heated very slowly for hardening, either in a muffler furnace, or in some receptacle to protect it from the action of the fire. When the die is heated to a uniform low red it may be immersed in a bath of lukewarm brine and worked back and forth to insure hardening the threads. The temper should be drawn to a full straw color. If it is an adjustable die the portion marked B, Fig. 115, should be drawn to a blue color in order that it may spring without breaking; this may be done by placing this portion of the die on a red hot iron plate, or the jaws of a heavy pair of tongs may be heated red hot, the die may be grasped in the tongs and held until the desired color appears. Do not allow the blue color to extend to the threads or they will be too soft. When the desired color has been obtained the die may be dropped into oil to prevent drawing the temper more than is desired.

TOOL MAKING.

Spring Screw-threading Dies. This form of die is adjusted by means of the clamp collar shown in Fig. 117; the die is shown in Fig. 118. In some shops it is the only form of screw-threading die used for screw machine work. When so used it should be fitted to one of the holders on hand, provided there be one of the proper size.

Average proportions of spring dies are given in the following table; these sizes are used by a manufacturing concern using a great many screw-threading dies of this description. It is not necessary to follow the proportions given, as they are intended only as a guide, and may be changed to suit circumstances. All dimensions are in inches.

SPRING SCREW-THREADING DIES.

Size of Screw.	Outside Diameter.	Length.
$\frac{1}{8}$ to $\frac{1}{4}$	$\frac{1}{2}$	$1\frac{1}{4}$
$\frac{1}{4}$ to $\frac{3}{8}$	$\frac{3}{4}$	$1\frac{3}{4}$
$\frac{3}{8}$ to $\frac{1}{2}$	1	2
$\frac{1}{2}$ to $\frac{3}{4}$	$1\frac{1}{4}$	$2\frac{1}{4}$
$\frac{3}{4}$ to 1	$1\frac{5}{8}$	$2\frac{1}{2}$
1 to $1\frac{1}{4}$	2	3
$1\frac{1}{4}$ to $1\frac{1}{2}$	$2\frac{1}{2}$	$3\frac{1}{2}$
$1\frac{1}{2}$ to 2	$3\frac{1}{4}$	4

For uniform and well-finished threads, two dies should be used, one for roughing, and one for finishing.

Where many dies of a size are made it is best to have a holder with a shank fitting the center hole of some lathe. The stock can be machined to size and cut to length. The clearance hole in the back of the die should be first drilled somewhat larger than the diameter of the screw to be cut. For dies up to and including $\frac{1}{8}$ inch the clearance holes should be $\frac{1}{32}$ inch large; for dies $\frac{1}{8}$ to $\frac{1}{4}$ inch it should be $\frac{3}{64}$ inch large; for dies $\frac{1}{2}$ inch and over, it should be from $\frac{1}{16}$ to $\frac{1}{8}$ inch large. After drilling the clearance hole, the die should be reversed in the holder, and drilled and tapped the same as a round die, using a hob to finish the threads to size. For general work, the die should have four cutting edges making the lands about one-sixteenth the circumference of the screw to be cut. Chamfer about three threads. The length of the threaded portion of the die should not exceed one and one-quarter times the diameter of the screw to be cut. To produce the cutting edges, use a 45° double angle milling cutter shown in Fig. 119; this cutter should be of sufficiently large diameter to produce a cut as shown in Fig. 120.

The chamferred edges should be relieved and the cutting edges finished with a fine file. Stamp the size and number of threads on the back end of the die as shown in Fig. 120 and then harden. The die should be heated in a tube and hardened in a jet of water coming up from the bottom of a tank in order that the water may enter the threaded portion. It should be hardened a little farther up than the length of the thread, moving up and down in the bath to prevent a water line; the temper should be drawn to a full straw color.

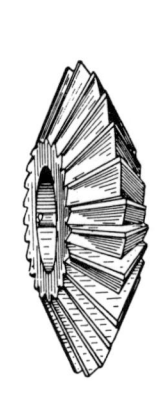

Fig. 119. 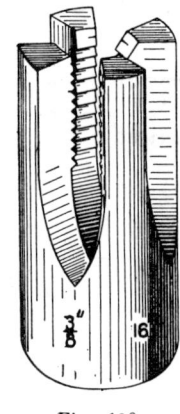   Fig. 120.

Where many clamp collars are used, castings of malleable iron or gun metal may be made from a pattern; the hole should be cored to within $\frac{1}{16}$ inch of finish size. The hole may then be drilled and reamed. When the screw hole has been drilled and tapped and the collar split, it is ready to use. If the surfaces are finished it adds very materially to the cost.

Die Holders. When cutting threads in screw machines and turret lathes, dies are held in die holders which are constructed in two parts as shown in Fig. 121. The shank A fits the hole in the turret, while the die holder B has a stem that fits the hole in the shank. While the die is cutting, the pins D and C are engaged, thus preventing the holder B from turning. When the turret slide of the screw machine has traveled to its limit, the holder is drawn out of the shank until the machine is reversed when the pins engage on their opposite sides. A pin is put through the stem of the holder at E; this strikes the end of shank just at the time the pins D and C become disengaged.

Both shank and body may be made of machinery steel; the shank may be finished to size except the portion marked A, which should be left .010 inch large for grinding. The front end of the hole should be rounded as shown in Fig. 121, to allow the fillet in the shoulder of the stem to enter. This fillet is left for strength. The pin hole should be drilled and reamed. When the holders are to take dies not over $\frac{1}{8}$ inch in size, this pin hole may be $\frac{3}{16}$ inch diameter; from $\frac{1}{8}$ to $\frac{5}{16}$ in size, $\frac{1}{4}$ inch diameter. As the dies

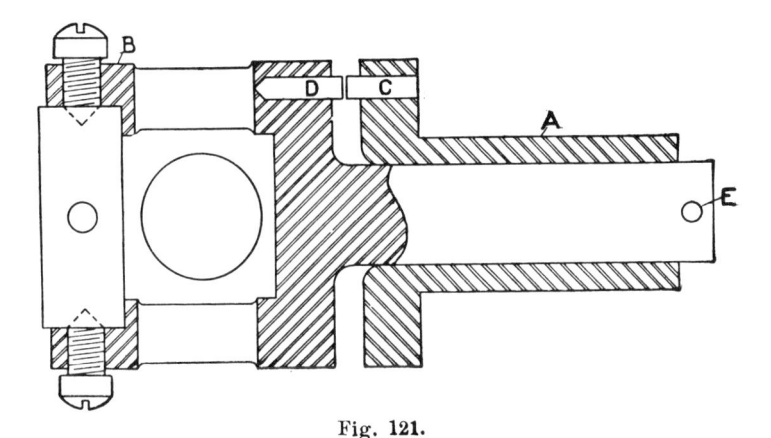

Fig. 121.

increase in size the pin must increase proportionately. The shank may be case-hardened in a mixture of granulated charred leather and charcoal; it should run about two hours and then be dipped in a bath of oil. The hole should be lapped straight and true. The outside ground to fit the hole in the turret. The pin C should be of tool steel hardened and drawn to a blue color, and forced into place.

The holder B may be made from a forging, or turned from a solid piece. After roughing to size somewhat larger than finish, the stem may be turned and fitted to the hole in the shank; it should turn *freely* in the shank. The larger portion (or body) should now be turned to size. This should be run in the steady rest, and the end drilled and bored for the die and for clearance back of the die as shown in Fig. 121. Three or four large holes should be drilled into the clearance hole in order that the chips and oil may find a way of escape, thus preventing injury to the threads of a screw long enough to reach through the die when being threaded.

Screw holes should be drilled and tapped as shown in Fig. 121; the screws are to hold the die in position in the holder and also to adjust to size dies that are split. The stem may be placed in the shank and the pin hole transferred through the pin hole in

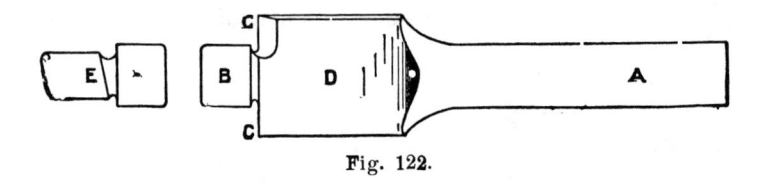

Fig. 122.

the shank into the body; this should be done before the pin C is pressed into place. The pin D should be hardened the same as C.

The pin hole for the pin E may be drilled in a location that allows C and D to become disengaged and yet have no play between the two

COUNTERBORES.

Counterbores are used for enlarging a hole without changing its relative position. For a *hurry up* job and for a small number of holes, it is advisable to make as cheap a form as is consistent with the work to be done. Probably the cheapest counterbore that will do satisfactory work is the flat form shown in Fig. 122. This can be forged to require but little machine work. After forging, turn to size; finish the shank A and pilot B with a fine file before taking from the lathe. The cutting edges C C should be faced true and smooth. The necking between the pilot and the body should be cut with a tool having the corners slightly rounded to decrease the liability of cracking when the counterbore is hardened. The flat sides D of the body may be finish filed; the edges should be draw-filed, removing more stock on the back than on the cutting edge to prevent binding. File the cutting edges C C for clearance, as shown at E, Fig. 122. The

TOOL MAKING.

pilot and the body should be hard the entire length or they will wear and rough up and consequently cannot cut a smooth hole; draw the temper to a full straw color. Unless intended for *accurate* work it need not be ground.

For permanent equipment, counterbores are usually made with four cutting edges as shown in Fig. 123 and Fig. 124. Fig. 123 representing a taper shank counterbore for a taper collect, while Fig. 124 has a straight shank to be used in a chuck, or collet having a straight hole the size of the shank.

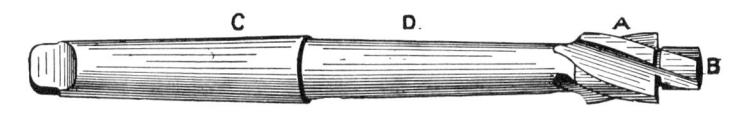

Fig. 123.

Counterbores for screw holes are usually made in sets of three, one for the head of the screw with pilot (or guide) of body size, one for head with pilot of tap drill size, and one to enlarge a tap drill hole to body size. The following instructions apply to counterbores with either straight or taper shanks. Take stock somewhat larger than finish size of counterbore.

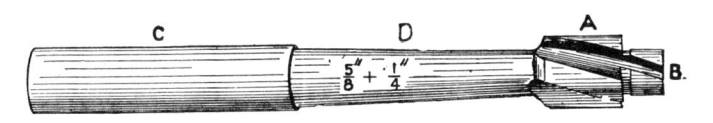

Fig. 124.

Turn a roughing chip all over the piece; turn the necked portion between the shank and body to size and stamp size of counterbore and pilot as shown in Fig. 124; turn shank C, body A, and pilot B .015 to .020 inch above finish sizes, to allow for grinding. In the case of the taper shank counterbore shown in Fig. 123 the tennon should be milled. The counterbore is now ready to have the grooves milled to form the cutting edges. One method is to cut them with a right-hand spiral of from 10° to 15°; the other method is to cut the grooves straight. The former has he effect of running chips back from the cutting edges and works very well on wrought iron and steel, while the latter method is considered more satisfactory for brass and cast iron and also works well on wrought iron and steel. The cutting edges are given clearance by filing, as shown at A in Fig. 125. If the counterbore is to be used for brass it is necessary to give clearance to the lands also as shown at A A A A, Fig. 126.

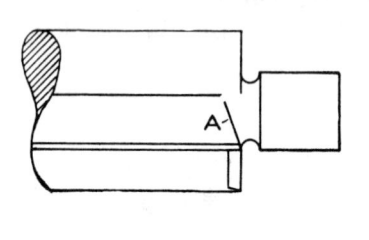

Fig. 125.

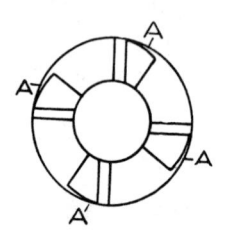

Fig. 126.

When centering counterbores or any tools whose centers are not to be used after the tool is finished, the drill should be small and the countersinking no larger than is necessary for good results in machining. If large centers should, by accident, be put in the ends, the one on the end to be hardened should be filled with fire clay moistened with water to the consistency of dough, or with graphite mixed with oil; this prevents steam forming in the

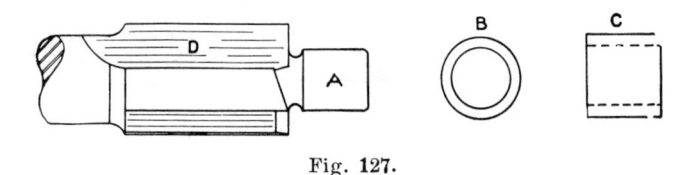

Fig. 127.

hole and cracking the tool when dipped in the bath. If the piece is to be heated in lead, the filling should be dried thoroughly before immersing in the red-hot lead.

Solid counterbores can be used with holes larger than the pilot by forcing a sleeve over it as shown in Fig. 127. B and C are two views of the sleeve which is to be forced on to pilot A. After hardening, the counterbore may be ground to size on the shank, body and pilot; the shank should be ground first as the length is greater, and in the case of a counterbore having a straight shank the grinder may be adjusted to perfect alignment by measurement.

Two lipped counterbores are sharpened by grinding on the flat faces marked D, Fig. 122. Grind a four-lipped counterbore on the flat side of the groove as D in Fig. 127.

Facing Tool with Inserted Cutter. Where a limited number of holes are to be counterbored, the tool shown in Fig. 128

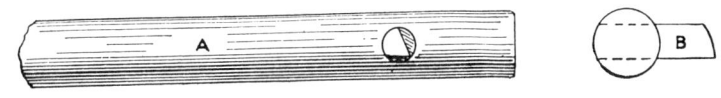

Fig. 128.

may be made. All that is necessary in making this tool is a piece of stock A, the size of the hole to be counterbored and a piece of drill rod for the cutter B; this may be filed to a cutting edge, hardened and driven in place. If accuracy is essential, a piece of drill rod must be cut off somewhat longer than the diameter of the required hole; it should be driven into the hole in the bar leaving an equal length on each side. It may be turned to the correct diameter and filed to shape. If several cutters are to be used in the same bar, or if the tool is to be used as a facing bar, to square a shoulder inside a piece of work as shown in Fig. 129, the cutter B is removed from the bar and after the bar is in place it is inserted and held by set screw C.

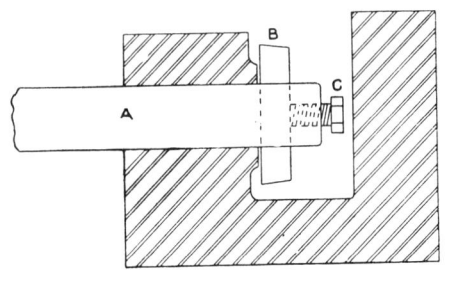

Fig. 129.

For large work, a counterbore may be made as shown in Fig. 130, A being the cutter bar which should be made of tool steel $\frac{1}{16}$ to $\frac{1}{8}$ inch larger than finish size. After taking a roughing chip, leaving it a trifle large, the slot should be made to receive the cutter C. This is done by drilling a series of holes as shown in Fig. 131. After prick punching the bar, it should be clamped to a drill press table, holding the bar in a pair of V blocks. The prick punch marks should be set in a position that will insure the

88   TOOL MAKING.

drill holes going through the center of the bar; this can be done as follows: place the square against one side of the bar, measure to the center, then place the square against the opposite side and measure in the same manner. When the distance is the same on each side from the square blade to the centers, the piece is in the proper position for drilling. The drill press table may then be swung around until the prick punch marks are in proper location

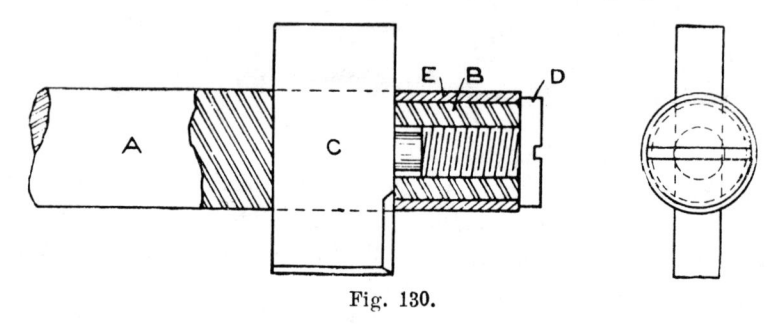

Fig. 130.

with the spindle of the press. After drilling, a drift may be driven through to break the walls separating the holes and the slot filed to size. The bar should be placed with one end in the steady rest and the other end strapped to the head center of the

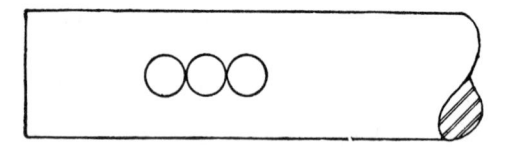

Fig. 131.

lathe. The screw hole in the end is now drilled and tapped into the slot in order that the screw may bind the cutter. The end should be countersunk to provide a center for finish turning. The bar may be turned to size at A and the pilot finished to size. The screw D should have a head $\frac{1}{16}$ inch larger than the part B in order that it may hold the sleeve in place, should it have a tendency to come off when removing the counterbore from the hole. The cutter C should be a close fit in the slot. A headless screw should be made short, so that it will not interfere with the dead center of the lathe when it is screwed to place against the cutter blank. It is intended to be used when turning the cutter to the right diameter, and should be kept for that purpose.

Counterbores with Inserted Pilots are useful when the counterbores need frequent sharpening, or when a variety of different sized holes are to be counterbored to the same size. A

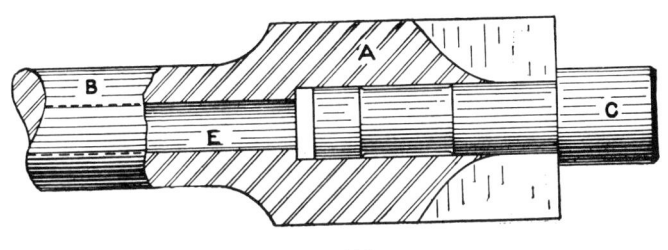

Fig, 132.

common form of counterbore having an inserted pilot is shown in Fig. 132.

When making this counterbore the stock should have a roughing chip taken off and the hole E drilled part way from the shank end. This drilling may be done in the speed lathe, holding the drill in a chuck in the head spindle; the center in the opposite end of the piece should be on the dead center of the lathe. If the piece is turned one-half revolution occasionally the drill will cut accurately enough, as perfect alignment is not necessary in this hole, since it is intended only for use when driving out the pilot.

After drilling, the shank end should be carefully countersunk. The piece may now be turned to grinding size which should be from .015 to .020 inch all over. After turning the outside, the hole for the pilot may be drilled and bored, running the large end of the counterbore in the steady rest. The counterbore should have four cutting edges for all ordinary work; these

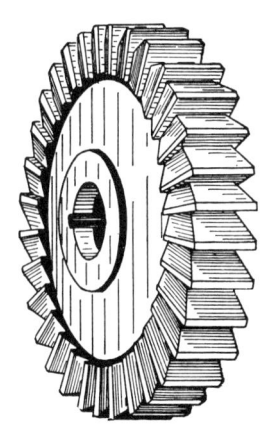

Fig. 133.

may be cut with a side milling cutter with a face sufficiently wide to cover the width of tooth. The form of cutter is shown in Fig. 133, while an end view of the teeth is shown in Fig. 134. When milling the teeth, the counterbore can best be held in the chuck on the spiral head. If a more stubbed form of tooth is needed than the one shown in Fig. 132, the spiral head may be tipped to the desired angle and the cutter fed through instead of sunk into the counterbore. After milling, the burrs should be removed, the counterbore stamped and hardened. While hardening, it should be heated to a red nearly the whole length of body; when dipped in the bath it should be inverted in order that the teeth may be uppermost, it should then be worked up and down rapidly in the bath until the red has entirely disappeared. It should be allowed to remain in the bath until cold. If larger than 1 inch diameter the *strain* should be removed immediately upon taking from the bath by heating over the fire as already explained. The pilot should be turned as shown in Fig. 135. A and BB should be left

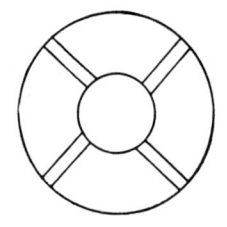

Fig. 134.

Fig. 135.

about .010 inch large for grinding after hardening; C should be turned $\frac{1}{32}$ inch smaller than the hole in the mill, as this does not bear when the pilot is in place. A slight depression should be made between the head and the first bearing point B for the emery wheel to pass over when grinding. When hardening, A is the only part that needs to be hard, but, unless a piece of tube is slipped over the stem B when the pilot is put in the bath it will be almost impossible to harden A the entire length and leave B soft. As A is likely to rough up when used it is best to harden a short distance on the stem B, unless there should be a great difference in size between A and B; in which case a tube, or a piece of iron with a hole drilled in the end the size of B and having the end beveled as shown in Fig. 136, should be slipped over B when the pilot is heated. This cover should be slipped over the stem and up against the shoulder of the head to prevent a *water line*;

TOOL MAKING.

if this precaution is taken there is no danger of pilot cracking under the head. After hardening and tempering, the pilot may be ground to size at A, and the portions B B ground to fit the hole of the counterbore. After grinding, the pilot may be forced into place. The counterbore may be ground with the pilot in position. When dull the pilot should be forced out of the counterbore and the cutting edges ground with an emery wheel.

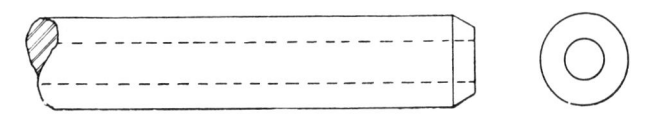

Fig. 136.

Combination Counterbores are made when it is necessary to change the size of counterbore and pilot frequently. A shank or bar is made to accommodate different sizes of cutters, and sleeves serve as pilots. In Fig. 137, A is the cutter, B the pilot which is tapped in the end to receive a screw which holds the sleeves, and C the shank which is held in a chuck or collet, when the counterbore is in use.

After taking a roughing chip off the bar, the end B is run in

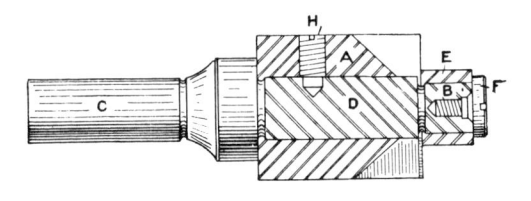

Fig. 137.

the steady rest and the hole for the screw F is drilled and tapped. The outside end is countersunk to a 60° angle to run on a center. When machining the holder, the portions B, C, and D should be left about .010 inch larger than finish size to allow for grinding. But if no grinder is at hand it may be left a few thousandths of an inch above size, and filed to finish dimensions.

The body (or cutter) A, should have a hole $\frac{1}{16}$ inch smaller than finish size drilled through it; the outside surface should be turned off, and the piece annealed. If a grinder having an inter-

TOOL MAKING.

nal grinding attachment is at hand, the hole in the cutter should be left .005 inch small for grinding. If such an attachment is not at hand the hole may be reamed to finish size. The outside diameter should be left about .010 large; the ends should be faced to length, and the teeth cut. If four teeth are to be cut, the work may be done with a side milling cutter as shown in Fig. 133. The counterbore should be held in a chuck on the spiral head

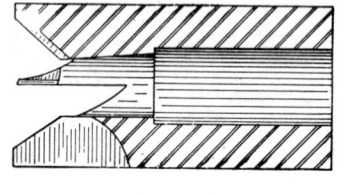

Fig. 138.

Fig. 140.

spindle, which should be tipped to produce a strong tooth as shown in Fig. 137. Before hardening, the hole should be drilled and tapped for the screw H which holds the counterbore to the bar. To harden, the counterbore should be given an even, low red heat, and plunged in water or brine in such a manner that the bath will come in contact with the teeth. If the teeth are stubbed

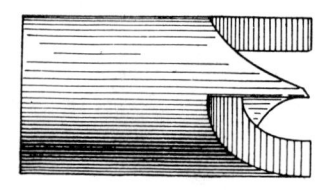

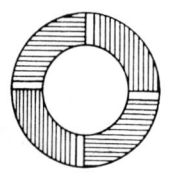

Fig. 139.

and strong the temper need not be drawn more than to a light straw color.

The screw H should be made of tool steel having a projection $\frac{1}{8}$ inch long on one end, turned to the bottom of the thread; this is to enter a hole drilled in the bar or holder, and keep the counterbore from turning. The end of the screw should be about .005 inch smaller than the hole. The screw should be hardened and drawn to a blue color. The sleeve intended to go on the pilot E should be made of tool steel, hardened and ground to size inside and out. The screw F may be made of machinery steel,

TOOL MAKING.

and case-hardened sufficiently deep by heating to a red and sprinkling with powdered cyanide of potassium, after which it is reheated and plunged in water.

HOLLOW MILLS.

Hollow mills are used in screw machines and turret lathes for roughing down and finishing. They are also used in drill press work in finishing a projection which must be in some given position; when thus used they are generally guided by a bushing in a fixture, to bring the projection in the proper location.

For roughing out work on a screw machine or turret lathe, solid mills having strong stubbed teeth are preferred for rigidity. For finishing they are made adjustable in order to get *exact* sizes. Fig. 138 shows a solid hollow mill having the cutting end hol-

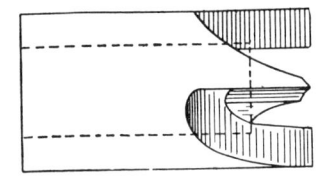

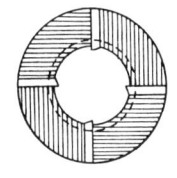

Fig. 141.

lowed out in the form of a V, in order that it may center itself when starting to cut. Fig. 139 shows a form of solid hollow mill intended for use in squaring up a shoulder at the end of a cut that has been made with a mill of the form shown in Fig. 138, or it may be used for roughing out a piece; however, it will not center itself as readily as the one shown in Fig. 138.

For small hollow mills some tool makers advocate three cutting teeth, while others claim better results with four teeth on all sizes.

The rear of the mill is bored somewhat larger than the cutting end, to allow it to clear on long cuts. The cutting end must be relieved or it will bind and rough the work, and probably twist it off in the mill. There are several methods of relieving mills; the more common one is to ream the hole tapering, making it larger at the back end, as shown in Fig. 140. Another method is to file back of the edges, as shown in Fig. 141.

For making hollow mills having the same outside diameter, it is advisable to use a holder of the form shown in Fig. 142, having a taper shank which fits the spindle of a lathe. The hole in the other end of the holder should be the size of the holder in the screw machine or turret lathe, which holds the mills when in use. The steel for the hollow mills should be cut to length and turned to the proper diameter to fit the holder. After putting the blank in the holder, the ends may be squared and the holes drilled and bored to the desired sizes. If the mill is to be of the form shown in Figs. 138, 139 and 140, the cutting end may be reamed with a taper reamer to give the necessary clearance. The reamer should be run in from the back end in order that this end of the hole be larger. For the form shown in Fig. 141, the hole at the cutting end should be straight and to finish size.

The mill is now ready for cutting the teeth. If four cutting edges are to be given, a side milling cutter may be used of a

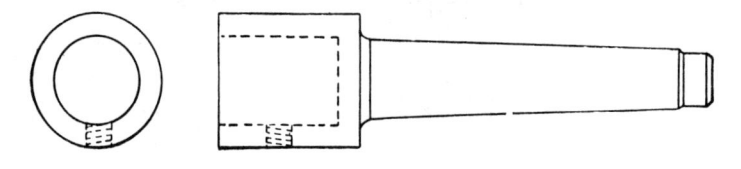

Fig. 142.

diameter about double the diameter of the hollow mill to be cut. The blank should be held in a chuck on the end of the spindle in the spiral head. For a strong tooth, the spiral head may be set at an angle that will produce a tooth as shown in Fig. 143, by feeding the milling cutter *through* the blank. If a deeper tooth is desired, the spiral head may be set so that the blank will be in a vertical position, and the milling cutter fed in until the desired form and depth of tooth is obtained.

An Adjustable Hollow Mill may be made by following the instructions given for *solid* hollow mills, except that the mill must be split as shown in Fig. 144, in order that the size of hole in the mill may be altered. There are two methods of adjusting the mill: the outside of the cutting end of the mill is tapered, and a collar having a corresponding taper hole is forced on the mill. The collar closes it, and causes it to cut smaller. The other method is to turn the outside of the hollow mill straight, and close by means of the clamp collar shown in Fig. 145. As adjustable hollow mills are generally used for finishing cuts, and are not used when taking heavy cuts, the teeth may be made finer than those of solid mills used for roughing. The teeth being nearer together will finish a cylindrical piece more accurately than if the teeth were cut farther apart. It is customary to give adjustable hollow mills to be used for finishing from six to eight teeth. The cutting edges should be cut radial for most work. Better results

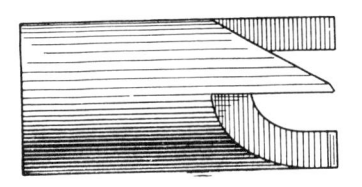

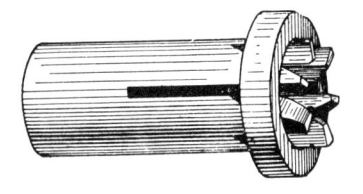

Fig. 143.

Fig. 144.

will be obtained if the hole in the cutting end of the mill is left .005 inch small, and ground to size after the mill is hardened.

The hollow mill, whether it be solid or adjustable, should be hardened a trifle farther up than the length of the teeth, and drawn to a straw color. The mill is sharpened by grinding on the ends of the teeth.

Hollow Mill with Inserted Blades. For large work, hollow mills are made having inserted blades. The hollow mill with removable blades, shown in Fig. 146, does good service on rough work; the blades

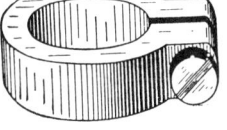

Fig. 145.

may be made of self hardening steel and inserted in a machine steel body. The grooves in the body to receive the blades should be milled with a cutter whose thickness corresponds to the size of the steel to be used for the blades. The grooves are cut somewhat deeper at the front end of the holder in order that the blades may have clearance to prevent binding. The edge of the slot corresponding to the cutting edge of the blade should be radial.

Two collars should be made of machinery steel having holes sufficiently large to allow their being placed on the mill when the blades are in the slots. Each collar should be provided with the same number of set screws as there are blades in the mill. One collar holds the blades in the holder, while the other is placed nearly at the ends of the blades to support them while cutting. This form of mill is used on cuts not exceeding one inch in length, as the blades must project beyond the holder to the desired length of the cut.

The size of cut may be changed somewhat by setting the cutters back or ahead in the slots, or paper may be placed in the slots under the blades to increase the diameter of the cut. The blades are set to an even length by bringing them against a surface perpendicular to the axis of the body of the tool.

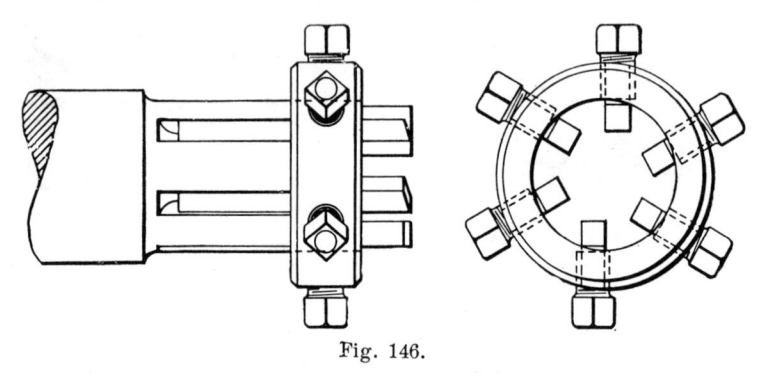

Fig. 146.

Hollow Mill with Pilot. It is often desirable to mill the outside of a projection central with a hole passing through it. This may be done very satisfactorily with a hollow mill having a pilot as shown in Fig. 147. It is advisable to hold the pilot in place by means of a set screw. In order to give clearance to the teeth to

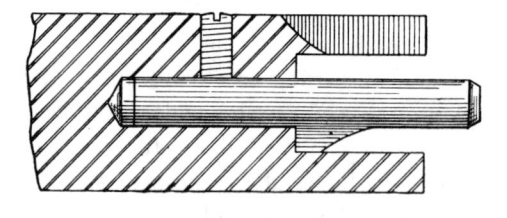

Fig. 147.

prevent the mill binding when cutting, the hole may be bored tapering .010 inch in $\frac{1}{2}$ inch of length, making it largest at the back end.

When hardening a mill of this description it is advisable to dip it in the bath with the cutting end *uppermost* working it up and down rapidly. After hardening, it may be drawn to a straw color. The pilot should be turned .010 inch above finish size, hardened, and drawn to a brown color, and ground to the desired dimensions.

FORMING TOOLS.

Forming tools are used when several pieces are to be made of exactly the same shape. They are particularly valuable for giving the desired shape to formed mills and similar tools and are extensively used in duplicating a given shape on work produced in the screw machine.

Forming tools are made flat and circular in shape. When used in the lathe for shaping milling machine cutters and similar tools they are generally made flat; for backing off formed milling machine cutters they are always made flat; for screw machines in duplicating a given shape they are made both flat and circular.

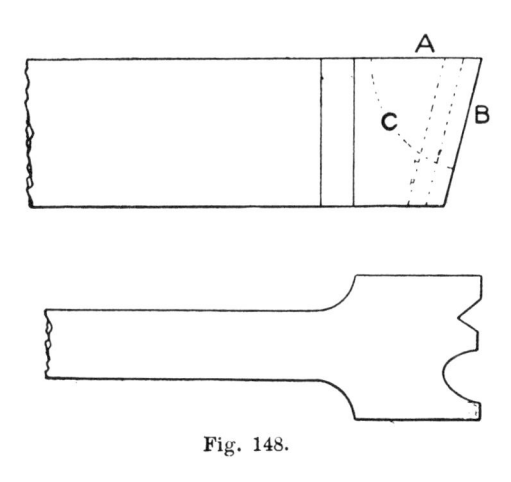

Fig. 148.

The flat forming tool is made as a solid cutter, the tool and shank being in one piece as shown in Fig. 148, or the cutter and shank may be made separate as shown in Fig. 149. When but one forming tool is to be made, that shown in Fig. 148 will be found to be inexpensive; but for making many tools, it will be found much cheaper to adopt the plan shown in Fig. 149.

On certain classes of work it is advisable to use a forming tool on a holder of the description shown in Fig. 150, which is known as a spring holder. On account of its design it may spring somewhat when used on heavy cuts, thus reducing the tendency to chatter. It is necessary to make these holders of tool steel, giving them a spring temper at point marked **A**. The slot

B allows the forming blade D to spring away from the work when under heavy strain. The blades may be planed up in long strips and cut off the required length. The tongue E should fit

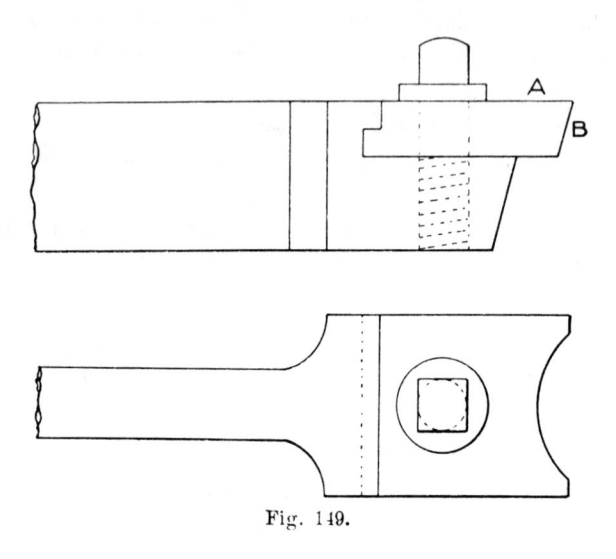

Fig. 149.

the slot O, which, with two cap screws through F and G, securely holds the blade in position.

In order that a forming tool may cut readily, it is necessary to give the surface marked B a sufficient amount of clearance.

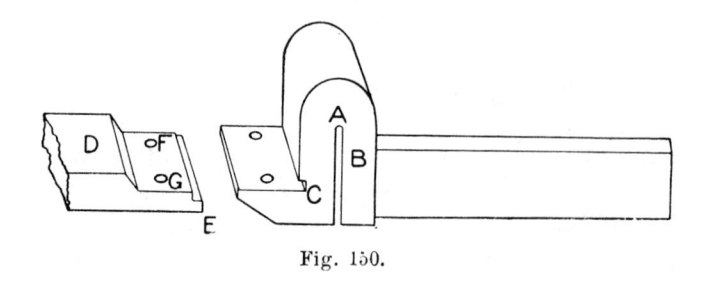

Fig. 150.

For tools to be used for shaping milling machine cutters and similar tools, a clearance of 10° to 15° will be ample; that is, the angle should be from 80° to 75°. But if the tool is to be used for backing off the teeth of formed milling machine cutters, it is necessary to give a clearance of 18° to 22°. When making a forming tool having the required angle at D, the shape can be produced by tipping the blank to the required angle and planing or milling with a tool having exactly the shape it is desired to produce. The tool used may be made of a shape enough different from that desired that it may produce the proper shape when the cutter is in a vertical position, and the blank at a given angle from that position as shown in Fig. 151. Or, the tool may be held in the tool post (or in a fixture made for the purpose) of the shaper or planer at the same angle as the blank being cut, as shown in Fig. 152, and it will produce a shape corresponding very closely with its own.

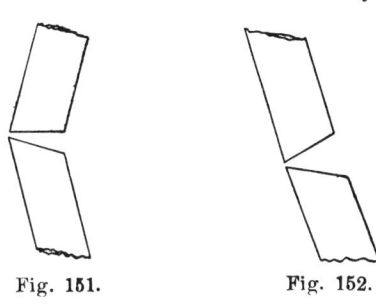

Fig. 151.   Fig. 152.

For screw machine and similar work for duplicating given shapes, a forming tool is made of the shape shown in Fig. 153. A represents a holder used by the Brown & Sharpe Mfg. Co. for use on their screw machines. B shows the forming tool blank. The desired shape is cut in the surface marked C.

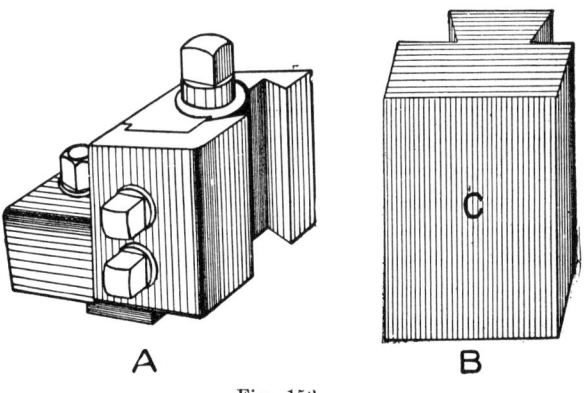

Fig. 153.

Circular Forming Tools are used very extensively on screw-machine and similar work. They are valuable on account of the ease with which any number of them may be produced, provided a forming tool is used in producing the shape on the face as shown in Fig. 154. After the blank has been formed to the desired shape, it may be milled as shown in Fig. 155 in order to provide a cutting edge. If it is desired to produce a shape on the piece being machined to correspond with the shape of tool, it is necessary to have the cutting edge radial as shown in Fig. 155. In order to feed the tool into the stock faster than can be done with the form shown in Fig. 155, it is given more clearance as shown in Fig 156. On a tool whose cutting edge is not radial and will not produce a shape corresponding to its own, it is necessary when cutting the edge with the rake shown in Fig. 156, to make the face of the tool slightly different in form from that desired.

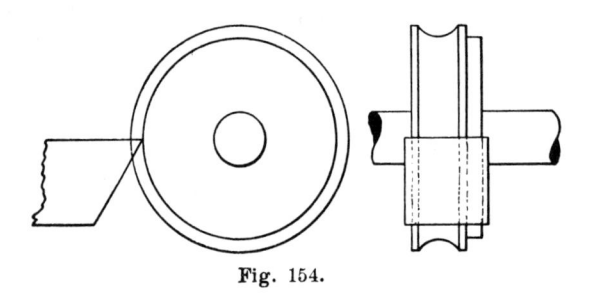

Fig. 154.

After milling the cutting edge, the name or number of the tool may be stamped on it, after which it is ready for hardening. When extremely high carbon steel is used, the tools sometimes crack while hardening from the strain incident to their shape. In order to overcome this tendency, some tool makers make two extra cuts in the edge as shown in Fig. 157, in order that the hardened edges may not be cracked from the contraction. Two cutting edges, as shown in Fig. 158 are often given tools in order that it may not need to be ground as often as when it has but one cutting edge. It is not necessary to stop the screw machine nearly as long to grind both cutting edges, as to stop the machine twice to grind the same edge on account of the time necessary to rig up the grinder.

When hardening, the tool should be heated to a low red and plunged in a bath of water or brine from which the chill has been removed; it should be worked around well in the bath. If

TOOL MAKING. 101

the temper is not to be drawn after hardening, the tool may be held over the fire after removing from the bath and heated sufficiently to remove the tendency to crack from internal strains.

On account of some weak projection, which, because of its

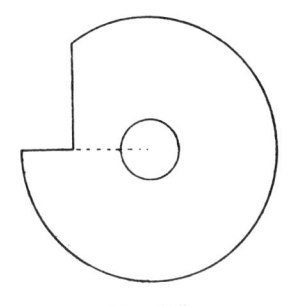

Fig. 155. 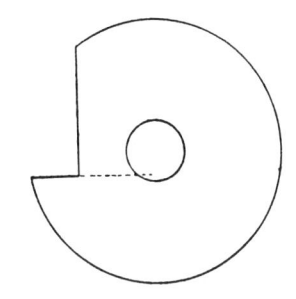   Fig. 156.

shape is likely to break when used, it is sometimes necessary to draw the temper. It is not always necessary to draw the temper to a straw color, and as a light straw is the first temper color visible, some other means must be employed. The tool may be placed in a kettle of oil, and by means of a thermometer any

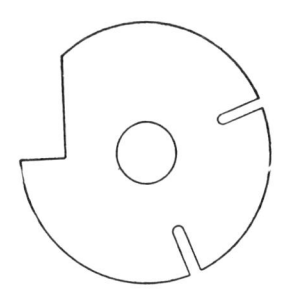

Fig. 157. 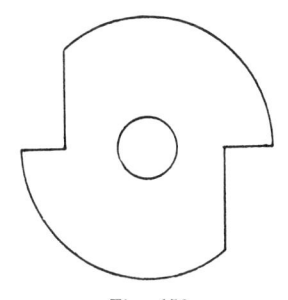   Fig. 158.

degree of heat may be obtained. The writer recalls a certain forming tool which was too brittle when left as it came from the hardening bath, yet was not hard enough when drawn to even the faintest straw color. When taken from the hardening bath, it was placed in a kettle of boiling water and left there about five minutes. The heat of the water at 212° reduced the brittleness so that the tool stood up in a good shape, yet it did not perceptibly soften it.

The following is an excellent plan: Use a bath of water having about one inch of oil on top; the tool after being heated red hot is plunged down through the oil into the water. Enough oil adheres to prevent the sudden shock which the steel received when plunged into the cold bath.

"Pack Hardening" also gives excellent results.

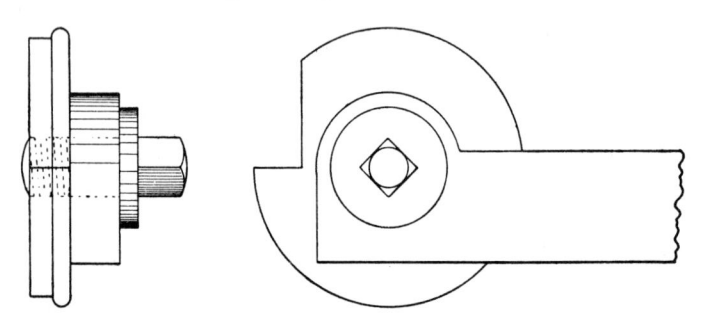

Fig. 159.

Tool Holders. The form of the holder for the tool depends on the class of work to be done and the machine in which it is to be used. Fig. 159 shows a design commonly used for hand screw machine work. If the cuts are comparatively light, the side of the tool and holder may be flat as shown. If, however, heavy cuts are taken which would have a tendency to turn the tool, it is often made with a taper projection on one side as shown in Fig. 160, the holder having a corresponding taper hole to receive the projection. This projection should be a good fit in the taper hole, but should not go in far enough to strike the bottom, neither should the side of the tool bear against the side of the holder.

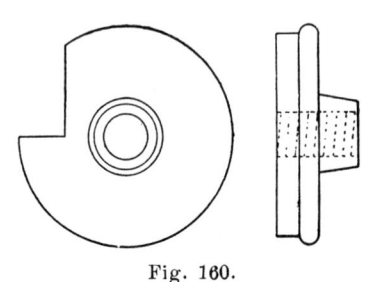

Fig. 160.

When used in automatic screw machines the holder is generally of a different shape from that used for hand screw machines.

A very common form is shown in Fig. 161. This holder is made in the form of an angle iron. The fixture (holder) is fastened to the tool rest by means of the bolt shown. The tool is fastened to the upright side of the holder by means of the bolt represented with its head let into the forming tool.

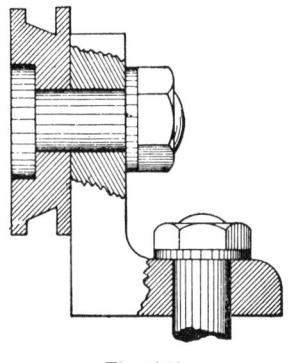

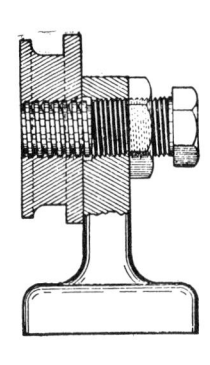

Fig. 161.   Fig. 162.

When extra heavy cuts are to be taken with a forming tool, it is sometimes considered advisable to make a holder of the form shown in Fig. 162. The holder is bolted to the tool rest in the same manner as the one represented in Fig. 161. A square thread having a pitch of five or six threads to the inch is cut in the forming tool; the thread should be right or left hand depending on which side of the machine the tool is to be located when in use, the thread being such that the tool will tighten by the pressure exerted by the cut. To get an adjustment, the thread in the holder must be of a finer pitch than that in the forming tool and of the same hand. If desired, this tool may be used in the ordinary form of holder shown in Fig. 161 by use of the bolt shown in Fig. 163.

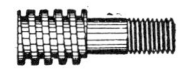

Fig. 163.

MILLING CUTTERS.

Milling machine cutters are made in two different forms: solid and with inserted teeth. It is customary in most shops to make cutters up to 6 or 8 inches in diameter solid, and above this size they are made with inserted teeth.

SOLID CUTTERS.

When making solid cutters it is advisable to use steel somewhat larger than the finish diameter of the cutter. A hole should be drilled in the blank $\frac{1}{16}$ inch smaller than the finish size of hole and the outside surface should be turned off. After annealing, it should be put in the chuck on the lathe, the hole bored and reamed to size and the hole recessed as shown at C in the sectional view of Fig. 164.

The piece should now be placed on the mandrel, and turned to the proper diameter and length. The teeth should be cut in the universal milling machine, or in a milling machine provided with a pair of index centers. The number of cutting edges for solid milling cutters varies somewhat according to the nature of the work to be done, but for general shop use the following table will be found satisfactory.

CUTTING EDGES FOR MILLING CUTTERS.

Diameter of Cutter.	No. of Cutting Edges.	Diameter of Cutter.	No. of Cutting Edges.
½	6	2½	20
¾	8	3	24
1	10 or 12	3½	26
1¼	14	4	28
1½	16	5	30
2	18	6	32

For most work it is desirable to have the faces of the teeth radial as shown in Fig. 164. However, when milling cutters are made to run in the direction of the feed or onto the work instead of against it, the teeth should be given a negative rake (cut ahead of the center) as shown in Fig. 165, as it has a tendency to keep the piece being milled from drawing toward the cutters.

When cutting the teeth, it is necessary to use a cutter that gives sufficient depth of tooth to provide a receptacle for chips, and also gives a form that supports the cutting edges. A cutter may be used that will produce an angle of about 50° between the face and back of the tooth as shown at A in Fig. 164. The cutter should cut deep enough to leave the lands about $\frac{1}{32}$ inch in width at the cutting edges.

The form of cutter shown in Fig. 164 is known as a Side

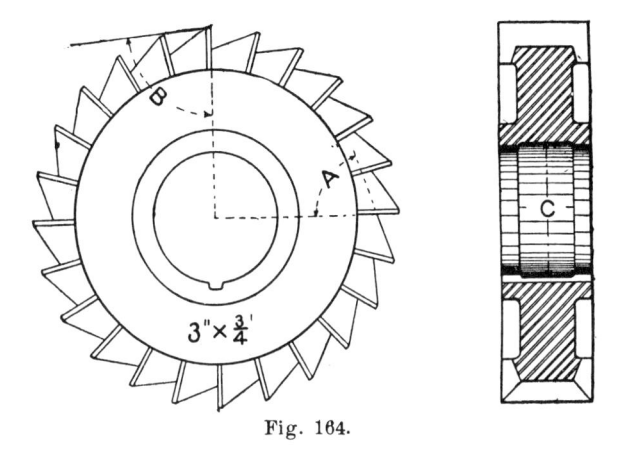

Fig. 164.

Milling Cutter. When cutting the teeth on the sides, it is necessary to put the cutter on a plug whose upper end does not project much above the top face of the cutter; this plug may be made straight and held in the chuck on the end of spindle in the spiral head. Such a plug is shown in Fig. 166 inserted in the cutter. If *many* cutters are made with teeth on the sides, it is advisable to make an expanding arbor, Fig. 167, whose shank fits the taper hole in the spindle of the spiral head. When milling the teeth on the sides, the index head must be inclined a little so that the side of the mill will stand at a small angle from the horizontal in order that the lands of the teeth may be of equal width at each end. The amount of this inclination cannot readily be computed.

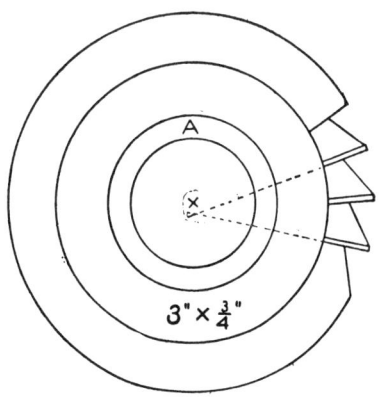

Fig. 165.

It is formed by first cutting a tooth leaving the cut somewhat shallow, then turning to the next tooth. After cutting the second tooth, the change in inclination will be apparent.

When the teeth are cut and the burrs removed, the diameter and length of the cutters may be stamped as shown in Fig. 164. The cutter is now ready for hardening. To successfully harden, it is necessary to have a *low, uniform* red heat; the teeth must be no hotter than the portion between the hole and the bottom of the teeth. When held toward the light there should be no trace of black in the interior of the cutter. When a uniform heat no higher than is necessary to harden the steel has been obtained, the cutter may be plunged into brine from which the chill has been removed; it should be worked around rapidly in the bath until the singing has ceased. It should then be removed from the brine and immediately plunged into oil and allowed to remain there until cold. When cold, the cutter may be taken from the oil and heated sufficiently to prevent cracking from internal strains. The cutter may now be brightened and the temper drawn to a straw color.

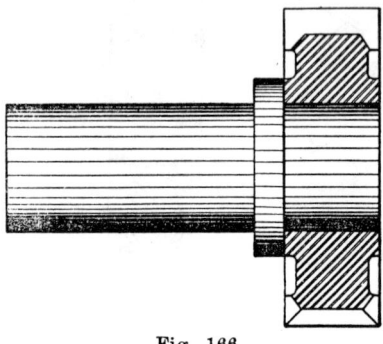

Fig. 166.

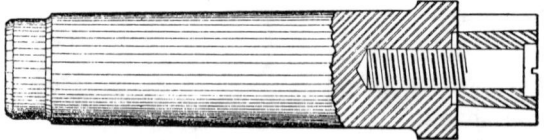

Fig. 167.

Grinding the Hole to Size. It is customary to ream the holes in milling cutters to size, and if the cutter contracts in hardening, the holes are brought to size again by lapping with a lead or cast iron lap, by means of oil and emery. However, this operation does not provide for the enlarging of the hole. While this is an unusual occurrence, it *sometimes* happens, and as a consequence the cutter does not fit the milling machine arbor and cannot do as good or as much work as it should.

On account of the necessity of having a correct fit on the milling machine arbor, it is advisable to ream the hole of the cutter with a reamer about .005 inch under the size of the arbor and finish by grinding after the cutter is hardened.

When grinding the hole to size, the cutter may be held in a chuck and ground with a small emery wheel, using the internal grinding attachment as shown in Fig. 168. This attachment is

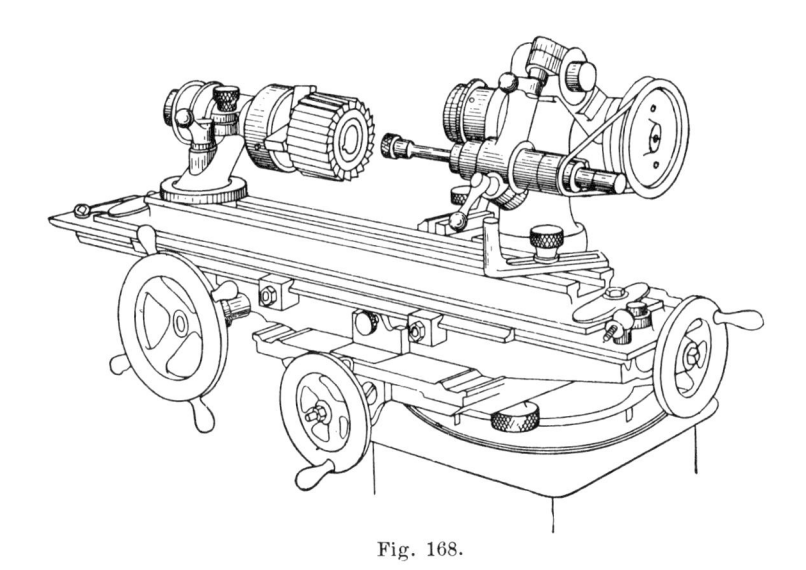

Fig. 168.

so designed that it may be swung out of the way when gauging the size of the hole as shown in Fig. 169. After grinding the hole to size it is advisable to grind the shoulders on each side of the cutter straight and true with the hole in order to prevent any possibility of springing the milling machine arbor by any untruth on the part of the cutter, and to prevent any possibility of the cutter running out of true. The shoulder (or boss) referred to is shown in A, Fig. 164.

There are two methods of grinding the shoulders. By one method the outer shoulder and the hole are ground at the same setting; if this is done properly this shoulder will be true with the hole. The chuck is now removed from the grinder and a face plate having an expanding plug is put in its place. The shoulder that has been ground is placed against the face plate with the expanding plug in the hole of the cutter. The outer shoulder may be ground after the plug is expanded until the cutter is held rigidly in place against the face plate which should run perfectly true.

By the other method both shoulders are ground while on an

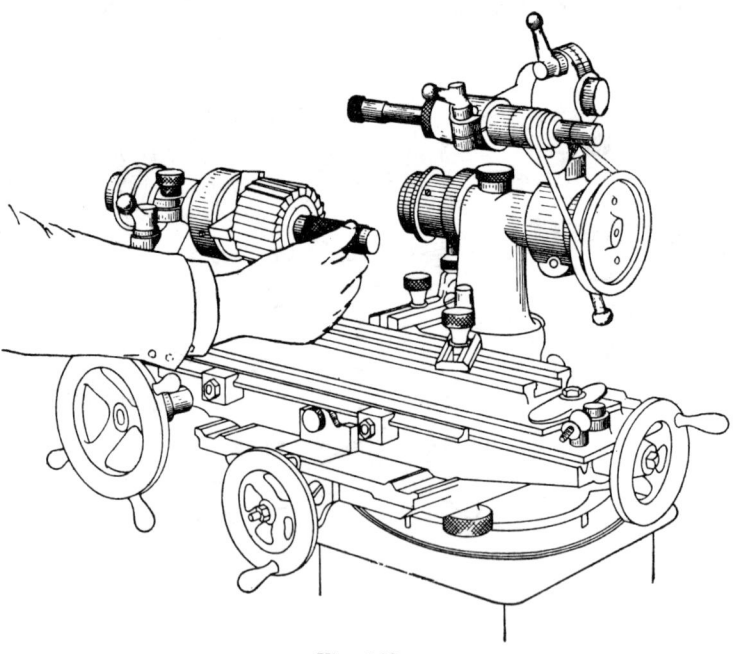

Fig. 169.

arbor which is necked down each side of the cutter as shown in Fig. 170. This necking allows the wheel to traverse the whole length of the shoulder and not cut into the arbor, as would be the case if an ordinary mandrel were used.

Grinding. In order to get the best results from a milling cutter it is necessary to use some form of grinder having a means of properly locating each tooth as it is presented to the wheel. This is usually accomplished by a finger which may be adjusted to the proper height to produce the required amount of clearance. The teeth may be given a clearance of about 3° as shown at B, Fig. 164. With this amount of clearance the cutter works freely and retains its edge; if more clearance is given the cutter is

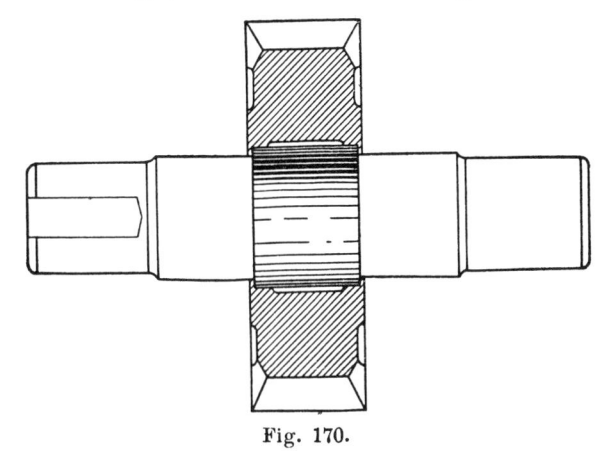

Fig. 170.

likely to chatter, and the edges of the teeth will become dull rapidly.

Fig. 171 shows a cutter in position for grinding the teeth; it will readily be seen that the tooth being ground rests on the finger or tooth rest; this finger may be adjusted to give any desired amount of clearance to the tooth. For grinding the teeth on the *side* of a milling cutter, a small emery wheel may be used in order to get the necessary amount of clearance without touching the tooth next to the one being ground.

If a grinder is used which will take a cup wheel as shown in Fig. 172, and whose table can be turned to bring the cutter in the position

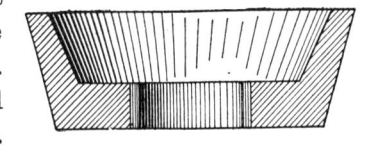

Fig. 172.

shown in Fig. 173, a form of clearance is given the tooth which is more satisfactory than if ground with a small wheel. With the cup wheel the line of clearance is straight, while with the small plain wheel it is hollowed out, and as a consequence the cutting edge is weak.

Spiral Milling Cutters. It is customary in most machine

shops to make all milling cutters of more than $\frac{1}{2}$ inch face with teeth cut spirally as in Fig. 174. The amount of spiral given the teeth varies in different shops and on different classes of work.

The object of providing spiral teeth is to maintain a uniformity of cutting duty at each instant of time. With teeth parallel to the cutter axis, the tooth on meeting the work will take the cut its entire length at the same instant, causing a jump to the

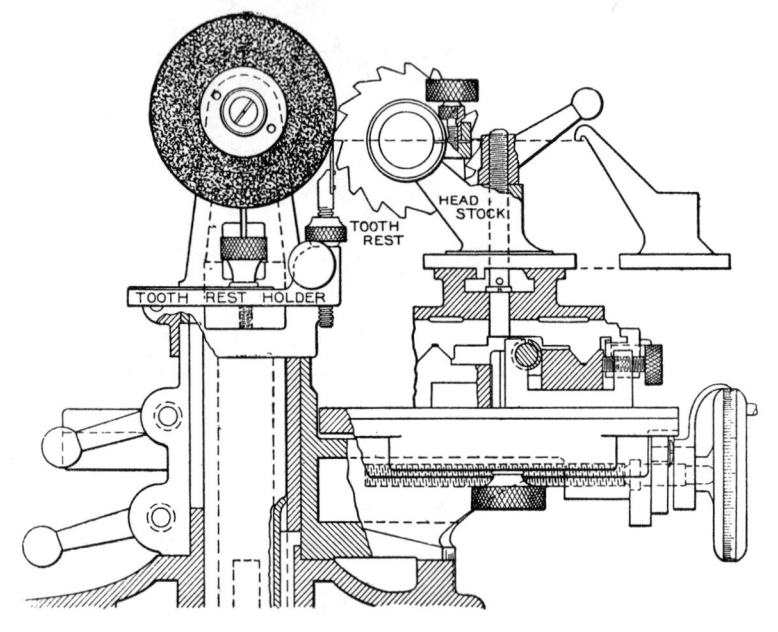

Fig. 171.

work on account of the springing of the device holding the work, and of the cutter arbor. If the teeth are cut spirally, the cut proceeds gradually along the whole length of the tooth, and after the cut is started a uniform cutting action is maintained, producing smoother work and a truer surface, especially in the case of wide cuts.

Milling cutters may be cut with either a right or left hand spiral, or helix, although it is generally considered good practice to cut a mill having a wide face with a spiral that will tend to force the cutter arbor into the spindle rather than to draw it out; then again, it is better to have the cutting action force the solid shoulder against the box, rather than to draw the adjusting nut against the box.

Where two very long mills are used on the same arbor and it is found necessary to cut them with a quick spiral, one cutter is sometimes cut with a right hand spiral and the other with a left hand spiral, in order to equalize the strain and reduce the friction resulting from the shoulder of the spindle pressing so hard against the box.

Special care should be taken in cutting spiral milling cutters

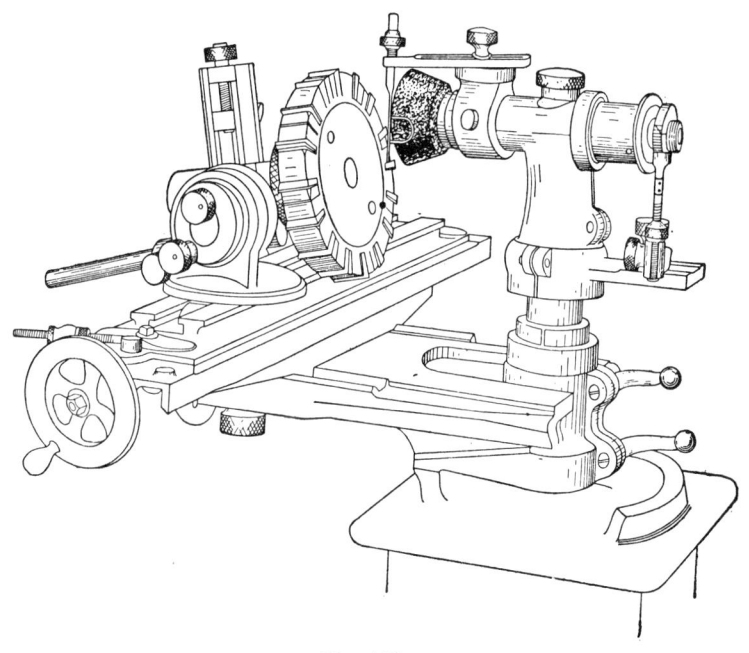

Fig. 173.

that the work does not slip. When a cut has been taken across the face of a cutter it is best to lower the knee of the milling machine, thus dropping the work away from the mill while coming back for another cut; the knee can then be raised to its proper position which may be determined by means of the graduated collar on the elevating shaft of the machine.

As it is important that the face of the cutting tooth be radial and straight, it will be found necessary to use an angular cutter of the form shown in Fig. 175, as cutters of this form readily clear the radial face of the cut and so remain sharp longer and produce a smoother surface to the face of the tooth than if cut with an angular cutter of the form used for cutting teeth which are parallel to the cutter axis.

The angular cutters for spiral mills are made with either 40°, 48° or 53° on one side and 12° on the other.

By setting the cutter, as shown in Fig. 175, so that the dis-

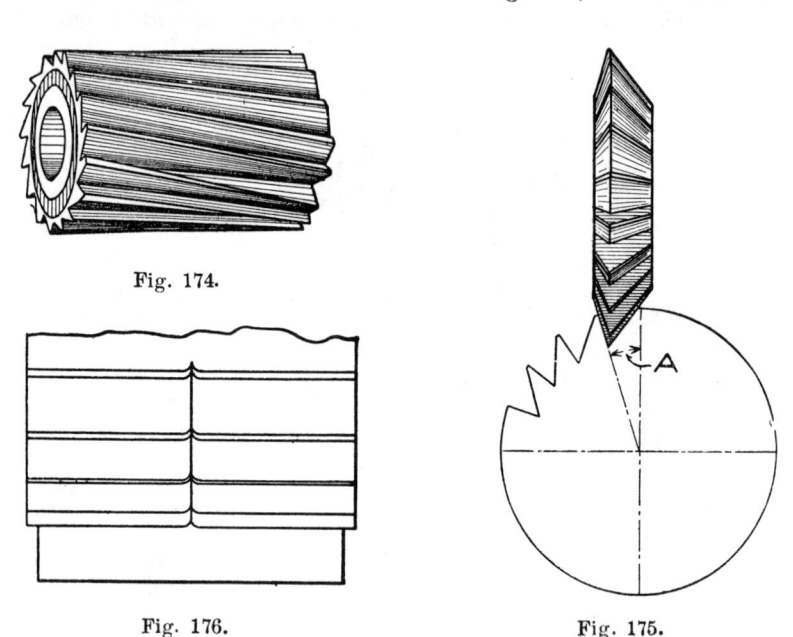

Fig. 174.

Fig. 176.

Fig. 175.

tance A is one twelfth the diameter, the face cut by the 12° side of the angular cutter will be nearly radial for the usual proportions.

The setting for cutting the teeth of a spiral cutter must be made before turning the spiral bed to the angle of the spiral.

Milling Cutters with Interlocking Teeth. When two milling cutters of an equal diameter are to be used on the same arbor in such a manner that the end of one cutter is against the end of the other, the corners of the cutting teeth are likely to break away leaving a projection — or fin — on the work as shown in Fig. 176. In order to overcome this, part of the teeth are cut away on the sides of the cutters; that is, a tooth will be cut away on one cutter and the corresponding tooth on the other cutter will be left full length to set into the recess formed by the cutting away of the tooth. In some shops it is customary to cut away every other tooth while in others two, three or four teeth, will be cut away and an equal number left. Fig. 177 represents a pair of mills having every other tooth cut away, while Fig. 178 represents a pair having four teeth cut away.

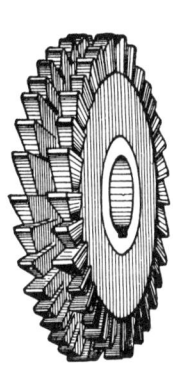

Fig. 177. Fig. 178.

In order to cut away the teeth to make the cutter of a form having interlocking teeth, the cutter should be placed on a plug or expanding arbor as described for milling teeth on sides of side milling cutters. By means of a milling cutter having the proper width, the teeth may be milled away, although in case a cutter having several teeth cut away as shown in Fig. 178, it is well to use a narrow cutter and after taking one cut turn the index head so that the next tooth is in position. Continue doing this until the desired number of teeth are cut away. The index head may now be turned to pass over the required number of teeth and the operation repeated.

It is necessary when making cutters with interlocking teeth (sometimes called dodged-teeth) that the milling be deep enough to prevent the corresponding tooth on the other part of the cutter from striking the bottom of the recess. The parts of the cutter should bear against each other on the shoulders, or hubs.

An excellent form of milling cutter to be used for milling slots or similar work may be made as shown in Fig. 179. This form is less expensive to make than one having interlocking teeth and answers the purpose as well. It is necessary to make an eccentric mandrel of the design shown in Fig. 180 having the eccentric centers on opposite sides of the regular

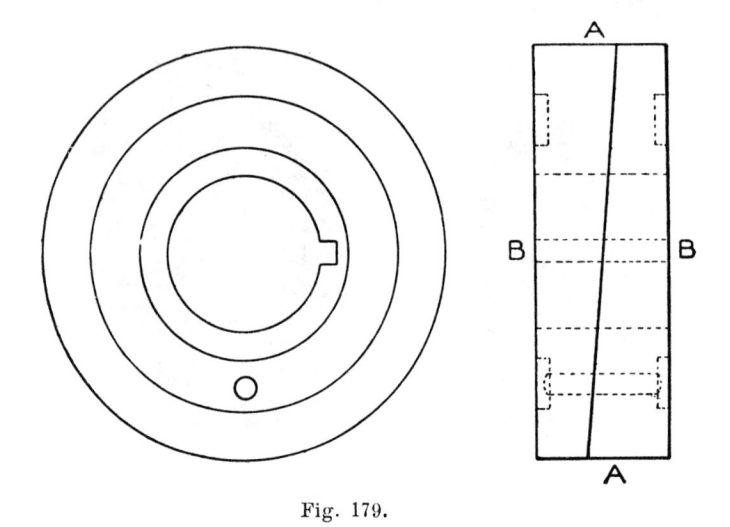

Fig. 179.

centers as shown. The two pieces which make the cutter should be cut from the bar long enough to finish the thickness of the heaviest part A A, Fig. 179. The hole is made $\frac{1}{16}$ inch smaller than finish size, the outside surface turned off and the pieces annealed.

After annealing, the hole may be made the desired size for grinding. One of the pieces may then be placed on the eccentric mandrel, forcing it on until the side that is to be beveled is exactly in the center of the mandrel. The side B may be machined with the mandrel running on the regular centers while the beveled side must be machined with mandrel running on the eccentric centers. When the arbor is running on these centers, a distance half way between the two ends runs true; it is at this point that the side of the blank to receive the bevel should be located as shown in Fig. 181 provided the eccentric centers are of an equal depth. After machining the two parts of the cutter to shape, they should be so placed on a stud that the two beveled sides will be next each other as shown in Fig. 179, and the thinnest part of one next to the thickest part of the other. The pin hole may now be drilled and reamed for a $\frac{3}{16}$ inch pin which should be inserted. The blank is next placed in the vise on the shaper or planer and the spline slot cut as shown. It is now ready

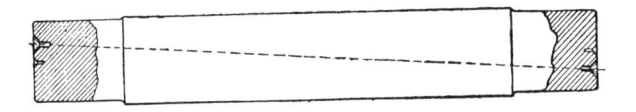

Fig. 180.

to be milled. After the cutter is hardened, the beveled sides may be ground true, the halves put together, hole ground to size, and the cutter ground to thickness, after which the teeth may be ground for clearance. If it is found necessary to increase the width of

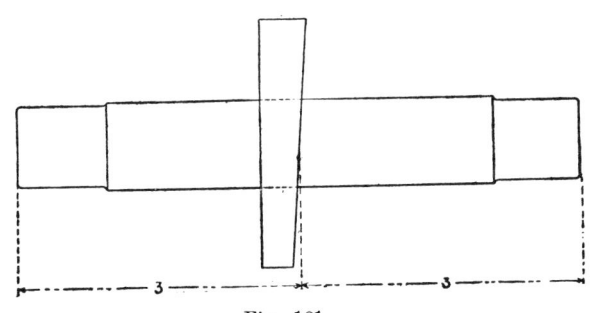

Fig. 181.

the slot, it may be done by shimming between the two parts of the cutter with paper or thin sheet metal; the design of the cutter allows this to be done without leaving any *fin* in the slot.

Nicked Teeth. Spiral cutters with nicked teeth, Fig. 182, are especially adapted for heavy milling. As the chip is broken up a much heavier cut can be taken than would be possible were an ordinary cutter used. The nicking may be done as follows: An engine lathe may be geared to cut a thread of the required pitch — two threads to the inch will be found satisfactory — and with a round nose tool $\frac{1}{8}$ inch wide cut a thread of sufficient depth that it may not grind out before the teeth will become too shallow to allow further grinding. This thread should be cut before milling the spaces to form the teeth.

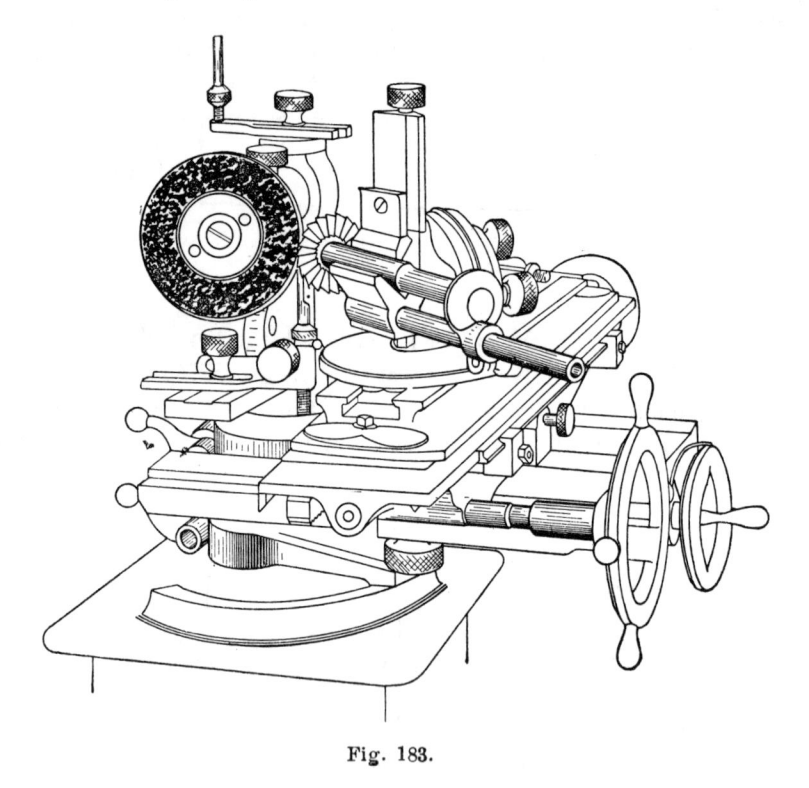

Fig. 183.

Angular Cutters. When making angular cutters the same general instructions given for making solid straight cutters should be followed except that the desired angle should be given.

When milling the spaces which form the teeth, the index head is set at an angle that will cut the edge of the tooth of an equal width its entire length. After removing the burrs the cutter may be hardened and tempered. The hole should be ground to size and the sides ground true with the hole. It should then be placed on a mandrel or stud and the teeth ground for clearance. Fig. 183 shows the method used in grinding the teeth of a mill of this form.

MILLING CUTTERS WITH INSERTED TEETH.

When milling cutters exceed 6 or 8 inches in diameter, it is generally cheaper to make the body of cast iron or machinery steel and insert in the periphery teeth made of tool steel. There is a variety of methods for holding the teeth in place. If the cutter is narrow, or is to be used as a side milling cutter, the grooves to receive the teeth may be cut straight (parallel to the cutter axis) as shown in Fig. 184. If the cutter face is over one inch long, the slots to receive the teeth should be cut in such a manner that spiral teeth may be used.

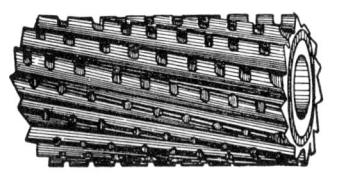

Fig. 182.

While it is a comparatively easy matter to cut the slots

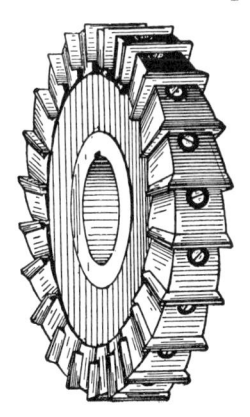

Fig. 184.

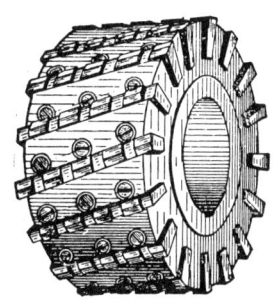

Fig. 185.

spirally, it is difficult to make the teeth of a shape that will fit the spiral slots without the aid of special tools. Consequently the slots are generally milled at an angle to the cutter axis, having the side of slot that corresponds to the face of the tooth equidistant from a radial line at each end of the cut. The face of the slot at one end would be ahead of the center, while at the opposite end it would be behind the center; this is termed a front rake, and a negative rake respectively.

The slots should be cut somewhat wider than would be necessary were the teeth to be made of a spiral form. After turning to size, the faces of the teeth may be milled spirally to make them radial.

If the mills are intended for heavy work, the teeth may be nicked as already described. The coarse pitch thread should be cut before the teeth are milled spirally.

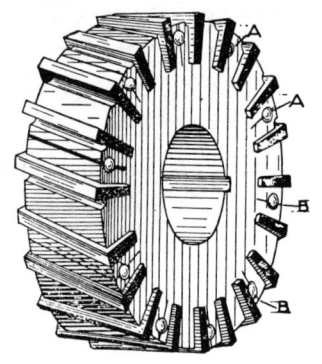

Fig. 186. 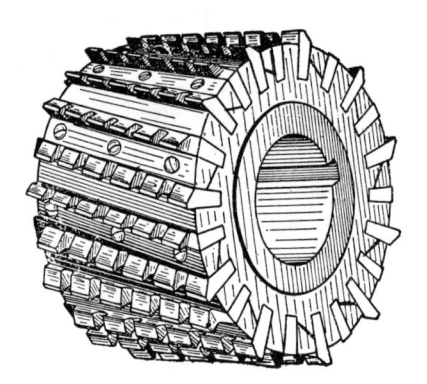   Fig. 187.

After hardening, the teeth may be put in place and fastened; they are now ready for grinding. The emery wheel for grinding milling machine cutter teeth should be of the proper grade as to hardness and coarseness; if the wheel is very *hard* or *fine*, it will be likely to draw the temper at the cutting edges of the teeth; the emery should not be coarser than No. 60 or finer than No. 90.

If the face of the wheel is glazed, remove the glaze with a piece of emery wheel somewhat harder than the wheel in use; this not only removes the glaze but makes the surface of the wheel more open and less likely to glaze. The emery wheel should run *true;* its face should not exceed $\frac{1}{4}$ inch in width. Generally speaking, the softer the emery wheel the *faster* it should run, but the peripheral speed should not exceed 5,000 feet per minute.

Fastening. There are several methods for fastening the

teeth in this form of cutter, any one of which gives satisfaction if the work is well done.

The method illustrated in Fig. 186 is in use in the works of the Pratt and Whitney Co., of Hartford, Conn. In this design, between every second pair of teeth a hole is drilled and reamed taper to receive the taper pins A A, after which the slots B B are cut with a thin cutter. After the cutters are in place the taper pins A A are driven into the holes, thus locking the cutters. To remove the cutters the pins are driven out.

A method of fastening the cutters which are used by the Morse Twist Drill & Machine Co., of New Bedford, Mass., is shown in Fig. 187. In this case the stock between every second pair of teeth is milled away not as deep, however, as the slots for the cutters. Wedge-shaped pieces of steel are fitted between the teeth as shown. When these are drawn to place by means of fillister headed screws they bind the cutters very securely. If the wedge-shaped binding blocks touch the bottoms of the slots they will not hold the cutters securely in place.

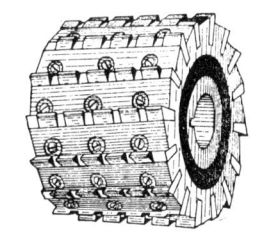

Fig. 188.

The method shown in Fig. 188 is used by Brown & Sharpe Mfg. Co. of Providence, R. I. The teeth are held in place by taper bushings and screws as shown.

Standard Key Ways. To prevent milling machine cutters turning on the arbor when cutting, it is necessary (especially when taking heavy cuts) to have key ways cut as shown in Fig. 189.

The arbor, of course, must have a similar slot to receive the key. It will be noticed that the dimension D refers to the diameter of the *hole* in cutter, and not to the diameter of the *cutter*.

Formed Cutters. As used by the Brown & Sharpe Mfg. Co., the term "Formed Cutter" applies to the cutters with teeth so relieved that they can be sharpened by grinding without changing their form. However, the term "Form Cutter" can be applied to any cutter cutting a form regardless of the manner in which the teeth may be relieved. Fig. 190 represents a formed cutter.

Formed cutters are used in many shops where work of irregular shape is milled in large quantities, as in sewing machine, gun and bicycle shops.

While this style of cutter can be made to better advantage in a shop equipped with machinery designed especially for this class of work, an ordinary engine lathe can be converted to a *backing-*

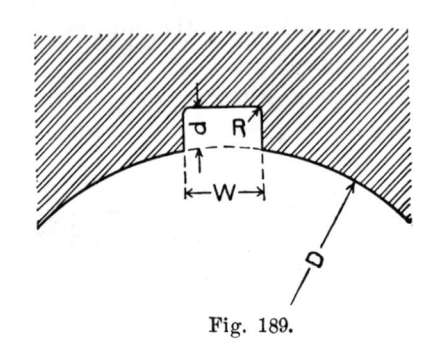

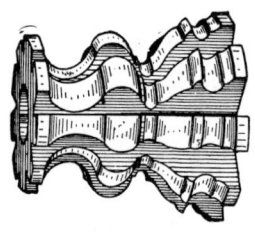

Fig. 189.

Fig. 190.

STANDARD KEY WAYS FOR CUTTERS.

Diameter (D), Inches.	Width (W), Inches.	Depth (d), Inches.	Radius (R), Inches.
$\tfrac{3}{8}$ to $\tfrac{9}{16}$	$\tfrac{3}{32}$	$\tfrac{3}{64}$	.020
$\tfrac{5}{8}$ to $\tfrac{7}{8}$	$\tfrac{1}{8}$	$\tfrac{1}{16}$	.030
$\tfrac{15}{16}$ to $1\tfrac{1}{8}$	$\tfrac{5}{32}$	$\tfrac{5}{64}$	.035
$1\tfrac{3}{16}$ to $1\tfrac{3}{8}$	$\tfrac{3}{16}$	$\tfrac{3}{32}$	.040
$1\tfrac{7}{16}$ to $1\tfrac{3}{4}$	$\tfrac{1}{4}$	$\tfrac{1}{8}$	.050
$1\tfrac{13}{16}$ to 2	$\tfrac{5}{16}$	$\tfrac{5}{32}$	.050
$2\tfrac{1}{16}$ to $2\tfrac{1}{2}$	$\tfrac{3}{8}$	$\tfrac{3}{16}$	.060
$2\tfrac{9}{16}$ to 3	$\tfrac{7}{16}$	$\tfrac{3}{16}$	.060

off lathe for relieving or backing off the cutters. Or, a comparatively inexpensive fixture (known as the Balzar backing-off device) may be used. However, a simple arrangement consists of an eccentric arbor operated by a hand lever, or a stud may be screwed in the faceplate of a lathe; the cutter is placed on this stud in a position that allows the teeth to be given the necessary amount of clearance. When backing off the teeth of cutters whose faces do not exceed 1 inch in width the Balzar backing-off fixture shown in Fig. 191 can be used to advantage. This device is held between the centers of a lathe in the ordinary manner, the backing off being such that the cutter can be ground without alteration of shape. The tool is so constructed that it is only necessary to place the cutter upon the arbor in the ordinary way. Place the arbor on the lathe centers as shown, start the lathe and feed the forming tool in by the cross-feed screw in order to take

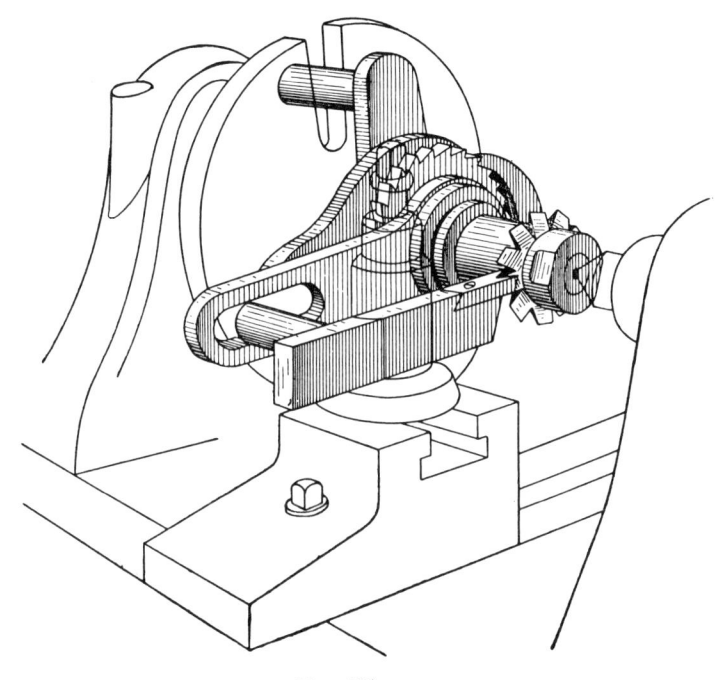

Fig. 191.

the desired cut in the same manner as in plain turning. The ratchet connected with the arbor, and actuated by the pawl, contains ordinarily thirty-six teeth and the stroke can be set to back off a cutter with 9, 12, 18 or 36 teeth.

Backing off by an Eccentric Arbor. An arbor may be made having a pair of centers located to give the cutter tooth the required amount of clearance; such an arbor is shown in Fig. 192. The eccentric centers are shown at the sectional portions at the ends. The amount of eccentricity depends somewhat on the size of the cutter to be backed off; but for cutters not exceeding 4 inches diameter, from $\frac{3}{16}$ to $\frac{1}{4}$ inch will give excellent results.

The screw at the end of the arbor should be of a fine pitch; about 12 threads per inch for arbors 1 inch diameter. The object in cutting a fine pitch thread is, the cutter being backed off may

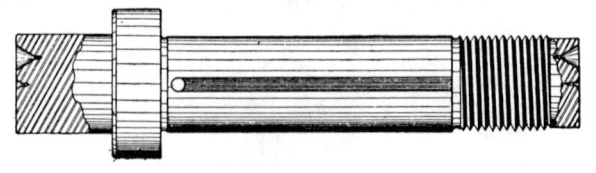

Fig. 192.

be held more securely with the same amount of power exerted in tightening the nut; again the depth of thread is not as great as for a thread of coarser pitch, and as a consequence, the plane portion at the end of the arbor (which is made the size of the bottom of the thread) may be left large enough to get in a center hole of good size having $\frac{1}{4}$ inch eccentricity.

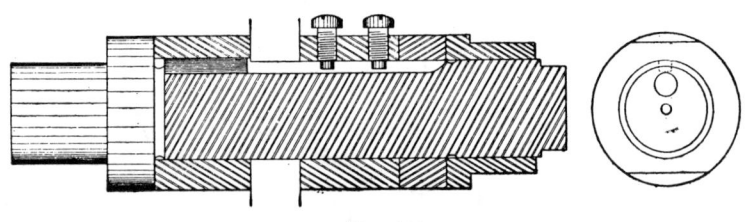

Fig. 193.

The spline cut should be at least $\frac{1}{8}$ inch wide and about $\frac{1}{8}$ inch deep; the walls of the cut should be parallel in order that the screws shown in Fig. 193 as passing through the collar and entering the slot in the arbor, may have a good bearing. These screws are to keep the collar from turning when the necessary power is applied to the nut when fastening the cutter in place. The collar on the opposite side of the cutter has a spline cut the same width as cut in the arbor, and is held in position by a spline as shown. The cutter cannot be held by a spline as it is necessary to move it each time a tooth is brought into position for backing off.

TOOL MAKING.

When machining the cutter blank, it is given the desired shape by means of a forming tool. If the shapes vary much in size the shape may be roughed out before using the forming tool. After it has been machined to the desired size and shape, it may

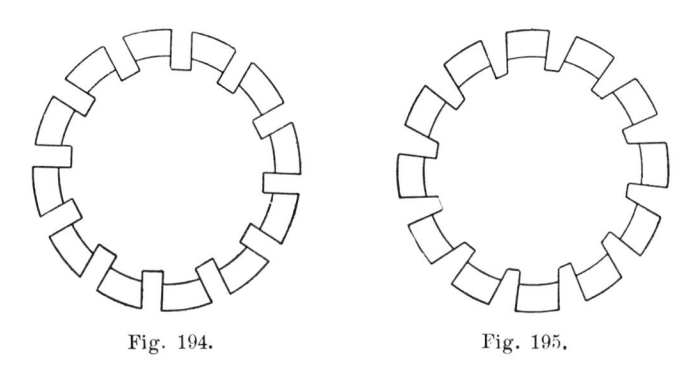

Fig. 194.   Fig. 195.

be placed between the centers of the milling machine, and a number of grooves cut the entire length of the cutter. The number of grooves must correspond to the number of teeth the mill is to have; these grooves cannot be cut to finish width until after the teeth are backed off, because the forming tool cuts a trifle deeper at the point of contact, making it necessary to mill a small amount from the face of the tooth after backing off. The grooves are sometimes cut with a thin milling cutter, or a metal slitting saw $\frac{1}{8}$ inch thick. When a groove of this description is cut, the cutter has the appearance shown in Fig. 194. Cutting a groove of this form makes more work for the operator than when cut as shown in Fig. 195, in which the distance across the tops of the teeth is decreased by using an angular cutter of the shape shown in Fig. 196. After cut-

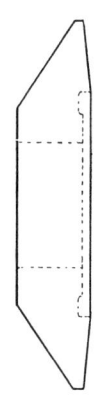

Fig. 196.

ting the grooves the cutter may be placed on the eccentric arbor which is held between the centers of the lathe in the ordinary manner. A forming tool that will produce the desired shape of tooth is placed in the tool post; the top face of the tool must be set at the exact height of the center of the lathe in order to produce the proper shape. Fig. 197 shows an eccentric arbor in a lathe in position to back off the teeth of a formed mill. The arbor is operated by means of the lever. The arbor is entirely independent of the spindle in its action, the eccentric centers being placed on the centers of the lathe, and the necessary motion given by means of the lever which strikes the carriage at the end of the stroke. In order to avoid bruising the lathe a strip of leather is attached to the lever as shown.

To set the cutter tooth in the proper location before backing

Fig. 197.

off, a piece of thin sheet metal is placed on the top face of the tool, as shown in Fig. 198. The lever is brought down on to the carriage, the tooth of the cutter is brought down on to the sheet metal and the nut tightened. The tooth to be backed off is the one below that set to the thickness of the strip above the tool. The object in raising the tooth a given distance above the face is to prevent the one being backed from and striking the tool at the end of stroke. Again the teeth are set alike. This operation must be repeated for the setting of each tooth before backing off. The forming tool is fed by means of the cross-feed screw, a tooth

TOOL MAKING.

is backed off nearly the desired amount leaving a little for a finish cut; the tool is withdrawn, the nut loosened and the cutter turned on the arbor to bring the next tooth in position to be backed off. This operation may be repeated until all the teeth are backed off alike. The amount of backing off must be determined by the cross-feed stop, or a graduated dial on the cross-feed screw. After the roughing cut has been taken on all the teeth, the forming tool may be sharpened by grinding, or by oil stoning, and the finish

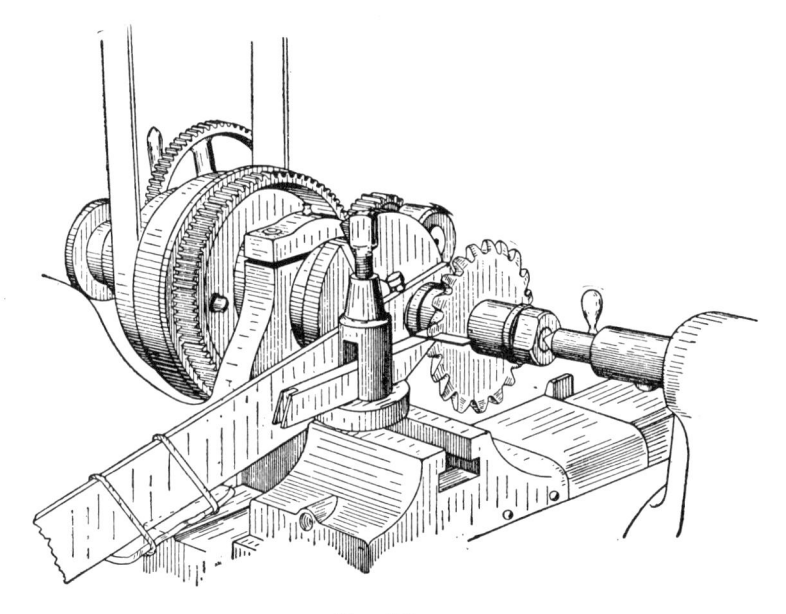

Fig. 198.

cut taken on the teeth. Another method of backing off cutter teeth is shown in Fig. 199. A stud is screwed in the faceplate of a lathe near the outer edge as shown. The cutter which must be a fit on the stud is clamped by means of the nut shown. The finger A is movable in the slot in the stationary block B which is located on the face plate to bring the tooth to be backed off in its proper location, and keeps it from turning when being operated on. The forming tool is fed in gradually until the tooth is formed. The finger is then disengaged from the space in the cutter, which is revolved by means of the set screw until the next is in position.

Each tooth is machined seperately, that is, the forming tool is fed in the required distance for each tooth when it is in position. The cutter is turned until the next tooth is in position, and the process repeated until each tooth has been backed off.

In backing off cutters in this device it is necessary to cut the notches (spaces between the teeth) somewhat wider than the teeth.

When backing off the teeth for clearance by any of the means described, it is first necessary to form the blank, then gash it or cut the notches as described; the teeth are now backed off.

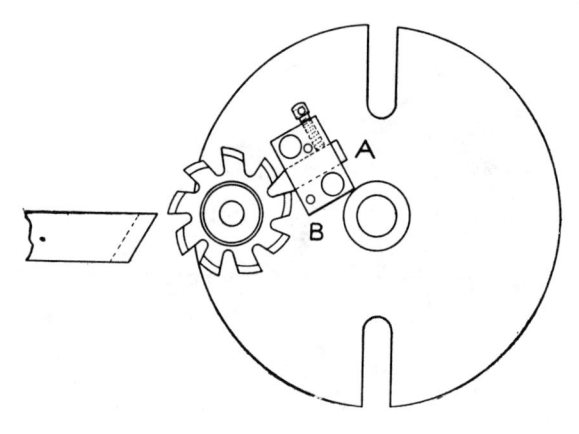

Fig. 199.

After backing off it is necessary to mill the face of the tooth back $\frac{1}{32}$ inch or so to cut away "the jump" (as it is termed) caused by the forming tool drawing in a trifle when it first strikes the edge of the tooth.

Threaded Holes. It is often necessary to make milling cutters with threaded holes. This happens in the case of *small* angular cutters, and many styles of cutters for use on profiling (edge milling) machines.

The same general instructions for making the other forms of cutters apply to those with threaded holes, except that instead of reaming the hole to a given size the thread is cut with a tap of the proper size and pitch or it is chased in the lathe. After threading, the cutter should be screwed on to a threaded arbor.

Fig. 200 shows an arbor of this description. The end A is threaded slightly tapering for short cutters about .002 inch in 1 inch of length. On the taper end of the arbor a thread should be cut of a size that will not allow the cutter to screw on the arbor quite the entire length, that is, the cutter should overhang the threaded

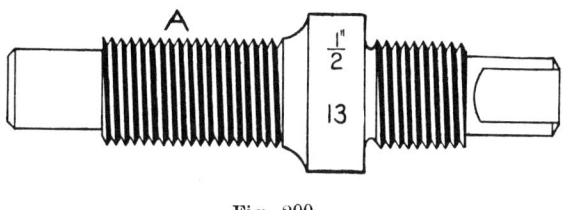

Fig. 200.

portion of the arbor a trifle (say one thread); this allows the outer end to be squared up without mutilating the threads on the arbor. The reason for using the *taper* end of the arbor when squaring the first end of the cutter is that the shoulder is true with the thread in the cutter. After squaring this shoulder, the cutter blank may be removed and placed on the opposite end of

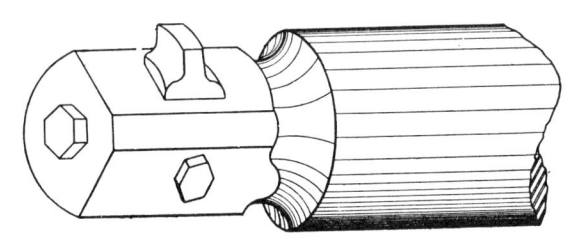

Fig. 201.

the arbor with the side that has been squared against the shoulder of the arbor. This method of machining pieces of work having a threaded hole, where it is desirable that the outer surfaces be true with the hole, is applicable to all classes of work. The cutter may be machined to length and shape on the straight end of arbor.

Fly Cutters. The simplest form of milling machine cutter is known as a fly cutter. It has only one cutting edge but is particularly valuable when making but one or two pieces of a kind for experimental work, and when making and duplicating screw-machine and similar tools of irregular shape.

As these cutters have but one cutting edge, they produce work very accurate as to shape, but cut very slowly and do not last as long as those having more teeth. However, they are used on *special work* on account of the small cost of making. It is necessary to hold the cutters in a *fly cutter arbor* which is shown in Fig. 201.

The cutter to be used in a fly cutter arbor may be filed to a templet, giving the necessary amount of clearance in order that the back edge, or keel, may not drag. If it is desirable to make the impression in the fly cutter with a milling cutter of the regular form, the piece of square steel from which the cutter is to be made may be held in the milling machine vise and the shape cut with the milling cutter. The desired amount of clearance may be given by holding the piece in the vise at an angle of a few degrees.

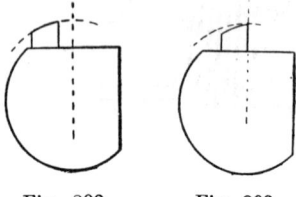

Fig. 202.   Fig. 203.

To make a fly cutter from a forming tool, the piece of steel may be held in the fly cutter arbor in such a position that the face is somewhat back of a radial line as shown in Fig. 202. After hardening the cutter may be set so that the cutting edge will be radial and the clearance will be as shown in Fig. 203.

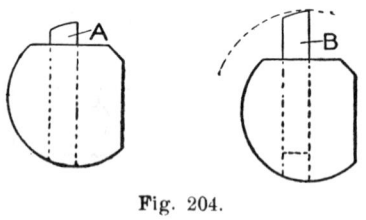

Fig. 204.

Another method of getting the clearance for the cutter is to place the top of the cutter blank as near the arbor as possible and then cut the desired shape. If the cutter is set in the arbor so that it projects from the surface it will have the necessary clearance as shown in Fig. 204. A represents the position of the blank while being cut and B the cutter in position for cutting; the dotted line showing the circle through which the cutting edge travels, the amount of clearance is apparent.

TOOL MAKING. 129

End Mills. This form of milling machine cutter (Fig. 205) is familiarly known as a **shank mill**. The term is used on account of the shank B which in small milling cutters fits into a collet. This collet in turn fits the hole in the spindle of milling machine. The collet referred to is used to save stock in making the cutters as otherwise it would be necessary to use steel large enough to make a shank of the size of hole in the spindle of the milling machine.

The cutter shown in Fig. 205 is what is termed a *left hand* mill; if the teeth run in the opposite direction, it is called a *right hand* mill.

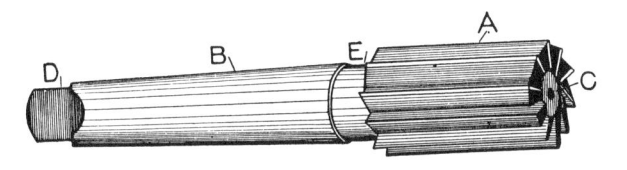

Fig. 205.

In making a shank (or end) mill of the form shown in Fig. 205 stock should be selected enough larger than the cutting end A to allow of turning off the decarbonized surface of the steel. After facing the ends to length, and turning the roughing chip, the end A may be run in the steady rest of the lathe and the center cut away — or recessed — as shown at C. The blank should be recentered and countersunk to furnish a center to use in turning the mill to size and shape. The object in cutting the center out as shown is to furnish a cavity for the angular cutter used in cutting the teeth on the end of the mill. Without this it would be impossible to grind satisfactorily.

After recentering the end C, the tenon D may be turned to size and milled to thickness, which should be a trifle ($\frac{1}{32}$ inch) less than the width of the center key slot in the collet. The taper at B should be turned enough larger than finish size to allow for grinding after the milling cutter is hardened. The cutter end A should be turned .010 inch larger than the required diameter. The portion E should be turned $\frac{1}{32}$ inch smaller than the large end of B or to dimensions if any are given on the drawings.

In order to insure teeth strong enough to resist the strain of cutting, an angular mill should be selected that will give the required shape. In Fig. 206 is shown a form of cutter tooth too weak for actual service; this tooth is the result of using an angular cutter with a cutting face forming an acute angle with the side. Fig. 207 shows a cutter whose teeth are strong, yet deep enough to be practical; these teeth were cut with an angular mill of less angle. Fig. 208 represents a cutter whose teeth were cut

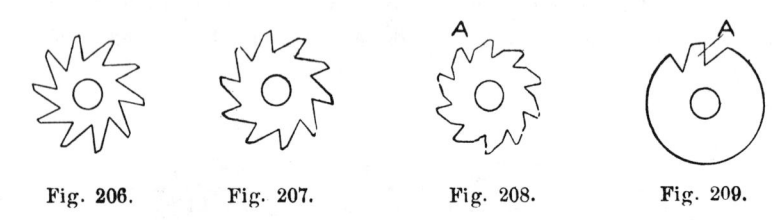

Fig. 206.   Fig. 207.   Fig. 208.   Fig. 209.

with the same cutter used for Fig. 206. The teeth were cut to the required depth first; this of course leaving them too thick at the cutting edges as shown in Fig. 209. After cutting the teeth as shown at A, Fig. 209, the index head was turned sufficiently to cut the teeth as shown at A, Fig. 208.

After cutting the teeth around the circumference of the mill,

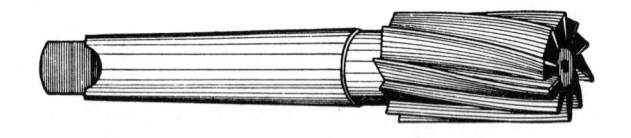

Fig. 210.

it should be placed in the collet and the collet put in the spindle hole in the spiral head in order to cut the teeth on the end.

When cutting the teeth on the end of the mill, the spiral head is turned until the cutter is in a horizontal position. The angular cutter used should not have a very acute angle or the teeth will be weak. An 80° angular milling cutter will be satisfactory.

Spiral End Mills. It is sometimes advisable to cut the teeth of end mills spirally as shown in Fig. 210. As there is no support at the outer end of this form of mill it will be necessary to cut the teeth of a spiral that will have a tendency to force the mill into the collet rather than draw it out. Fig. 210 represents a left hand end mill cut with a right hand spiral.

End Mills with Center Cut. This form of End Mill is useful when it is necessary to cut into the work with the end of the

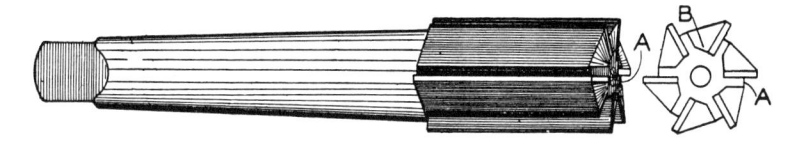

Fig. 211.

mill, and then move along as in dies, cams, and grooves. The teeth being sharp on the outside, cut a path from the point of entrance. The coarser teeth allow a heavier cut, especially in cast iron. Fig. 211 shows two views of an end mill with center cut.

After cutting the teeth on the end with an angular cutter, a

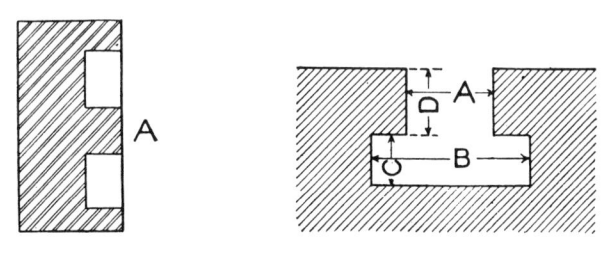

Fig. 212.   Fig. 213.

thin straight faced cutter of small diameter should be run through close to the face of the cutter tooth making a cut as shown at A; this cut should be of sufficient depth to permit of backing off the inner edge of the tool as shown at B. This clearance allows the mill to cut away the slight projection left in the center of mill when it is fed into a piece of work. Such a projection is shown at A in Fig. 212.

T-Slot Cutters. In cutting T slots in various parts of machines, such as milling machine carriages, etc., it is necessary

132   TOOL MAKING.

to use a form of shank mill known as a T-Slot Cutter. Fig. 213 shows the ordinary form of T-slot; while Fig. 214 shows the cutter. A portion of the stock below the teeth is cut away as shown at A A in the sectional view Fig. 215. This is necessary in order to back off the teeth on the sides of the cutter for clearance, and to do away as far as possible with unnecessary friction when the cutter is working.

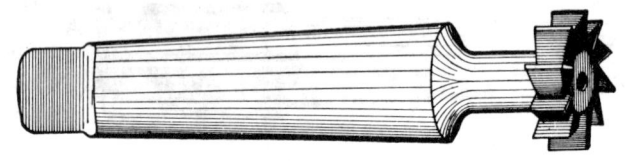

Fig. 214.

T-slot cutters are usually made $\frac{1}{32}$ inch larger in diameter than the size designated on the cutting portion to allow for sharpening; that is, a mill intended for cutting a slot $\frac{1}{2}$ inch wide is made $\frac{1}{2} + \frac{1}{32}$ or $\frac{17}{32}$ inch diameter, unless intended for cutting a slot to given dimensions.

It is advisable to harden mills of this description the entire length of the neck, especially if the neck is of small diameter; otherwise they will be very likely to spring when in use. After hardening, the neck should be drawn to a blue color, while the cutting part should be drawn to a straw color.

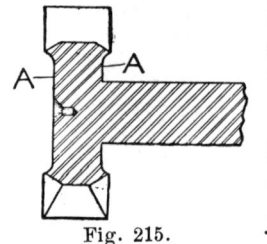

Fig. 215.

When grinding end mills, the shank in all cases should be ground first to fit the collet or holder, allowing it to enter *far enough* to key out readily, yet not enough to allow the shoulder above the tenon to strike the shoulder in the collet.

After grinding the teeth for clearance on the diameter, the teeth on the end should be ground. Most universal and cutter grinders are provided with a fixture for holding the mill by the shank while grinding these teeth; such a fixture is shown in Fig. 216.

Face Milling Cutters. This form of cutter is used in milling surfaces too large to be cut with the ordinary form of milling cutter held on an arbor passing over the work. As the full diameter of the face of the cutter may be used, it may have less than one half the size that would be necessary for a side milling cutter. A side milling cutter must be double the diameter of the surface to be cut plus the diameter of the collar on the arbor. For instance if a surface as A, Fig. 217, were to be milled, it would be necessary to use a cutter somewhat larger in diameter than twice

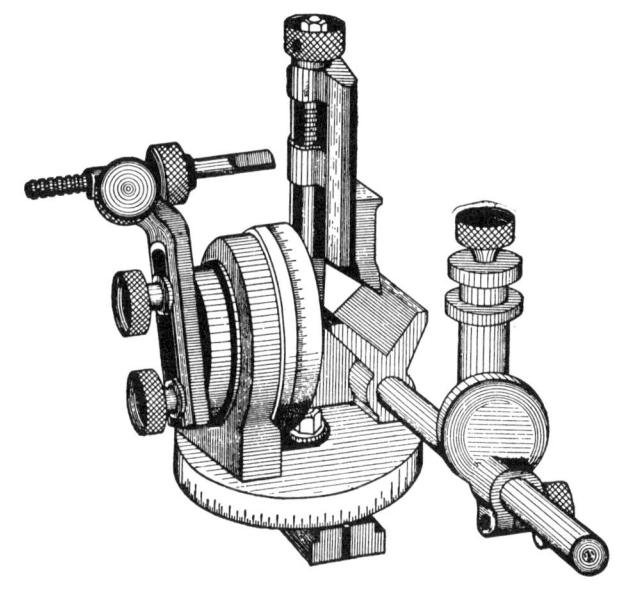

Fig. 216.

the height of the surface plus the diameter of collar B. Whereas if a *face* milling cutter of the form shown in Fig. 218 were used the diameter need not be much greater than the height of the face of the piece of work being milled.

Generally speaking, cutters of this description are necessarily of a diameter that makes it advisable to use inserted teeth as shown in Fig. 218. The body may be made of cast iron, having a taper hole and key way, and held in place on the arbor by a screw.

The teeth may be made of tool steel and hardened, or of self-hardening steel if the cutter is to be subjected to rough usage. In either case they may be fitted to the slots by grinding on a surface grinder, and held in place by taper bushings and screws as explained under "Milling Cutters with Inserted Teeth." The construction of the body may be readily understood from the sectional view given in Fig. 219. The letters A, B, and C represent the diameter of cutter, width of face, and number of taper of the hole respectively, while D represents the key way.

The following table gives the dimensions of Face Milling Cutters of different diameters.

FACE MILLING CUTTERS.

A	B	C
5½"	2"	No. 10 Brown & Sharpe Taper.
6½"	2"	" 12 " " " "
7½"	2"	" 12 " " " "
8½"	2⅜"	" 12 " " " "
9½"	2⅜"	" 12 " " " "

After boring and reaming the taper hole, the body of the cutter may be placed on a taper mandrel fitting the hole, and the ends and circumference finished to size. It should then be placed in the vise on the shaper or planer at the proper angle and the spline slot cut of an equal depth at each end of the taper hole. After removing the burrs it should be placed between the centers on the milling machine, and the slots cut for the teeth.

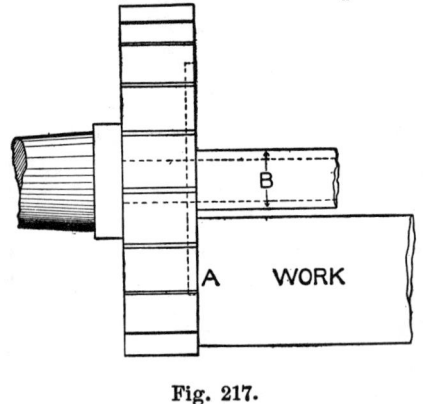

Fig. 217.

When the teeth are firmly secured in their proper places, they may be ground for clearance; the same general instructions given for grinding other forms of milling machine apply to this form.

Arbors For Face Milling Cutters. In. Fig. 220 is shown an arbor to be used in connection with *face* milling cutters. The shank A fits the hole in the spindle of the milling machine. B is the body which fits the taper hole in the cutter; this portion of the arbor has a spline which fits a spline slot in the cutter. A screw C enters the body of the arbor and is used in holding the cutter

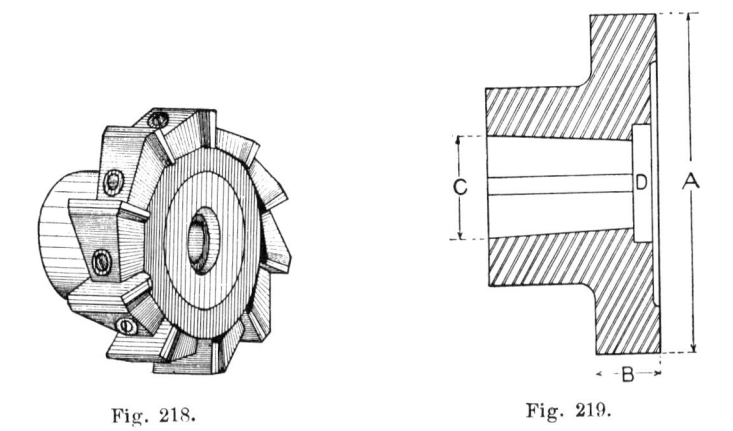

Fig. 218.

Fig. 219.

on the arbor. D is a nut used to force the cutter off the arbor when it is necessary.

Stock used in making an arbor for a face milling cutter should be strong and stiff, and on this account tool steel is generally used. After squaring the end and roughing out the cir-

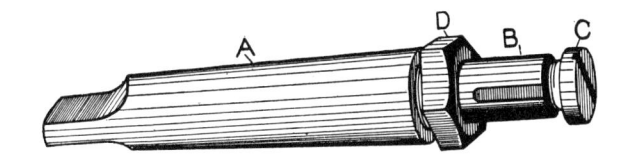

Fig. 220.

cumference, one end should be run in the steady rest and the screw hole in the end drilled and tapped, after which it should be countersunk at the end to furnish a center for use in turning and finishing. The tenon should now be turned to size and milled to thickness. If necessary to harden the end of the tenon it should be done before finish turning the arbor to prevent springing when heating. After turning the taper to fit the hole in the milling machine spindle, and on the opposite end to fit the cutter, the thread may be cut for the nut D, Fig. 220, after which the arbor may be cut for the spline as already explained.

The result will be more satisfactory if the two tapers are left a trifle large until after cutting the spline cut and are then ground to fit. Although the spline is intended to fit snugly in the slot in the arbor, the fit should not require pressure enough to endanger the truth of the arbor when it is pressed to position.

DRILL JIGS.

A drill jig is a device for holding work so that one or more holes may be accurately drilled; the locations of the holes may be governed by hardened bushings (guides) through which the drills run.

The design of a jig depends entirely on the shape of the piece and the nature of the work to be done. Jigs should be so designed that work may be placed in and taken out of them as quickly as possible. The fastening device should allow rapid manipulation, yet be capable of holding the work without danger of a change of location.

The construction of drill jigs calls for as great accuracy as any branch of the tool-maker's business; but no undue accuracy should be indulged in. If the location of a hole is near enough when within a limit of variation of $\frac{1}{16}$ inch it is a waste of time to attempt to get it within .0005 inch. Yet if the work is of such character that it is necessary that the holes be within a limit of variation of .0001 inch or even closer, every effort should be made to locate the drill bushings as accurately as possible.

While the design of the jig and the character of the work to be drilled must necessarily determine the method of construction, a few general points may not be amiss. The amount of *finish* given the exposed surfaces of a jig must be determined by the custom or requirements of the individual shop. In many shops it is not considered necessary nor advisable to finish the surfaces any more than to allow of their being wiped without the waste sticking to the jig.

A jig should be constructed so that it may be easily cleaned. Chips or dirt between the piece of work and the seating surface, or between the work and the stops, or locating points, throw the work out of true. As a result the holes will be at a wrong angle to the working surface, or they will be improperly located. Either condition would make the pieces unfit for use on most work, consequently bearing surfaces (wherever possible) should be cut away leaving several small seating surfaces, rather than one large one. A, Fig. 221, shows a piece of work resting on its entire seating surface; while B shows a surface cut away to leave six bearing points. If the seating surface is to be cut away as described, the raised portions should be so located that the article

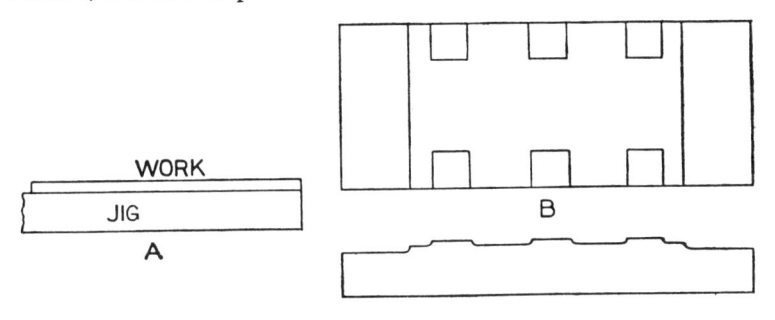

Fig. 221.

cannot be sprung by the action of the cutting tools or from any pressure that may be applied by any fastening device; otherwise the work will be thrown out of true as badly as though chips were lodged between the work and the seating.

It is advisable, whenever possible, to divide a long, locating bearing into several short surfaces, thus decreasing the chance of holes becoming inaccurately located. When making jigs for pieces that are likely to have burrs at any given point, it is well to cut a depression in the seating or locating surfaces for the burr to set in, thus preventing the work being incorrectly located.

Seating surfaces should be made smooth so that chips and dirt may not stick to them, but they should not be polished nor finished as this would necessitate unnecessary cost and might cause the surface to get out of true.

A jig must be handled by the workman, and a clumsy jig cannot be handled as readily as one designed so that the workman can use it to advantage.

Sharp corners should be avoided wherever possible, and all handles or similar devices should fit the hand. If not, the amount of work done will not be the maximum, as the operator cannot do as much work with a jig which tires the hand and wrist.

As already stated the accuracy with which a jig should be constructed depends entirely on the nature of the work to be done, yet it should be borne in mind that any inaccuracy must of necessity be duplicated in the work.

EXAMPLES OF JIGS.

A few designs of jigs will now be considered to show the general requirements and the methods of construction.

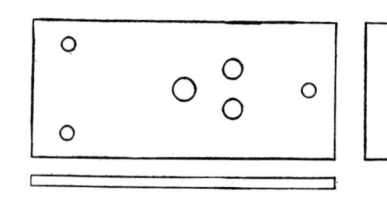

Fig. 222.

The slab jig, shown in Fig. 222, is the simplest form in use; it consists of a piece of flat stock of suitable thickness and of the same general outline of the piece of work to be drilled. The work may be clamped to the jig by means of U clamps, or parallel jaw clamps. If the jig is made of machinery steel the walls of the holes may be case-hardened by heating the jig red hot and sprinkling powdered cyanide of potassium around the hole, reheating in the fire and plunging in water; it should be worked back and forth in the bath so that the water will circulate through the holes. While this form of jig answers very well where but a few pieces are to be drilled, it is not suitable for permanent equipment on account of the wear of the holes. To overcome this, the holes may be made sufficiently large to receive hardened bushings having holes the size of the drill to be used. Fig. 223 shows this construction.

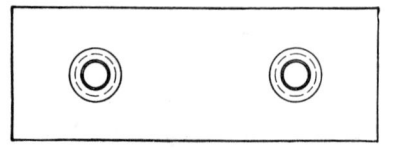

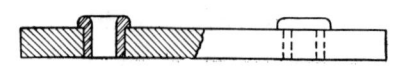

Fig. 223.

When holes are to be drilled at certain distances from one or more edges, it is necessary to have stops against which the work may rest. These stops may be pins, a shoulder, or a rib.

If the outline of the work has been finished by any process — as milling, punching or profiling — that insures uniform lengths and widths, the locating points may be placed on all sides of the piece as shown Fig. 224, in which pins are used as stops or locating points. It is necessary to flatten the pins on the sides that come in contact with the work to prevent wear.

When a jig is to be used constantly, it is advisable to have a shoulder or rib for the work to rest against, rather than pins, as the former will not wear as rapidly. Fig. 225 shows the same form of jig as Fig. 224 except that ribs are substituted for pins.

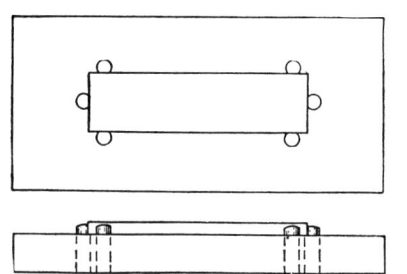

Fig. 224.

When there is no surety that the dimensions of the different pieces are exactly alike it is advisable to locate the pieces in the jig from certain portions. The work must be forced against the locating points by means of a screw, cam or wedge. With a screw the work may be forced to position and held there even when the dimensions of the piece vary considerably. The cam is operated much more quickly than the screw and holds the work firmly when the size of the pieces vary but little. For certain purposes the wedge is an admirable holding device, but it is not generally used. Fig. 226 shows a jig in which the work is located from one side and end; the work being forced against the stops by means of a screw.

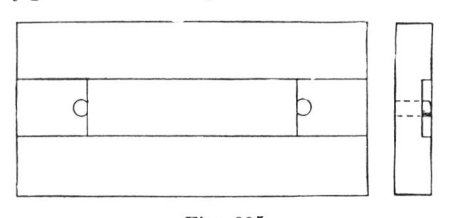

Fig. 225.

Fig. 227 represents the same jig having a cam instead of a screw.

When making any of these styles of jigs, the holes to contain the bushing may be located by several methods. If extremely accurate work is not necessary, a templet may be made, or a model piece used having the holes properly located; this piece may be placed in the jig and by means of drills the holes are transferred to the jig. If the bushings are to be used the holes may be enlarged by a counterbore having a pilot which fits the drilled hole and a body of the desired size of the bushing. While this method is cheap and good enough for certain classes of work, it is not advisable to use it for a very accurate job.

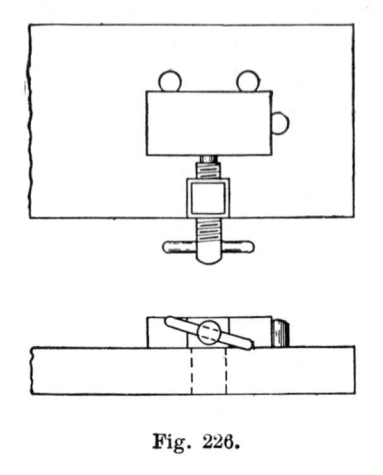

Another inexpensive method which insures *fair* results is to drill the holes as described above, then run a drill or reamer a trifle larger than the holes in the templet through the holes in the jig. Now place the templet in position and by means of a counterbore having a pilot which fits the hole in the templet counterbore the jig to the templet as shown in Fig. 228. Better results will be obtained if the ends of the teeth of the counterbore are made of the shape shown in Fig. 229, especially if the drilled hole should have run from its proper location.

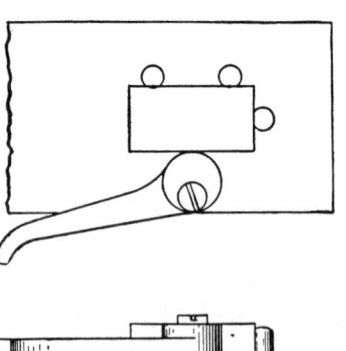

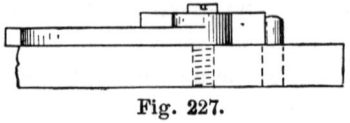

Fig. 226.

Fig. 227.

A third method is used when the bushing holes must be located by measurement, or when there is no templet or model piece. By means of a surface gauge having the point of the needle set at the proper height from a scale attached to an angle iron, as shown in Fig. 230, scratch a dimension line on the surface which has been colored with blue vitriol. The needle is first set to the height of the locating rib. The scale attached to the angle iron is adjusted so that the needle is at the exact height of one of the inch lines if possible, if not, at one of the half of quarter inch lines. The needle may then be raised to locate the center of the first hole and a line scratched while the jig is on edge. The centers of the other holes may now be laid off on this plane, after which the jig may be turned one quarter way around to

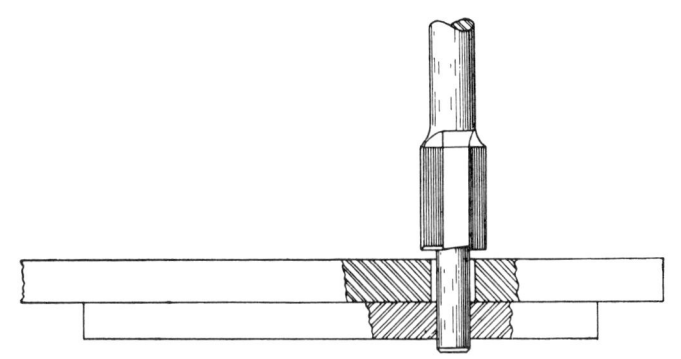

Fig. 228.

locate the hole from the other measurements. Where the lines intersect prick punch the surface of the jig. For this work *do not* use the center punch made for centering work to be turned in the lathe. Use the prick punch which should be much lighter than the ordinary center punch; Fig. 231 shows the two punches. The point of the prick punch should be ground in some form of

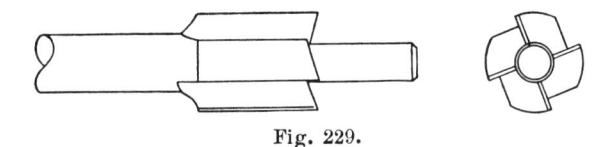

Fig. 229.

grinder in which it may be held and revolved in order that the point may be perfectly round. If this is not done it will be impossible to get the point of the center indicator to run true when attempting to true the jig on the face plate of the lathe.

While the above method might be properly classed as an approximate measurement, an experienced workman can locate the bushings within a small limit of variation. More accurate work will result if the height gauge is used in laying off the dimension lines. The bottom surface of the extension is set to the height of the locating rib, as shown in Fig. 232; then by means of the vernier it may be raised to the exact height of the

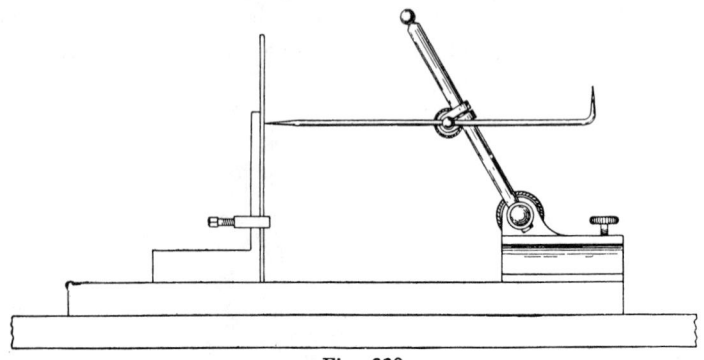

Fig. 230.

dimension desired, and the line scribed by means of the point of the extension.

While this method insures greater accuracy in laying off dimension lines and is sufficiently accurate for most work, it is open to the objection that the tool maker may change the location of centers somewhat when prick punching.

When *precise* measurements are desired many tool makers

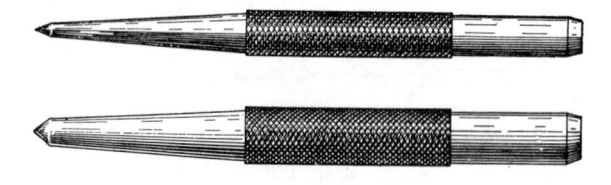

Fig. 231.

determine the location of bushing holes by means of hardened discs or buttons. A very common size, Fig. 233, if $\frac{1}{2}$ inch diameter, $\frac{3}{16}$ inch thick and having $\frac{1}{4}$ inch hole. While it is not essential that the diameter be any particular size, it must be some fraction divisible by two without a remainder, as one half the size of the disc is considered in all computations. If the disc is .500

inch diameter, .250 inch is the decimal to be considered; but if the disc were $\frac{9}{16}$ (.5625) inch diameter it would be necessary to consider the decimal .28125 in all computations. In locating the disc most of the measurements are made with the vernier caliper, and as the tool is not graduated to read closer than .001 inch it would be impossible to consider the fractions of a thousandth of an inch; consequently discs .500 inch diameter are generally used.

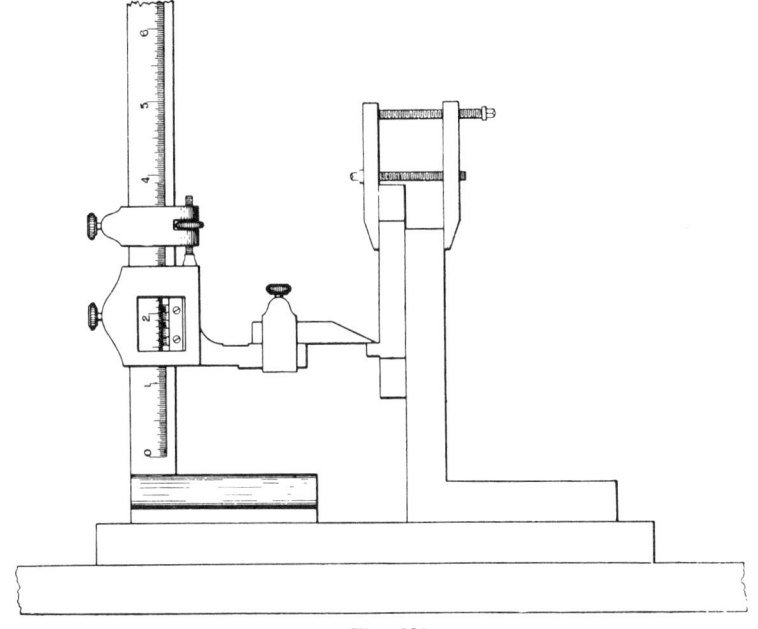

Fig. 232.

The locations of the different holes are laid off by means of the surface gauge, setting the needle to the scale fastened to an angle iron as already described. The holes are drilled and tapped for a screw somewhat smaller than the hole in the discs. The discs are now attached to the jig by means of screws. As the screws do not fill the holes in the discs, they may be moved until properly located. Fig. 234 shows a jig having the discs located in relation to the stops.

After properly locating a disc at each point where a bushing is desired, the jig may be fastened to the face plate of the lathe.

144   TOOL MAKING.

The jig must be so located on the face plate that one of the discs will run *perfectly* true. This may be determined by a test indicator operating on the outside of a button, as shown in Fig. 235. After locating so that the disc runs exactly true, the disc may be removed and the hole bored to the required size. The jig may now be moved to bring another disc to the proper location, after which it may be removed and the hole bored; this operation may be repeated until all the bushing holes are bored.

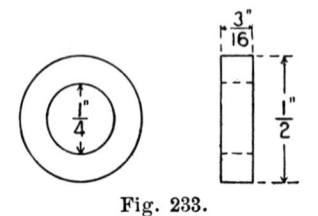

Fig. 233.

When jigs are made for permanent equipment, or if they are to be used constantly, it is well to provide some means of raising them from the drill press table to avoid inaccurate work occasioned by chips. When the jig is made of cast iron, the legs are sometimes cast solid with the jig as shown in Fig. 236. In order to grasp a jig handle in a manner that will not be tiresome to the

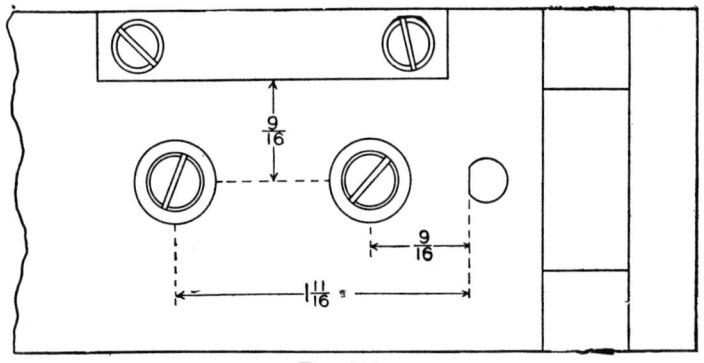

Fig. 234.

wrist or hand, and allow sufficient room between the handle and the table of the drill press so that the fingers may not be cut by chips, the legs are made of a length that will raise the handle about $1\frac{1}{8}$ inches above the table. As cast-iron legs of this length would be too weak, it is customary to make the legs of tool steel hardening the ends that come in contact with the drill press table.

While the form of jig shown in Fig. 222 would give satisfaction on certain classes of work, the process of putting the work in,

TOOL MAKING. 145

and taking it out of the jig would be very slow, as it would be necessary to clamp the work securely to resist the pressure of the cutting tools.

In order that work may be handled rapidly during these operations, jigs are designed so that the work will rest on the base

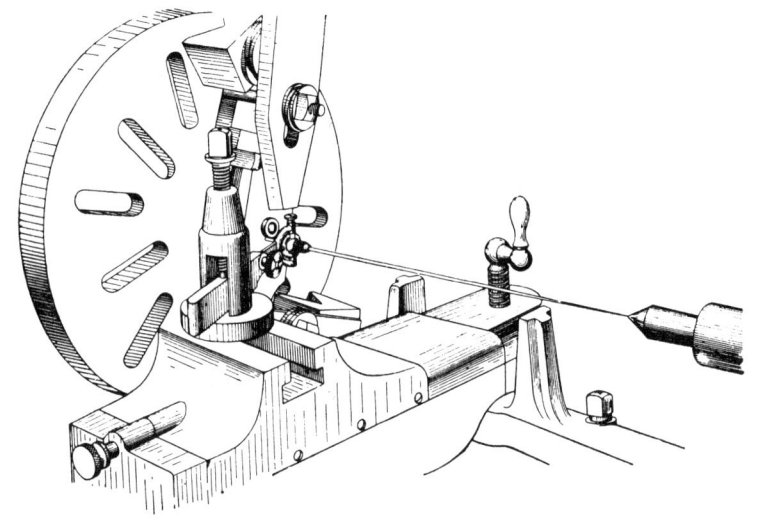

Fig. 235.

of the jig as shown in Fig. 237. A leaf or cover containing the bushings can be raised when putting the work in place and taking it out.

When the pieces to be drilled are of a uniform thickness the

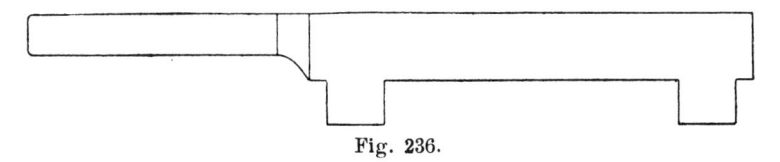

Fig. 236.

leaf may be made to rest on the piece. But should the pieces vary in thickness the leaf would not be parallel to the base; consequently the hole in the bushing would not be at right angles to the piece to be drilled. For this reason a little space is left between the top of the piece to be drilled and the bottom of the leaf, as shown in Fig. 238; a steady pin having a shoulder is located at the handle end of the jig. The upper end of pin may project into a hole in the leaf as shown thus relieving any strain on the joint of the jig occasioned by the action of the cutting tools.

When holes are to be drilled from opposite sides of a piece

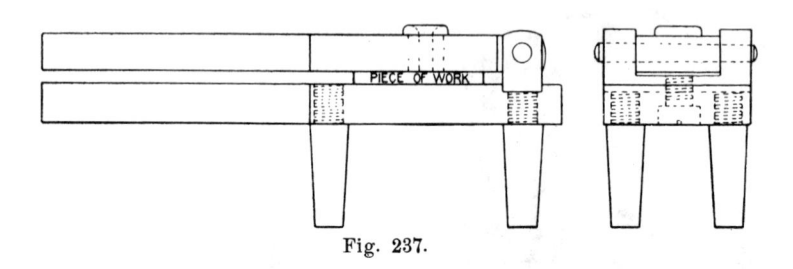

Fig. 237.

of work, as shown in Fig. 239, a jig may be constructed having legs on both upper and lower sides, but both sets of legs should be solid with the base as shown in Fig. 240.

If the two end holes in Fig. 239 are of the same size and it is necessary to use a drill press having but two spindles, the legs on each side should be of a length that would make it possible to

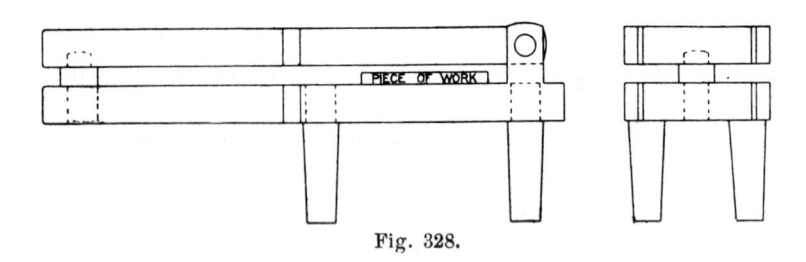

Fig. 328.

set the stops so that the drill would cut the required depth on each side. If a drill press having three or more spindles is to be used, the jig legs may be of a convenient length, as two drills of the same diameter can be used in two different spindles, each one to drill the required depth when the stop is set.

Drill jig legs are generally made of tool steel and are screwed into the base of the jig: the thread on the legs should be a good

TOOL MAKING. 147

fit in the base. After screwing in place the ends of the legs should be machined to length by milling or planing; the legs may then be removed and the ends that come in contact with the drill press table hardened. The legs may now be polished (if that is allowable) and then screwed in place. The ends should now be ground to such a length that the surface where the work is seated will be of the correct height above the drill press table.

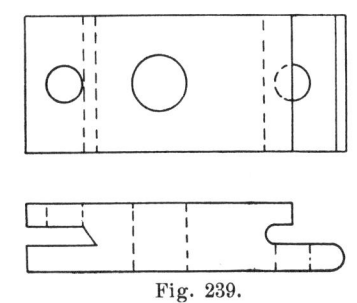

Grinding the ends of the legs can best be done in a surface grinder, or some form of universal grinder designed for surface grinding. After grinding, the ends of the legs may be lapped to

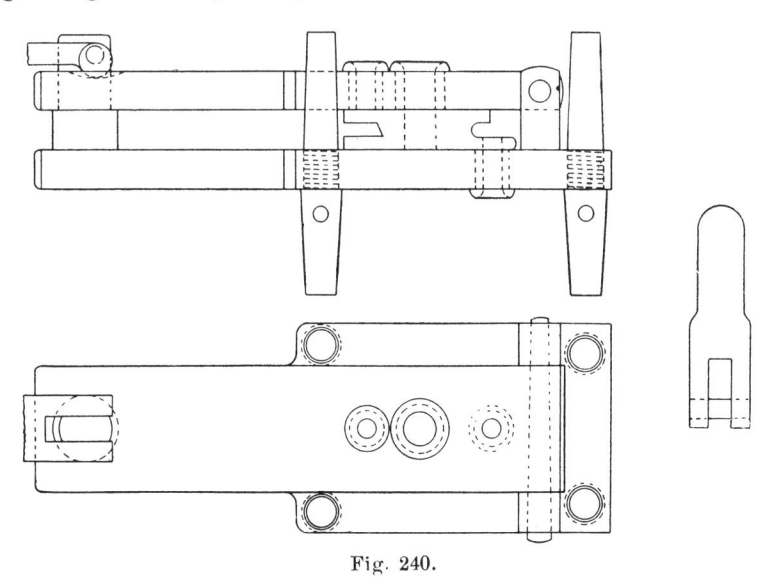

Fig. 239.

Fig. 240.

remove any irregularity that may result from grinding. A very good lap may be made from a flat plate or block of cast iron. The surface to be used may be planed flat and smooth, then a series of grooves cut to form squares, as shown in Fig. 241. These grooves may be cut with a V-shaped tool and should be $\frac{1}{4}$ inch to $\frac{1}{64}$ inch to $\frac{1}{32}$ inch deep. The grooves catch the emery and feed it to the work being lapped. If the pressure is not equal one leg may be

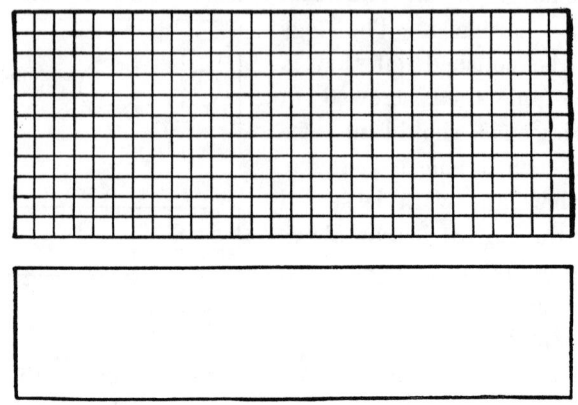

Fig. 241.

cut shorter than the other, or may be lapped out of true, causing the jig to rock.

TOOL MAKING.

PART III.

DRILL JIGS.

Fastening Devices. Various devices are used to fasten the leaf of a jig to hold the work in place or to clamp the leaf in position. The forms used depend upon the class of work being operated on.

If the leaf must be fastened solidly and the amount of time consumed is not of great importance, some form of screw clamp may be used. If, however, the work must be handled rapidly, the clamping device is generally operated by some form of a cam. However, a screw clamp may be designed to work quite rapidly.

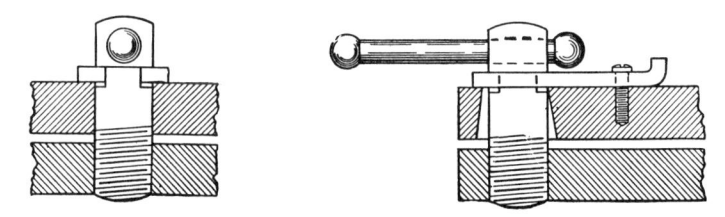

Fig. 242.

Fig. 242 shows a screw clamp which consists of a screw which has a hole drilled through it to receive a pin which is used as a lever to operate the screw. The screw is necked $\frac{1}{16}$ inch deep, the necking being $\frac{1}{8}$ inch wide; a flat washer is attached to the leaf of the jig by a small screw as shown. A slot of the width of the screw is cut in this washer in order to allow it to slide back and forth. In the end of the washer is a slot the width of the bottom of the necking in the screw. The other end of the washer is turned up as shown, in order to furnish a means of pushing back and forth. When the jig leaf is closed, the washer is pushed forward and the ends engage in the slot in the screw. One turn of the screw binds it very tightly. When the screw is given one turn to loosen it, the washer may be pushed back and the jig leaf raised.

If a quicker form of clamping is desired a cam may be used. The form represented in Fig. 240 is rapid and powerful.

Were it not necessary to use much power, but extreme rapidity of action is desired, a hinged cam lever of the design

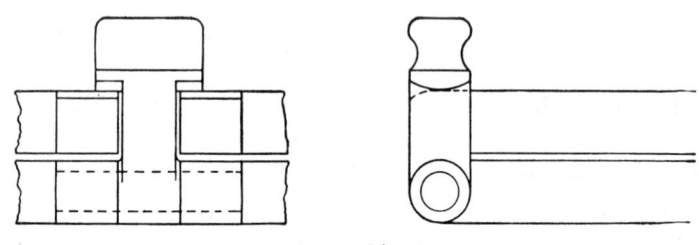

Fig. 243.

shown in Fig. 243 may be used. The cam lever is pivoted to the base of jig by means of a pin as shown. The lever passes into a slot in the leaf and the bearing surfaces on the under part of the head come in contact with the inclined surfaces at the end of the leaf.

Bushings. Bushings of hardened tool steel are made for a

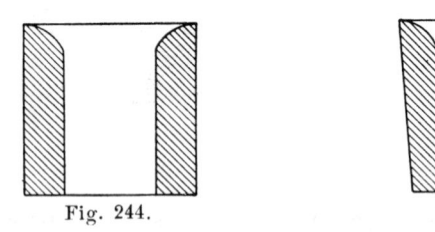

Fig. 244.   Fig. 245.

permanent means of guiding the cutting tools. The hole in the bushing is made to fit the cutting tool that is to be guided. There are various forms of bushings; the plain straight form shown in Fig. 244 is sometimes used, but is objectionable because it may be pushed into the jig if the cutting tool is too large to pass through the hole.

To overcome this tendency they are sometimes made **tapering** on the outside as shown in Fig. 245, but as this is an expensive form

TOOL MAKING.

to make, and as it is an extremely difficult operation to bore the bushing hole in the jig, this form is not generally used for permanent bushings.

The most common form of bushing is straight with an enlarged portion or head. When no allowance is made for grinding on the outside it is commonly made of the form shown in Fig. 246. If the shoulder under the head is square, it is likely to crack at the sharp corner, or the head may be broken off when being forced in position. In order to avoid these difficulties a fillet is left under the head as shown in Fig. 247.

When it is essential that the location of the drilled hole or portion of the piece being machined in the jig be exact as to location, the tool must fit well in the bushing; and as the size and shape of the bushing is likely to change when hardening, it is

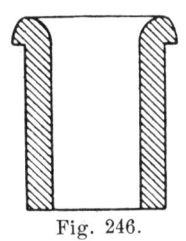

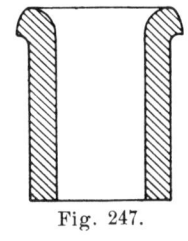

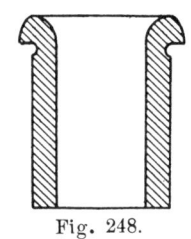

Fig. 246.   Fig. 247.   Fig. 248.

advisable to leave enough stock to grind to size both inside and out. It is essential that the outside of the bushing be exactly concentric with the inside. After grinding and lapping the hole to size, the bushing may be placed on a mandrel which runs true and the outside ground to size. When machining a bushing which is to be ground on the outside it is necessary to neck in, under the head, as shown in Fig. 248, in order that the emery wheel may pass entirely over the part being ground and insure a straight surface. The under side of the head which rests on the upper surface of the jig should be ground in order that it may be true with the surface of the jig.

When grinding a bushing, a mandrel should be used which has been tested for truth. The mandrel should be straight or of very slight taper. If the taper is considerable, one end of the hole in the bushing, will not fit and the outside of the bushing will not be concentric with the hole. Consequently no matter how careful the tool maker might be in laying out his work and in boring the holes for the bushings the jig will not be accurate.

Size of Bushings. The outside diameter of a bushing is often determined by the design of the jig; for instance, two holes are often located so near each other that it is impossible to make the bushings much larger than the holes through them. Wherever possible the outside diameter should be made enough larger than the hole to leave a reasonably thick wall. A bushing with thin walls is likely to close in when being pressed to its seating; then again, if a cutting tool binds in a bushing with thin walls, the bushing becomes loose and turns in the jig.

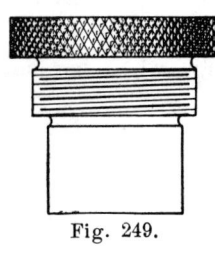

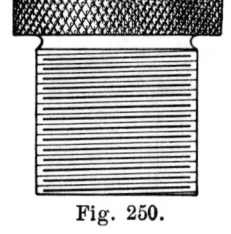

Fig. 249.   Fig. 250.

Removable Bushings. It is sometimes advisable to do two or more operations in the same jig. After drilling a hole it may be considered good practice to counterbore or tap it, or possibly it may be better to do the three operations while the work is seated in the jig. In such cases the bushing having a hole the size of the drill must be removed and one with a hole fitting the tool to be used inserted.

A very simple way of making a removable bushing consists in boring the hole in the jig large enough to receive a hardened bushing with a hole the size of the outside of the bushing to be used. If the hole in the large stationary bushing and the outside surface of the removable bushing are lapped smooth after grinding, they may be used for a long period before wearing enough to appreciably affect the location.

Tapered removable bushings are sometimes used; but on account of the expense of producing them and the fact that chips and dirt readily throw them out of their true locations, they are not very common.

Fig. 249 shows a form of removable bushing threaded on the outside to fit a threaded hole in the jig. If the thread on the outside of the bushing runs the entire length the process of screwing it in and out of the jig is necessarily very slow; consequently it is advisable to have but few threads. The balance of the length may be made to fit a bearing in the jig. If it is advisable to thread the entire length as shown in Fig. 250, the hole should be ground true with the thread to prevent change of shape in

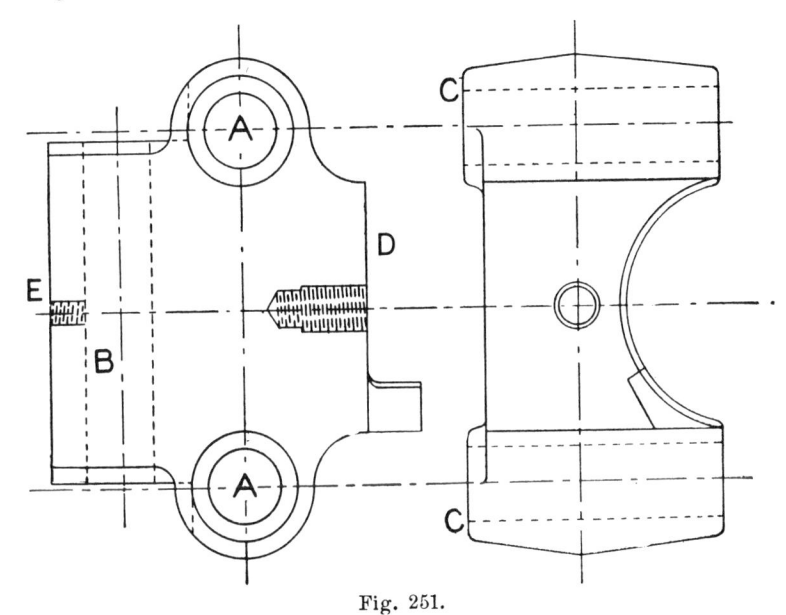

Fig. 251.

hardening. As it is not well to attempt to grind between the lands of the thread with the facilities in the ordinary machine shop, it is necessary to grind the hole true with the thread. This can be done satisfactorily by placing a piece of stock in a chuck on a lathe having a grinding attachment.

After drilling and boring the hole to tapping size, the thread may be chased so that the bushing is a good fit in the hole. It may then be screwed in and the hole ground to size.

If the piece of work is of a shape that makes it necessary to operate on all sides and the outline prevents the use of a clamp jig of the forms shown, a box jig must be used.

154   TOOL MAKING.

A Box Jig is made in the form of a box; the work is located in the jig by means of stops or locating points which differ according to the nature of the work. It is often advisable to design this form of jig so that all the holes in the work may be drilled at one setting; that is, if there are twenty holes in the piece, the jig is designed to allow drilling all the holes while the piece is in the jig. For other work it is advisable to make two or more jigs to

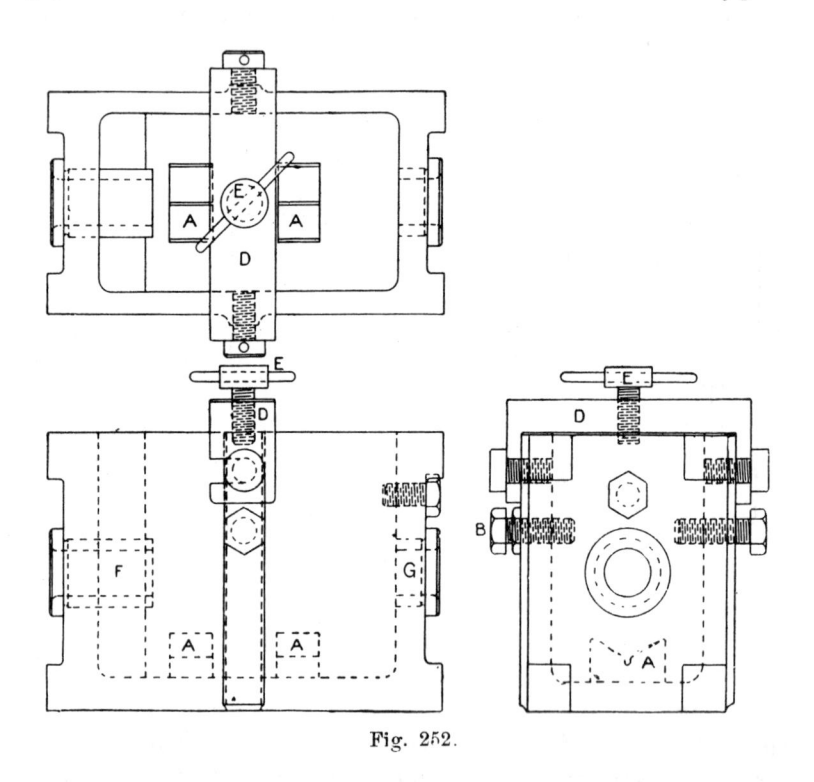

Fig. 252.

drill the holes; this is the case when some part of the piece is to be machined after one or more holes are drilled but before drilling the others.

In Fig. 251 a piece of work is shown (three eighths size); through the piece it was necessary to drill three 1-inch holes as shown at A, A and B. As it was necessary to have the holes A A an *exact* distance from B it was found by experience that much better results could be obtained if the hole marked B was drilled and reamed in a jig, the piece taken out of the jig and the portions marked C and C milled in exact relation to the hole B and as nearly at right angles with the side of casting marked D as possible. After milling the portions C C, as described, the piece was placed in another jig locating it by the hole B and the surfaces C C; the holes A A were then drilled and reamed. In order to drill the hole B the jig shown in Fig. 252 was used.

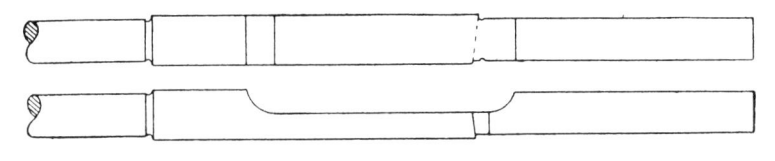

Fig. 253.

The piece was placed in the jig with the rounded surface E resting in two V blocks as shown at A. It was located by means of the fixed stop screw B and forced against A by the screw; it was held in position by the screw E which was located in the strap D. This strap was removed when putting a piece of work in the jig, or taking it out. As it was necessary to have the hole straight and true with the locating points, it was reamed with a single lip

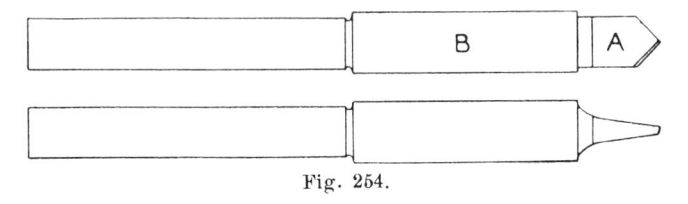

Fig. 254.

reamer having a pilot as shown in Fig. 253. The hole was drilled somewhat smaller than finish size ($\frac{1}{64}$ inch); the reamer was entered in the hole, the pilot fitting the bushing G. While the body of the reamer fits the bushing F, as previously explained, the single lip reamer acts on the same principles as a boring tool used in the engine lathe; the result being a hole straight and true. As it is necessary to have the hole in the upper bushing of the size of the body of the reamer, and as a drill $\frac{1}{64}$ inch smaller than this size must be used in drilling the hole, it was advisable, in order to properly start the drill, to use a transfer drill shown in Fig. 254, the cutting portion A of drill being the size of the drill to be used in drilling the hole, while B fits the hole in the bushing. By means of this drill a hole the size of the drill to be used was started in the casting perfectly true with the hole in the bushing yet somewhat smaller. When the hole had been drilled to a depth of $\frac{3}{16}$ or $\frac{1}{4}$ inch, the transfer drill wss removed and a twist drill of the proper size used to finish the drilling. When the piece of work was taken from the jig the portions marked C C, Fig. 251, were milled as explained. The piece was then placed in another jig, a pin which fits the reamed hole passed through the locating bushings and through the hole; by this means it was located to properly drill the other two holes. The second jig so closely resembles the first it is unnecessary to illustrate it.

PUNCH AND DIE WORK.
THE DIE.

A die used for punching a blank from a sheet of metal is termed a blanking die, and is generally considered as belonging to one of three classes: plain (or simple) die, gang die or compound die.

A set of blanking dies consists of a male die or *punch* and a female die or *die block*. The die block is that part of the die which has a hole of the same outline as the desired blank; the male die, or punch, is of a shape that fits the impression, or hole, of the die block.

When punching work on a punching press, the stock is placed on the die and the punch forced through it into the die; this drives a piece of stock of the same outline as the hole down into the die block. Now as the punch is forced through, the metal in the sheet closes on the punch and is raised by it. In order to prevent this the die block is provided with a *stripper plate* (or stripper). The stripper is fastened to the die or to a shoe holding the die at a height that allows the metal to be punched to pass freely between it and the die. The stripper must be strong enough to force the stock from the punch without springing, especially if the punch is slender and the stock thick, because under these conditions the punch would be sprung or broken.

In order to guide the stock over the die and leave the proper amount of margin or scrap at the edge of the sheet, a *guide* is furnished. The guide is usually made of stock sufficiently thick to bring the stripper the proper height above the face of the die.

A *gauge pin* (or stop) is usually provided; this pin is located so that the proper amount of scrap is left.

In Fig. 255, A is the die block, B the hole through the die

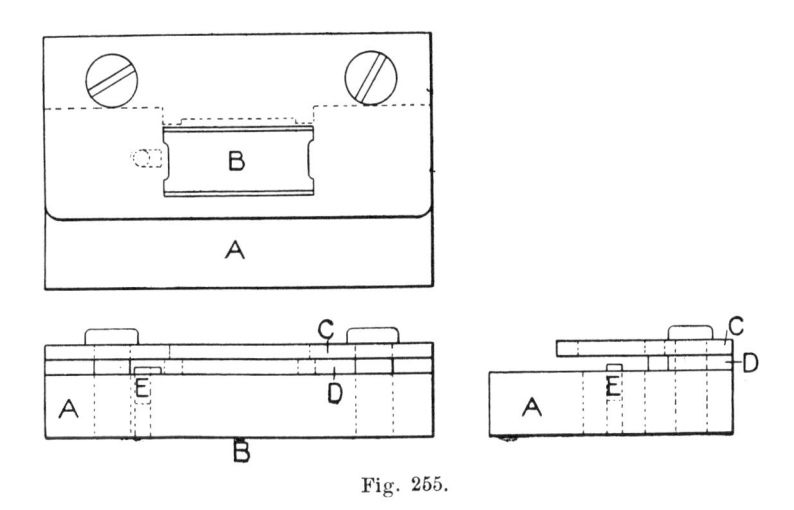

Fig. 255.

block of the shape of the piece to be punched, C the stripper, D the guide and E the gauge pin or stop.

Dies are held in position on the punching press bed by various methods, the most common of which is by means of the forms of hold-fast shown in Figs. 256 and 257. These die holders are known by various names, such as chair, bolster, chuck and die holder. Large dies are clamped to the bed of the press.

Dies are usually beveled on the edges that come in contact with the die holder to prevent their rising from the seat. The angle given to the edges varies according to the ideas of the designer. An angle of 10° from the vertical gives satisfaction, although some mechanics insist on an angle of 15° or even 20°.

Fig. 258 shows a die, whose edges are at an angle of 10°, in a die holder; the die being held in place by set screws. It is generally considered advisable to place a gib between the set screws and die as shown. Sometimes the gib is omitted, the set screws bearing directly on the edge of the die. Some tool makers prefer a die holder without set screws, the die being held in place by the gib which is made wedge-shaped and is driven to place, thus securely holding the die.

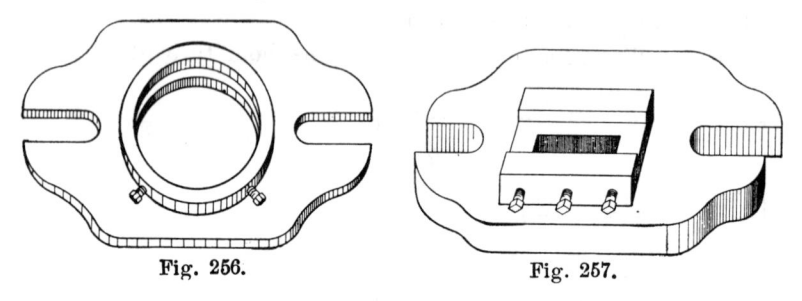

Fig. 256.   Fig. 257.

Fig. 259 shows a method of holding dies which allows the die to be easily set in position when rigging up. The die may be placed on the seating of the die holder and brought to the proper location; the set screws may then be brought against the edge of the die, or against strips of steel which may be placed between the edges of the die and the set screws.

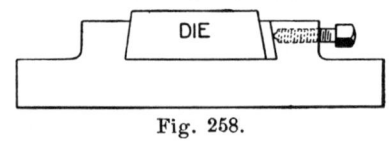

Fig. 258.

When making several dies of equal width and thickness a good method is to plane the two sides of a bar to remove the outer surface, then bevel the edges to the required angle. Pieces may then be cut off to any required length as wanted.

The upper surface of the die may be finished smooth by planing with a smoothing tool; it may be ground in a surface grinder, or it may be finished with a file. It is necessary to have the surface smooth in order to lay out the correct shape of hole, as it cannot be laid out correctly or distinctly on a roughly machined surface.

The face, or upper surface of the die is now covered with blue vitriol solution and the outline of the piece to be punched laid out. A die should be laid out in such a manner that the stock to be punched may be readily fed to the die. The *grain* of the stock should run in the proper direction if the product is to be a tempered spring or any article where the grain of the stock must be considered.

After the die has been carefully laid out from a templet, or drawing, all round corners should be drilled with a drill of the proper size, and reamed from the back side of the die with a taper

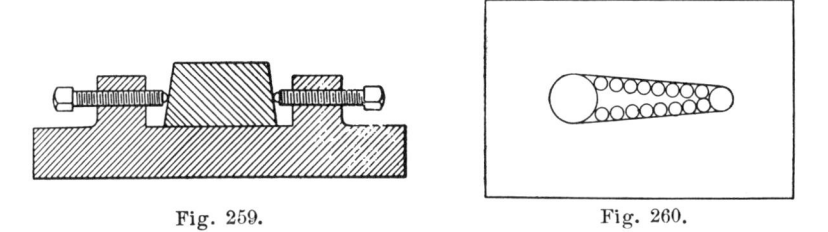

Fig. 259.   Fig. 260.

reamer to give the desired clearance; the balance of the stock is removed by drilling, as shown in Fig. 260. The method of removing the center, or core, depends on the custom practiced by the individual die maker; one may drill the holes so that they break into one another. When this method is adopted it is advisable to use a straightway (straight fluted) drill. Another will drill

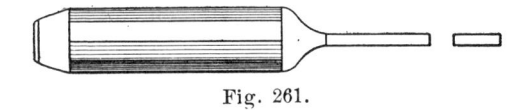

Fig. 261.

small holes and use a counterbore to enlarge to size; the counterbored holes breaking into each other.

Usually the holes are drilled with at least $\frac{1}{64}$ inch to $\frac{1}{32}$ inch between them, and then the intervening stock is cut out with a flat-ended "hand broach." Fig. 261 shows a tool of this description.

Generally speaking, the last mentioned method is the safest and quickest. After removing the center, the die may be placed in a die milling machine or a die sinking machine, and by using a milling cutter of the proper taper, the desired angle of clearance may be given; the amount of clearance varies with the nature of the work to be done.

160   TOOL MAKING.

When a die is milled on a die milling machine of the form shown in Fig. 262, the cutter spindle is underneath the die, the face of which is uppermost, consequently the milling cutter can be made largest at the shank end of cutting part, the required taper being given as shown in Fig. 263. If the outline of the hole is milled on a die sinking machine, it is necessary to use a cutter of the shape shown in Fig. 264 in order that the face of the die having the lines will be uppermost. After working the impression as near to shape as possible by milling, it can be finished by filing. In order to give the die the proper clearance the walls may be gauged with a bevel gauge of the form shown in Fig. 8. As the amount of clearance differs in various shops, and on different classes of work, no stated amount can be given for all cases; the amount varies from $\frac{1}{4}°$ to 3°. The latter is excessive and is seldom given unless it is necessary that the piece punched drop from the die each time.

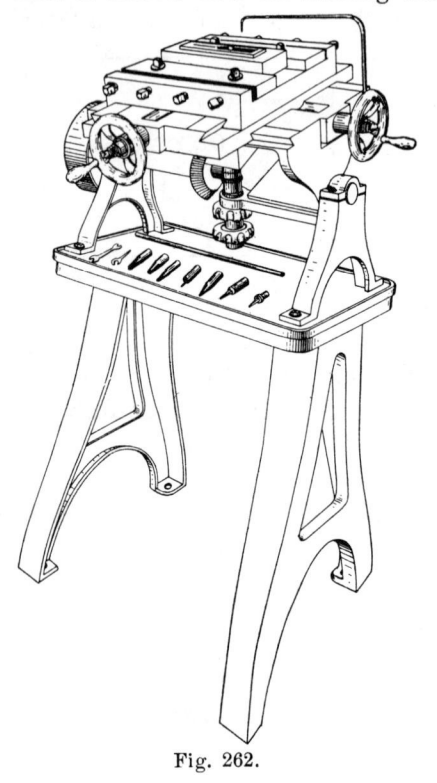

Fig. 262.

If the die is milled as described above it will be necessary to work all corners to shape with a file. If a universal milling machine having a slotting attachment is used, the corners can be properly shaped and the necessary clearance given by using suitably shpaed cutting tools, and turning the fixture to the proper angle.

Fig. 265 shows a slotting fixture attached to a universal milling machine, while Fig. 266 shows a fixture known as a die shaper which is also attached to a milling machine.

Die blocks have their cutting edges beveled in order that the

TOOL MAKING. 161

blank may be cut from the stock by a shearing cut. *Shear* is given the face of the die to reduce the power necessary to cut the blank from the stock; thus enabling a press to punch a blank from thicker stock. It also reduces the strain on the punch and die.

The face of the *die* is sheared when the blank, or piece forced through, is the product to be saved. But if the piece surrounding the blank is to be saved, and the blank is of no use, the face of the die is left perfectly flat and the end of the *punch* is sheared.

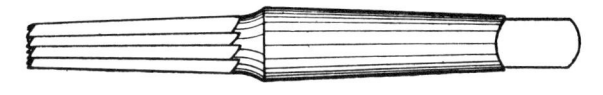

Fig. 263.

The cutting face of the die may be sheared by milling or planing to the desired angle which depends on the thickness of the stock to be punched and also the power of the press. A common method of shearing a die is shown in Fig. 267, which shows a section of a die used for punching a heavy spring. The end of the *punch* is left flat. The punching commencing at the center A, is continued with a gradual shearing cut as the punch descends until it reaches the ends BB, of the opening. The blank punched will be straight while the stock will bend somewhat unless it is quite stiff, in which case it springs back to shape when the pressure is removed.

Fig. 264.

When the punching requires an amount of power in excess of the capacity of the press, as in the case of the forging shown in Fig. 268, it is necessary to trim the flash occasioned by the process of drop forging, and at the same time punch the end to shape as shown in Fig. 269. It is obvious that the material removed is of no value as a product, and as it is necessary to use a light press, the die may be given a shear as shown in Fig. 270; thus making it possible to do the punching on a press whose capacity is not equal to the job if the die had been sheared as shown in Fig. 267.

In order to facilitate the operation of grinding the face of a die, it is frequently made with a raised boss around the hole as shown in Fig. 271.

Sectional Dies. In order to make it easier to work dies to shape, they are sometimes made in two or more pieces; these are fastened together when in use. In the case of a plain die of the form shown in Fig. 272, the die is made in two pieces which are held in their relative positions by the dowel pin at each end as shown at A and B. When in the die holder they are held together in such a manner that they cannot spread. Dies of this form should have the surfaces that go together finished true; the pieces should then be clamped together and the dowel-pin holes drilled and reamed. They should then be taken apart and any burrs caused by drilling and reaming removed. The pins should now be inserted and the top and bottom of the die planed. The outlines of the piece to be punched may now be laid out and the round hole at one end drilled; after which it should be reamed from the back with a taper reamer to give clearance. The die may now be taken apart, and the opening cut out on the planer or shaper; the sections of the die being held at the proper angle to give the desired amount of clearance. After placing the two pieces together the opening may be finished with a file and scraper to the templet.

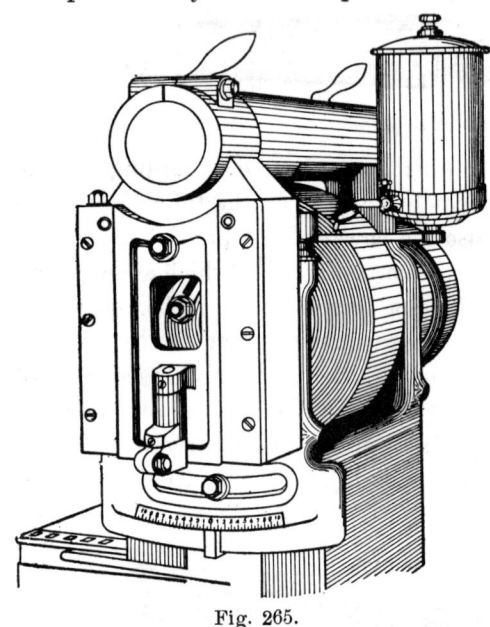

Fig. 265.

To hold the die together securely it is necessary to use a die holder of the form shown in Fig. 273. The die is represented in place in the holder which is held in the bolster which is in turn attached to the bed of the press. When the die is finished to the

TOOL MAKING. 163

templet and the proper clearance given, make sure that the walls of the opening are straight (not crowning), although it is not always considered advisable to carry the clearance to the edge, as the size of the opening would then increase every time the die was sharpened. In such cases the clearance extends from the bottom to within a short distance (about $\frac{1}{8}$ inch) of the cutting surface as shown in the sectional view, Fig. 274. In this figure the clearance is exaggerated in order to illustrate the idea.

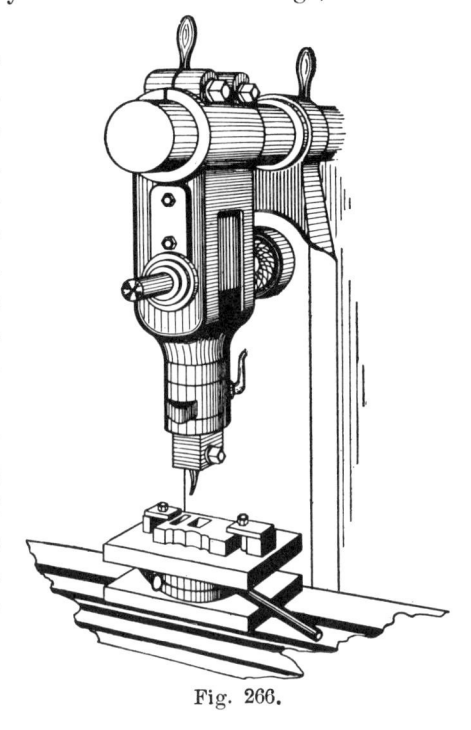

The walls of the upper part of the opening are at right angles to the base of the die, but they must be straight, that is, not crowning; because if the opening is wide enough to allow the punch to pass through the crowned part, the stock, if thin, would be likely to leave the blank with ragged edges which would extend up on the sides of the punch and have a tendency to burst the die.

Fig. 266.

Before hardening, the stripper and guide-screw holes should

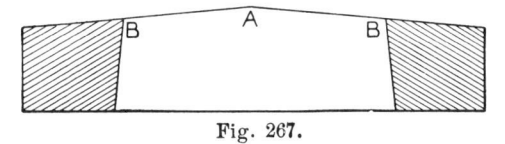

Fig. 267.

be drilled and tapped and the hole drilled for the gauge pin, or stop. If the name of the part to be punched, or the shelf number of the die are to be stamped it may be done now. After all screw holes, stop-pin holes, etc. are filled with fire clay mixed with water to the consistency of dough, the die is ready for hardening. Extreme care should be exercised when heating a die for hardening: it should be no hotter than is necessary to accomplish the desired result, and the heat should be uniform throughout; the corners must be no hotter than the middle of the piece and the outside surface must be of the same temperature as the interior of the

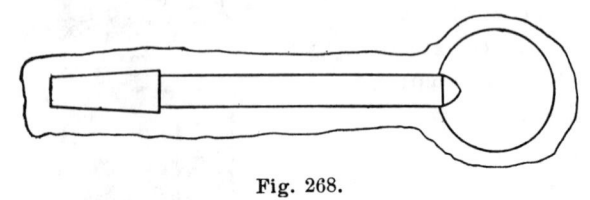

Fig. 268.

steel. The water in the bath should be slightly warmed to prevent any tendency to crack. The die should be lowered into the bath and swung back and forth gently so that the bath may pass through the opening, and harden the walls. As soon as the "singing" ceases it may be removed and plunged into a tank of

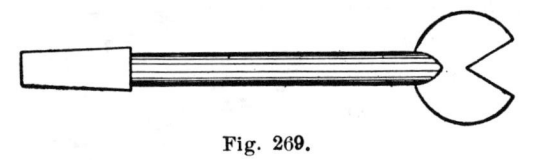

Fig. 269.

oil and allowed to remain until cold. It may then be brightened and the temper drawn. If more than a few minutes is to intervene between the time the die becomes cold, and commencing to draw the temper, it should be held over a fire or placed where it

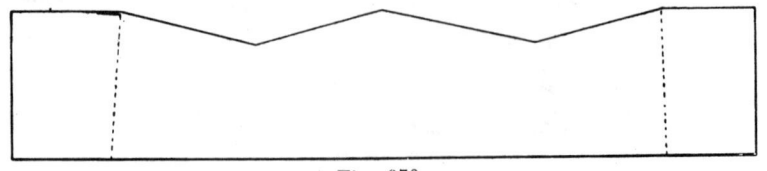

Fig. 270.

can be heated to remove the internal strains which have a tendency to crack the piece.

A very common method of drawing the temper of dies and similar pieces, is to heat a piece of iron to a red heat and place the

TOOL MAKING.

hardened piece on it leaving the face of the piece uppermost. Experience has taught the writer, however, that this method of treatment is too harsh for hardened steel, especially if the job is in the hands of one not thoroughly experienced. One side of the piece is subjected to an i n t e n s e heat while the opposite side is exposed to the cooling effects of the air. If an open fire is used a plate may be set on the fire, and the die placed on the plate before it is hot; now the temperature of the plate may be raised gradually, turning the die occasionally. In this manner the temper may be drawn to the desired degree with safety. When such a fire is not available two plates may be used, one heating while the other is in use. The first one should not be very hot,

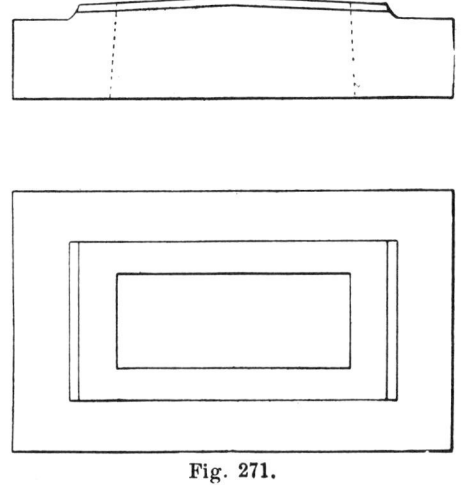

Fig. 271.

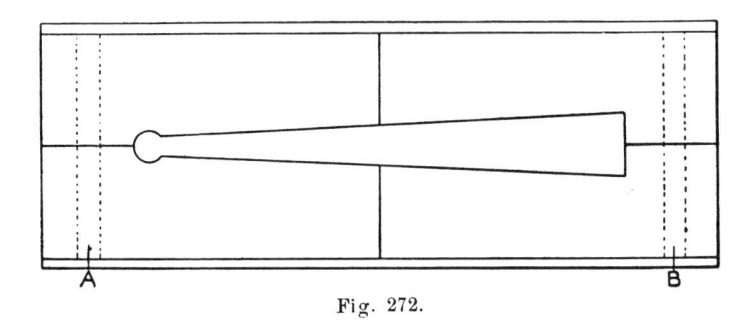

Fig. 272.

the next somewhat hotter, and so on until the die is drawn to the desired color.

When a die of such a shape that is likely to give trouble, is to be hardened much more satisfactory results will follow if the "Pack Hardening" process is used. Run the dies from 1 to 5 hours in the fire after they are red hot, then dip in raw linseed oil.

THE PUNCH.

The punch is used to force the metal through the die thus producing pieces of the desired shape.

In the case of small plain dies the punch is generally made of the form shown in Fig. 275. The end A is of the same outline as the opening in the die, the shoulder B which bears against the shoulder of the punch holder takes the thrust when the punch is working. The shank fits the hole in the punch holder, or in the ram of the press.

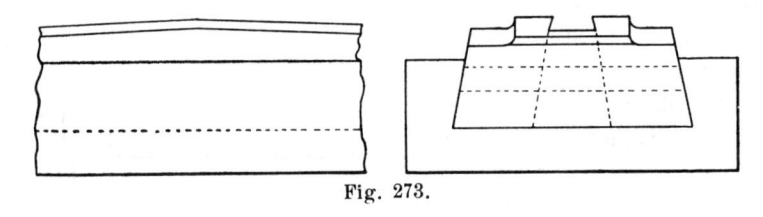

Fig. 273.

It is customary in most shops in this country to make the die to a drawing, or templet, and then harden it; after which the punch is fitted to it.

In the case of a punch for a plain die, the templet may be used in laying out the punch. If the shape of the opening in the

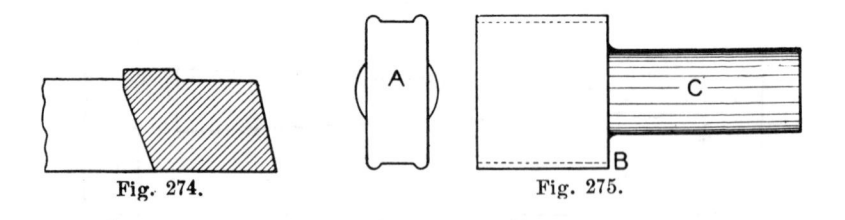

Fig. 274. Fig. 275.

die is the same on each side as shown in Fig. 276 and the die does not change shape in hardening the templet may be used either side next to the face of punch, but if the outline is of the form shown in Fig. 277, it will be necessary to exercise care when laying out the face of the punch from a templet, because the side of the templet placed against the face of the punch when laying it out will be opposite the one that would be placed against the face of the die when laying *that* out.

In order to obviate this trouble many tool makers lay out the face of the punch from the opening in the die before beveling the face for shear. In order to hold the punch and die together so that there will be no danger of the punch slipping while the required shape is being transferred, a die clamp of the form shown in Fig. 278 should be used.

The punch blank should be machined on both ends and the shank turned to size; the end which is to fit into the opening in the die should be finished with a smooth flat surface which should be colored with blue vitriol. After coloring, it may be clamped to the face of the die by means of the die clamp and the outline of the punch marked on the face by scribing through the opening in

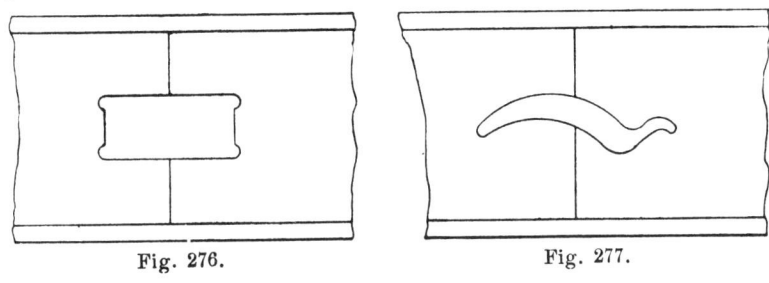

Fig. 276.   Fig. 277.

the die. This outline should be accurately marked with a sharp pointed prick punch as the scribed line is likely to become obliterated by the various operations of machining the punch to shape.

After the outline has been carefully prick punched, the punch may be milled or planed to shape leaving stock enough at all points to fit the die. If the die is to be beveled for shear, it should now be done and then hardened before fitting the punch.

The punch should be machined close to the lines and then placed over the hardened die and forced into it a little (about $\frac{1}{16}$ inch). This is termed "shearing in," and is the custom generally employed in this country.

After the punch has been sheared in for a short distance it may be removed and worked to size by means of chisel, file and scraper to the "witness" mark as the portion sheared in is termed, the operation of shearing may be repeated until the punch enters the entire length.

Fit of Punch and Die. If the material to be punched is

thin or soft, it is necessary to make the punch a closer fit in the die than if the stock is heavy or very stiff. Thin stock requires a punch nicely fitted to the die in order to avoid ragged edges on the punched blank. When punching stock $\frac{1}{8}$ inch in thickness, the punch may be $\frac{1}{64}$ inch smaller than the die; if the stock to be punched is very stiff there may be a greater difference, however, the exact amount depends on the nature of the material to be used and the character of the tool.

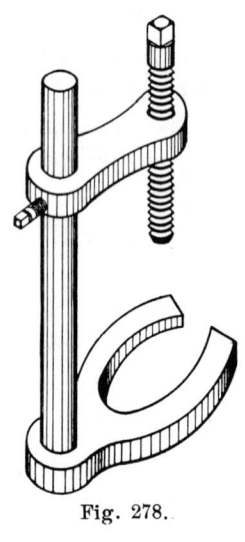

After the punch has been fitted to the die, the cutting end should be faced off to insure a good working surface and sharp edges. Any distinguishing names or marks necessary should be stamped on it, after which it is ready for hardening.

Hardening the Punch. Punches are hardened by heating in a muffler furnace, or in a clear charcoal fire, to a *low red* and cooling in water or brine, preferably the latter. Punches whose form insures strength need be hardened only on the end; the hardening should not extend quite back to the shoulder or shank. Small, slender punches are sometimes hardened the *entire* length; especially if they are to punch stock nearly as thick as the diameter of the punch; in which case the punch would become upset when used, if it were not hard the entire length.

Fig. 278.

It is generally considered good practice to have the punch softer than the die; on this account the punch is generally drawn to a color that insures this result. If a die is drawn to a straw color, the punch is drawn until it assumes a distinct purple, or even a blue color.

The punch is sometimes left soft, not hardening it at all. When this is done, it can be upset, and refitted when worn. As this would not work satisfactorily in many cases, it can be advocated only when it would be considered advisable to use a *soft* punch.

It is sometimes necessary to punch a hole in a piece of work that has been machined to some given shape. The piece is placed on the face of the die against locating points, or in an opening in a gauge plate; the opening being of the same outline as the piece of work. In Fig. 279 is shown a blank intended for a gun-sight leaf; A shows the blank before the rectangular hole is punched, while B represents the leaf after punching. The hole is punched

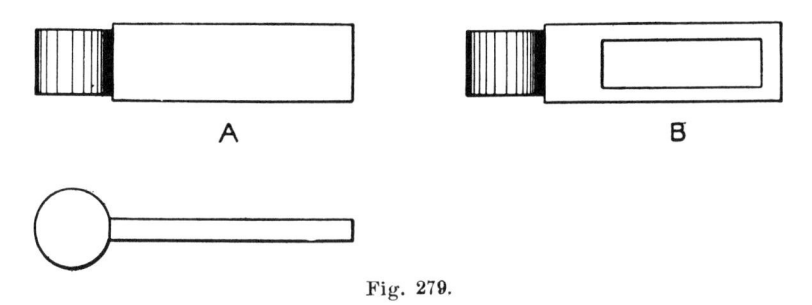

Fig. 279.

somewhat smaller than finished size, enough stock being left to work to size with broaches.

When punching work of this description, it is necessary to leave the face of the die flat; the punch is sheared as shown in Fig. 280. The piece punched from the leaf is of no value in this

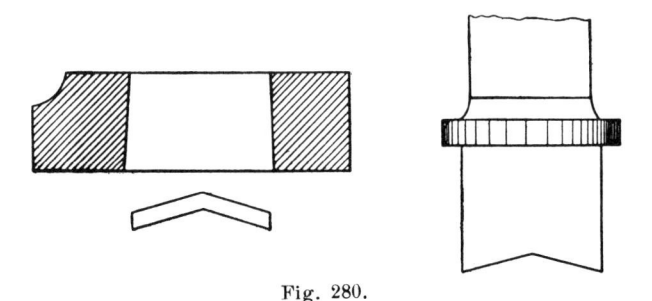

Fig. 280.

case, consequently the face of the punch is beveled, and the face of the die is left flat in order that the sight leaf may be straight after punching.

When a die and punch are to be used for an operation similar to the one described above, it is necessary to make a stripper of a form that allows the pieces to be easily placed in position and removed. As the piece which is punched is likely to increase in width from the operation, it is advisable to have stops or a guide on one side only in order to allow the piece to be readily removed after it is punched. Fig. 281 shows the same die with stripper and guide attached. The stripper is raised sufficiently from the die to allow the work to be readily inserted. A gauge pin is furnished for the end of the piece to determine the position of the slot in relation to the end. On one side is furnished a guide against which the piece rests to bring the slot central. The piece is held against the guide by means of a screw driver, a thin piece of steel, or a piece of wood.

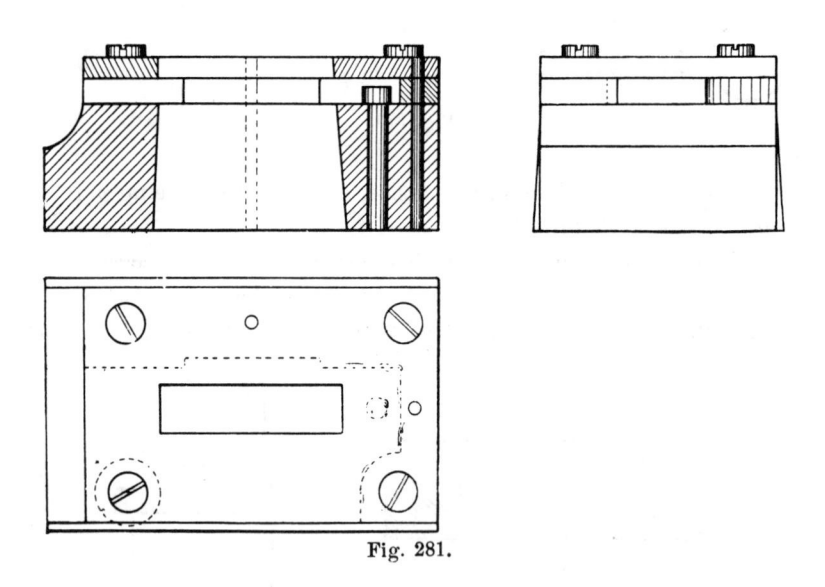

Fig. 281.

When a piece is to be punched and its size does not allow of a stripper being attached to the die as in the previous example, the stripper may be attached to the punch as shown in Fig. 282. It is made in such a manner that the stripper plate descending with the punch comes in contact with the piece being operated on and remains stationary. Between the stripper plate and the punch holder are coil springs which are compressed. The punches pass through and return. The stripper being forced downward by the action of the springs forces the blank from the punches. The gauge plate which is securely fastened to the die by means of screws and dowel pins as shown, has an opening of the same general outline as the blank but somewhat larger in order that the blank may be easily put in place and removed.

GANG DIE.

The gang die is used when punching a blank, together with any holes it is necessary to have in the blank, without being obliged to handle the pieces twice as would be the case if they were "blanked" at one operation and the holes punched at another. Two operations would be necessary if a punch and die of the form shown in Fig. 282 were used.

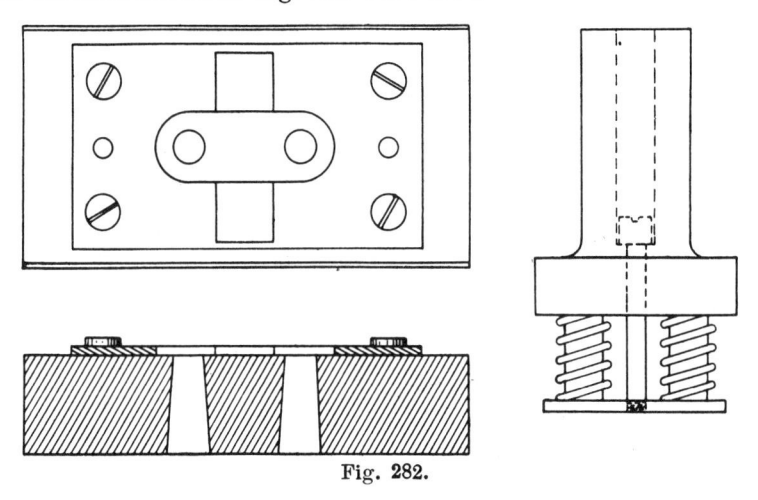

Fig. 282.

A common design of a gang die is shown in Fig. 283 which represents the piece operated on in Fig. 282. This die not only punches the holes but cuts the blank from the sheet. The stock is fed from right to left. The two holes are punched first and the stock is then fed along and the blank punched. At the same time the two holes are punched for the next blank to be cut. When the first two holes are punched in a strip of stock, the sheet is placed against the guide C, the end projecting slightly over the edge of the opening E. As the punches descend the holes F and F[1] are punched, and the end of the sheet is trimmed to length to stop at gauge pin D, which should be located about .010 inch farther to the left than the proper location for punching. The center pins as they enter the holes draw the stock

172   TOOL MAKING.

back to the proper location. It is obvious that the punch A must be a trifle longer than the punches B^1 and B. Were the small punches longer than A or even of the same length they would hold the stock in such a manner that the centering pins could not locate it, and, again, the centering pins striking on one edge of the hole would spoil the blank punched and probably the pins

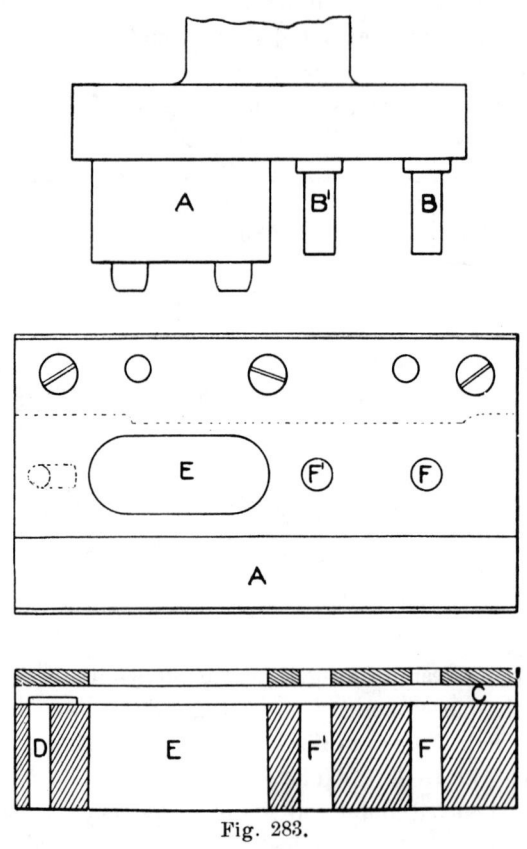

Fig. 283.

would be broken. The centering pins must not be a tight fit in the holes or the punched blank will stick to the pins and return with the punch. By carefully fitting the pins to a punched hole they may be fitted close enough to insure punching within a very small limit of variation. In fact for most classes of work it is possible to punch near enough to standards for all practical purposes.

TOOL MAKING. 173

When punching work with gang dies of the design shown in Fig. 283, it is easily seen that in the case of work being punched from strips wider than is necessary to get out two punchings, the scrap left between must be removed by some means. This is fre-

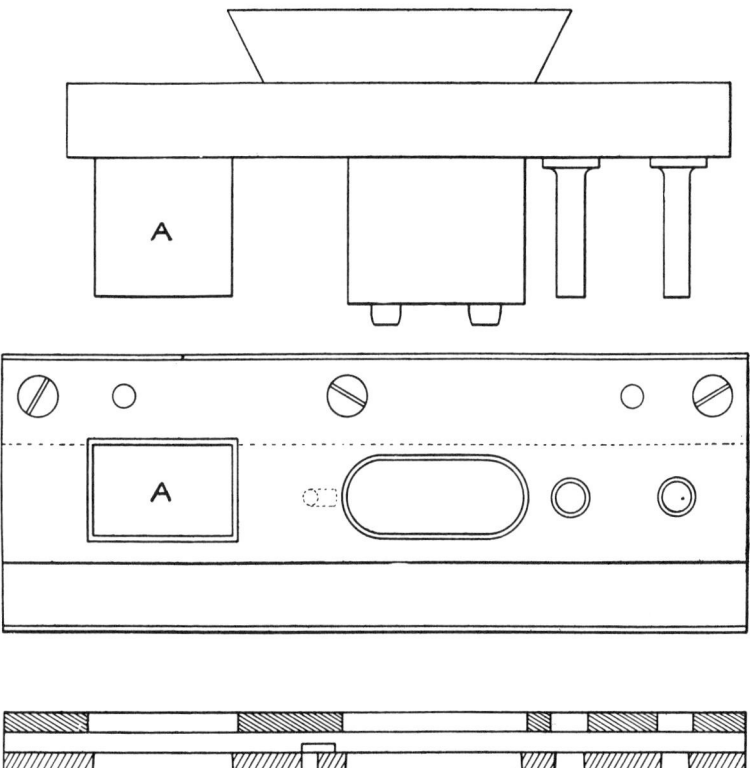

Fig. 284.

quently done by a large lever shear, or a pair of power shears; this is a costly operation where many pieces are punched at a time. To do away with this extra cost, dies are made having an extra opening and a punch working into this cuts away the surplus stock, or scrap, leaving the edge of the sheet straight and in condition to rest against the guide. In Fig. 284 the opening A is the trimming die; the punch working in this cuts away the scrap leaving the edge of the sheet straight.

MULTIPLE DIE.

When making a die for punching pieces whose outline will allow it, it is sometimes advisable to make several openings of the same outline so arranged that as many pieces may be punched at a time as there are openings in the die block. If the work is punched in large quantities a great saving can be effected in the cost of production by the use of this form of die.

Where perforated sheet metal work is manufactured it is customary to make dies having as many as 500 punches working into one die block at a time, but as this is an unusual application of this principle it will not be considered.

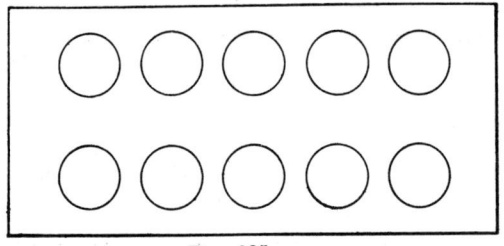

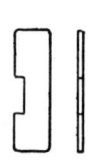

Fig. 285.   Fig. 286.

If it is necessary to punch 10 holes in the piece shown in Fig. 285 a die can be made having this number of openings. Then by making a punch holder having an equal number of punches properly located all the holes can be punched at one stroke of the press.

While in the case just cited the piece of stock which had the holes punched in it is the product, the punchings being scrap, the same principle may be applied to punching blanks from a sheet of stock by means of a multiple die.

The design shown in Fig. 286 is the product in a shop where many thousands of this piece are used monthly. The die produces a dozen or more blanks at each stroke of the press; but for convenience in illustrating the die and punches, it shows but four openings in the die with a corresponding number of punches. See Fig. 287.

If a die were made with the openings near enough together to punch the stock as shown in Fig. 288 there would be so little stock between the openings that the die would not stand up when used; for this reason the openings are located in such manner that every other opening shown in Fig. 288 is omitted. When the punch descends four blanks are punched; the stock is moved until the first opening strikes the gauge pin. This leaves the stock in

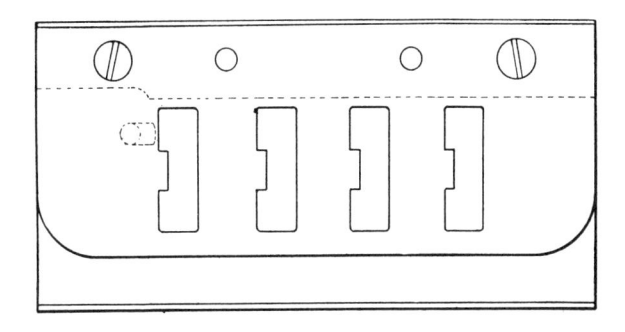

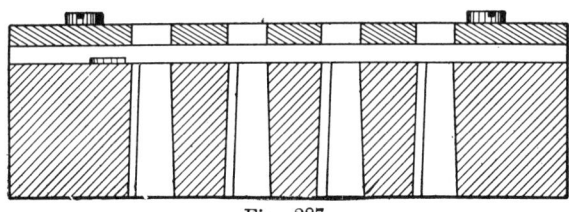

Fig. 287.

position to punch between the openings already made, thus preventing waste. The next time the stock is moved until the gauge pin strikes the wall of the last opening to the right.

BENDING DIE.

In order to bend metals to various forms, dies are made for use in punching presses, drop hammers and various other machines. A simple form of bending die is shown in Fig. 289. The shape of the upper and lower parts of the die is such, that when the upper part is brought down on the blank B (shown by the dotted lines) it will be bent to the required shape. The shoulder A forms a locating stop against which the blank rests before bending.

When making bending dies for extremely soft metals, the

dies may be made of the exact shape of the model, or the shape the piece should be when finished; but if the pieces are made from stiff material which bends with difficulty, it will be necessary to make the die of a form that will give the article **more** bend than is required as it will spring back some as soon as released by the return of the upper part.

Compound Bending Die. In Fig. 290 is shown a form of bending die used in bending bow spring and looped wire for armature connections or other looped wire work. The work is placed in the die, and the punch, as it descends, bends the wire to the shape of the die. The spring just back of the punch is compressed thus allowing the punch holder to descend and force the side benders BB toward the punch by means of the wedge pins AA, thus forming the piece in a circle.

Fig. 288.

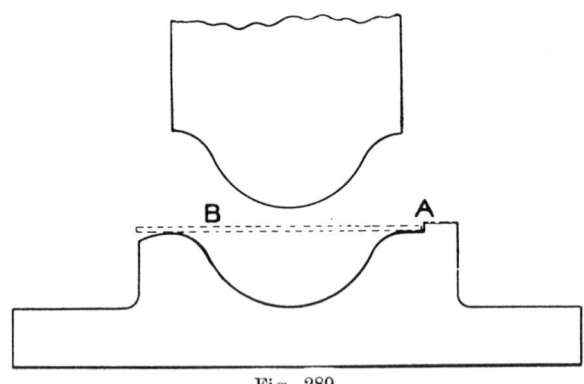

Fig. 289.

It is obvious that it is necessary to make the shape of the punch and die different. The lower die must have its bending surface, a curve of a radius equal to that of the punch plus the thickness of the material.

FORMING DIE.

This type of die is familiarly known as a *drawing die*. The most common examples of *forming* die is that used for drawing a flat circular blank, as shown at A, Fig. 291, into a cup-shaped

TOOL MAKING. 177

piece, as shown at B. This operation can be done in an ordinary punching press by means of a forming die of the shape known as a push through die, from that fact that the piece is formed to shape, and pushed through the die at one operation. This form of die is shown in Fig. 292. The face of the die is cut to receive the blank; this depression is known as the *set edge*. The opening

BOW SPRING

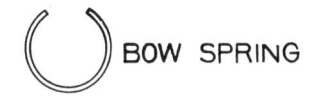

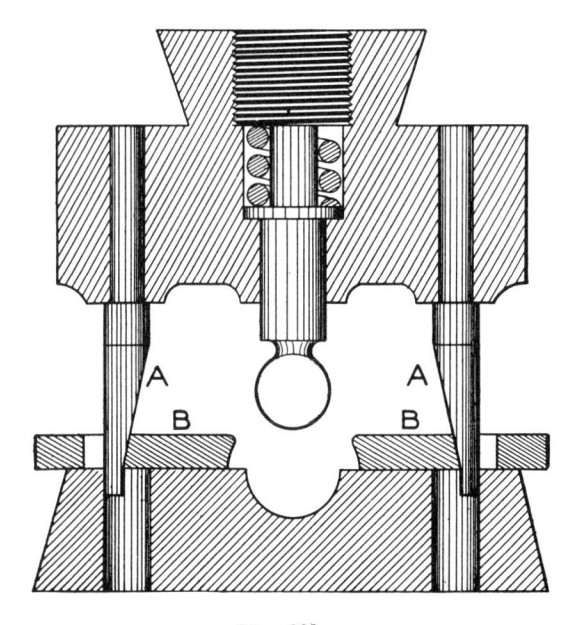

Fig. 290.

in the die is given a "draw" of $\frac{1}{4}$ to $\frac{1}{2}$ of a degree making it larger at the top, the upper edge is rounded over and left very smooth. The bottom edge of the opening is made very sharp in order that the piece may not be carried back with the punch as it returns.

This form of die is left as hard as possible, and the walls of the opening are made as smooth as they can be polished. It is sometimes advisable to finish the walls with a lateral rather than a circular finish.

MAKING GAUGES.

Gauges are used in machine shops in order that a part of a machine, apparatus, or tool may correspond with some other part, so that when it is assembled every part may go in its place with little or no fitting.

In shops where work is made on the interchangeable plan, that is, a piece of work made to-day will exactly duplicate a similar piece made at some time in the past, a very thorough system of inspection is necessary. In order that the inspection may accomplish the desired result, gauges are made that show any variation of the pieces from a given standard.

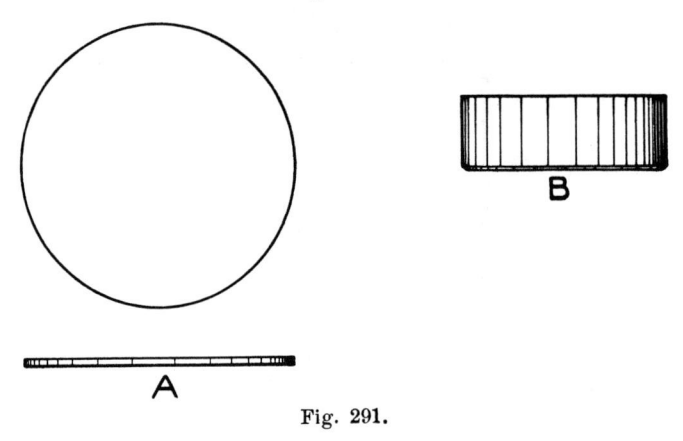

Fig. 291.

There are several forms of gauges in use for various classes of work, but only those in common use in the general machine shop will be considered here.

Gauges are generally made of *tool steel*; but *hardened tool steel* has a tendency to change its size or shape at a considerable time after the hardening takes place. This change is ascribed by acknowledged authorities, to a rearrangement of the minute particles or molecules of the steel, whose original arrangement had been changed by the process of hardening. While this change of size or shape is small, so small indeed, that it need not be considered except in the case of gauges where great accuracy is required, yet it has led some manufacturers to use machinery steel.

TOOL MAKING. 179

If tool steel is used, the tendency to change its shape may be overcome to some extent by grinding the gauge to within a few thousandths of an inch of finish size and allowing it to "season" as it is termed among mechanics; that is, it is laid aside for a few months or a year before finishing to size. This method is open to serious objection if one is in a hurry for a gauge.

To save time, it is customary in many shops to draw the temper to a straw color, allowing the gauge to cool off slowly;

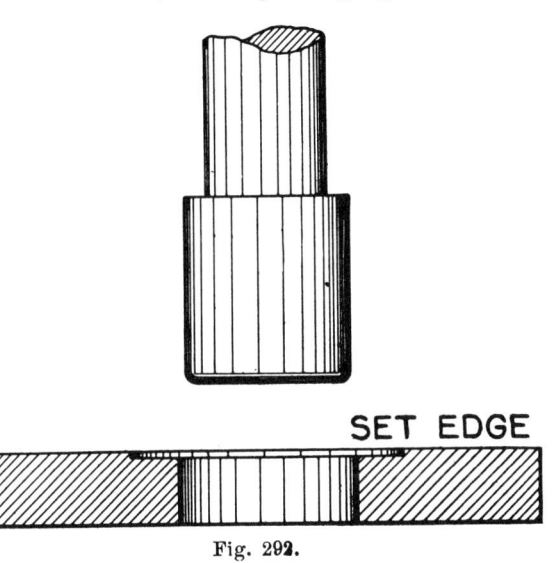

Fig. 292.

this operation is repeated several times. It is necessary to brighten the steel each time before drawing the temper in order that the colors may be readily seen; as this very materially softens the gauge it will not last as long as if left hard.

Accuracy in Gauge Making. When making gauges the workman should observe the points emphasized under "Approximate and Precise Measurements." While gauge making is generally considered very accurate work, unnecessary accuracy should not be used. If a gauge is intended for work where a variation of .005 inch is permissible, it is folly and a needless waste of time to attempt to make the gauge within a limit of variation of .0001 inch. On the other hand if the gauge is to be used as a test gauge on work requiring *great accuracy* it is necessary to use every possible effort to make it accurate.

If a gauge is to be made of tool steel, it is necessary to first remove all the outside portion (skin) of the stock, and "block" the gauge out some where near to shape; it should then be thoroughly annealed. If the gauge is flat, and should spring while annealing it *should not* be straightened cold, as it would be almost sure to spring when hardened.

It is necessary to stamp the name of the part to be gauged and the sizes of the different parts of the gauge. The workman should bear in mind that the effect of driving stamps, letters, or figures into a piece of steel will be to "stretch" it, consequently it is advisable to stamp the gauge before finishing any of the gauging portions to size, even if the gauge has an allowance for grinding.

PLUG AND RING GUAGE.

Plug gauges are used to gauge the size of a hole, while a ring gauge is for measuring a cylindrical piece of work.

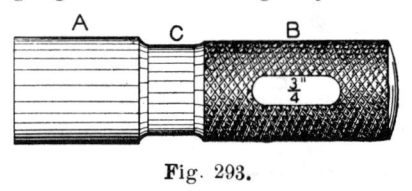

Fig. 293.

To make a plug gauge as shown in Fig. 293, stock should be selected enough larger than finish size to allow for turning off the decarbonized surface. After roughing out, the handle B should be turned to size and knurled, the portion C should be turned to size and finished, the spot in the center of the handle should now be milled and the size of the gauge and any distinguishing mark or name of the article to be gauged should be stamped as shown. Or, as is the custom in many shops, the stamping may be done at C. After stamping, the gauge end A may be turned to a size .010 or .015 inch larger than finish to allow for grinding. Plug gauges should be heated very carefully for hardening, remembering that the lower the heat, the more compact will be the grain, and a piece of steel whose grain is fine and compact will wear better than one whose grain is coarse. If the gauge is one requiring great accuracy, it may be left .0025 or .003 inch above size and allowed to season, provided this precaution is deemed necessary; if not it may be ground to a size .001 inch larger than finish, after which it must be lapped to finish size. When grinding a gauge of this description, it is advisable to use a grinding machine having a supply of water running on the work to keep it cool, but if this form of grinder is not available, the gauge should not be heated any more than is necessary. The gauge should be measured while cold, as steel always expands from the action of heat, and a gauge ground to size when heated would be too small after it had cooled.

When grinding work of this nature, it is advisable if possible to use a form of grinder having two dead centers, that is, one in which neither center revolves. This is mentioned on account of

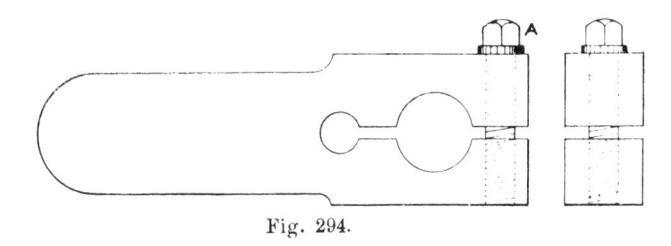

Fig. 294.

the tendency in some shops where there is no universal grinder, (and an engine lathe is to be used as a grinder) to select the poorest lathe in the shop for the purpose. Lathes that have been in use for some time are very likely to have become worn, so that accurate work is impossible; this is especially true of the head spindle which will duplicate its untruth on the piece being ground.

If obliged to use a machine of this description, it is advisable to leave a trifle more stock for lapping than if a suitable grinder is at hand. When grinding, a coarse wheel free from glaze should be used to grind within .004 of finish size, after which a finer wheel may be substituted to grind to lapping size.

A very simple method of making a lap for lapping a cylindrical surface is shown in Fig. 294; this consists of a piece of cast iron having a hole bored a trifle larger than the size of the gauge to be ground. It is split as shown, and is closed by means of the screw A.

If there is much gauge, or similar work, requiring lapping it is advisable to make a lap as shown in Fig. 295. The holder A has a hole bored to receive the laps which are made in the form of rings fitting the holder as shown; these rings are split in three places. One cut is carried *through* one wall, while the other two commencing at the inside, terminate a little distance from the outside surface. The laps may be held in place by means of the pointed screw shown at B.

The lapping should be done with flour emery mixed with oil. This operation has the effect of heating the gauge to a degree that would make it unsafe to caliper. On this account it is necessary to have a dish of water handy in which to cool the gauge

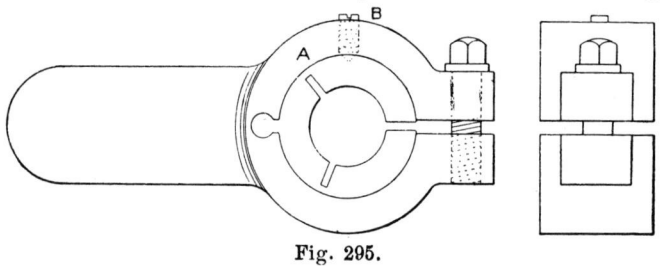

Fig. 295.

before measuring it. This water should not be *cold*, or incorrect measurements will result; it should be as nearly as possible the average temperature of the room in which it is to be used, (about 70 degrees).

When plug gauges are made of machinery steel they should be case hardened in the following manner. They may be packed as for "Pack Hardening"; that is, using charred leather as the packing material. They should run in the furnace for 7 or 8 hours; *after* they are red hot, the box should be taken from the furnace and allowed to cool, after which the gauge may be heated in an ordinary fire enclosing it in a piece of tube. When it reaches a low red heat, it should be plunged in a bath of raw linseed oil. It will not be necessary to draw the temper, and the danger of alteration as it ages is done away with.

The reason for not hardening when the gauge has run the required length of time in the furnace is that the effect of the *second* heat is to refine the steel, making the grain more compact, like *properly* hardened *tool steel*, thus increasing its wearing qualities.

After the gauge has been lapped to the required size, it may be placed in a chuck on the grinding machine and the end ground off to remove any portion that is slightly smaller than the balance of the gauge, as the lapping is likely to grind the extreme end slightly tapering. In order to save time when grinding the end, the gauge may be made as shown in Fig. 296. The sectional

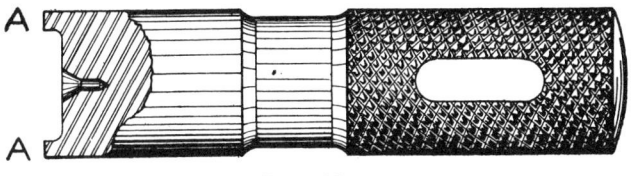

Fig. 296.

view shows the end cupped in, leaving a wall $\frac{1}{16}$ inch to $\frac{1}{8}$ inch thick according to the size of the gauge, the larger sizes having the thicker walls; the cupping should be about $\frac{1}{16}$ inch deep and the corner left slightly rounded as shown.

Another method is to cut a groove with a round nose cutting off tool leaving a disc on the end as shown in Fig. 297. If the

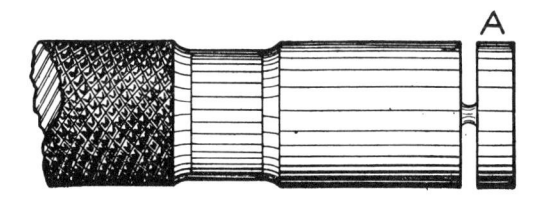

Fig. 297.

gauge has its end shaped as shown in Fig. 296, the projecting end A A is ground away until the end of gauge is straight across. In case it is made as shown in Fig. 297, the disc A is broken off and the end ground as described.

RING GAUGE.

Ring gauges intended for gauging cylindrical pieces smaller than 1 inch diameter are generally made of a solid piece of tool steel, or machinery steel which may be case hardened. For a gauge 1 inch or larger custom varies, some tool makers making it of a solid piece, while others make the body of cast iron, or machinery steel, into which is forced a hardened bushing which is the gauge proper.

It is advisable when making a solid gauge to use a piece of steel somewhat longer than finish dimensions as shown in Fig. 298. The dimension A representing the *finish* length of gauge; the projections B B being left until the gauge is lapped to size. The hole should be bored somewhat smaller than finish size in order to allow for grinding and lapping. If a grinder having an

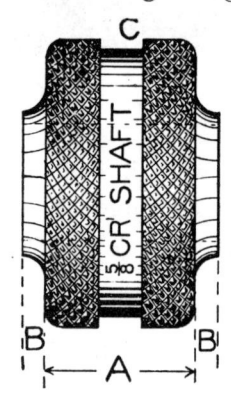

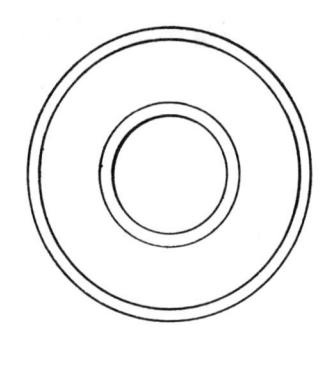

Fig. 298.

internal grinding attachment is not available, the allowance should be much less than if it were possible to grind the walls of the hole. If the gauge is to be ground to size an allowance of .005 inch will be sufficient; if not to be ground and the hole is bored straight and smooth, allow .0015 to .002; but the amount left cannot be given arbitrarily, as much depends on the condition of the hole, and the care used in hardening.

After boring the hole the blank may be placed on a mandrel the ends shaped as shown in Fig. 298, the outside diameter turned and knurled, and the portion C necked to the bottom of the knurling. The size and any distinguishing marks may be stamped on this necked portion as shown. The gauge is now ready for hardening; much better results may be obtained if the gauge is pack hardened. If this method cannot be used, the gauge should be carefully heated in a muffler furnace or in a piece of gas pipe or iron tube in an ordinary fire. When it reaches a *low uniform* heat it should be plunged in a bath of brine and worked around so that the bath may circulate freely through the hole; excellent results can be obtained if a bath is used having a jet of brine or water coming up from the bottom and passing through the hole with some force in order to remove any steam that may be generated.

If it is considered necessary to allow the gauge to "season," the hole may be ground enough to remove part of the allowance, and the gauge laid away. If it is not considered necessary to do this it may be ground .001 or .0015 inch smaller than finish size to allow for lapping.

When lapping a ring gauge to size, it is necessary to use a *suitable* lap. A poor lap is the cause of many of the failures when attempting to do satisfactory work of this description.

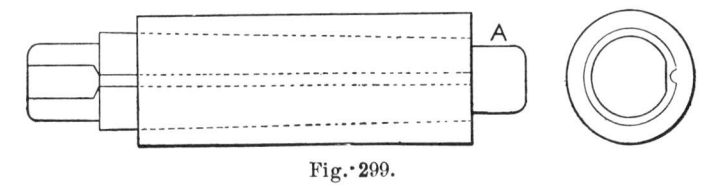

Fig. 299.

When a grinder having an internal grinding attachment is not available, and it is found necessary to leave considerable stock in the hole for lapping, many tool makers claim best results from using two laps; the first, a lead lap, for removing most of the stock; and the second, a cast-iron lap for finishing the hole to size. In either case, the lap should be in the form of a shell which should be held on a mandrel when in use. Fig. 299 shows a lead lap on a mandrel as described.

The mandrel should be made with the ends somewhat smaller than the body which should be tapering in order that the lap may be expanded as it is driven on. A groove is cut the entire length of the body with a convex milling cutter, or it may be cut in the shaper or planer, holding the mandrel between centers, or in the vise, cutting the slot with a round-nosed tool. A mold for casting the lead to shape may be made of two pieces of wood an inch or two longer than the desired length of lap which should be three times the length of the hole in the gauge. The two pieces of wood should be clamped together, and a hole bored with a bit about $\frac{1}{8}$ inch larger than the diameter of the finished lap; after boring to the required depth, a bit should then be used the size of the projection on the small end of the mandrel; the hole bored with this bit should be a trifle deeper than the length of the projection. After the hole has been bored in the mold as described, the mandrel may be put in position as shown in Fig. 300 with the mold in a vertical position. Two narrow strips of wood or metal are placed on top of the mold to hold the mandrel central in the mold. In order that the lead may *run* well, it will be necessary to heat the mandrel somewhat; this should be done before putting it in the mold.

After the lead has become cool the mold may be opened, and the casting removed. It should be placed in the lathe on the mandrel, and turned to a size .001 inch smaller than the hole in the gauge; it may then be charged with emery, using fine emery and oil.

For finishing the hole to size, or lapping a hole *ground* nearly to size, it is advisable to use a lap made of harder material than lead; for this purpose fine-grained cast iron answers admirably, although copper is preferred by some. In order to make a cast-iron lap, a mandrel is necessary, which should taper $\frac{1}{8}$ to $\frac{3}{16}$ inch per foot of length. The slight taper is used in order that the lap may not increase its size too rapidly when driven on the mandrel. The cast-iron lap (sleeve) should be bored with a taper corresponding to the taper of the mandrel, after which it may be forced on the mandrel and turned to size and split as shown in Fig. 301. One slot should extend through the wall as shown at A (end view), while the other two slots B B extend deep enough to allow the lap to expand readily. Before finishing the hole to size the lap should be forced a trifle farther on the mandrel, and

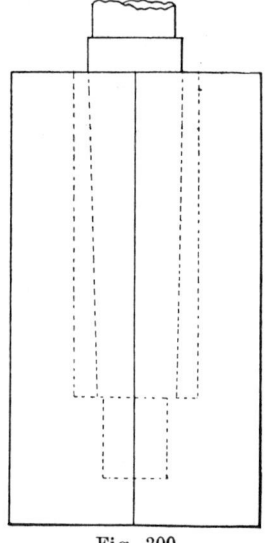

Fig. 300.

TOOL MAKING. 187

trued in the grinder using an emery wheel to cut the lap. The lap should be *perfectly round* and *straight*, in order to produce true holes. For the finish lapping the finest of flour emery should be used. The same precautions should be observed while cooling the gauge before trying the size of hole, as were noted under " Lapping Plug Gauges." In order to clean the gauge of the oil and emery, it should be dipped in a can of benzine, which readily removes any dirt. Extreme care should be exercised

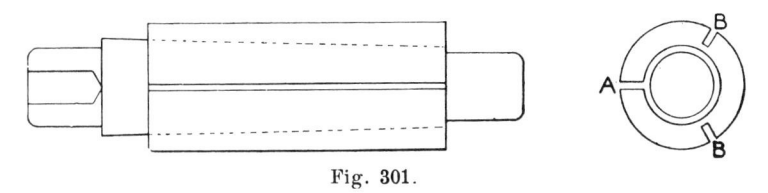

Fig. 301.

when washing work in benzine that it is not brought in the vicinity of a flame of any kind, as it is *extremely* inflammable, and very difficult to extinguish if it becomes ignited; should it become ignited it can be extinguished with a piece of heavy sacking.

The ring should be fitted to the plug gauge which has previ-

Fig. 302.   Fig. 303.

ously been finished to the correct size. It must be borne in mind that the temperature of the plug and ring should be as nearly the same as possible when testing.

SNAP GUAGE.

This form of gauge is used more extensively than any other for outside measurements; it is extremely useful in gauging a dimension between two shoulders as shown at A, Figs. 302 and 303; in the former case the piece being machined is flat while in the latter it is cylindrical.

Snap gauges may be designed to meet the requirements of the particular piece of work upon which they are to be used. When a gauge of this description is intended for use on a cylindrical piece, the opening should be made a trifle deeper than one-half the diameter of the piece to be measured.

When a snap gauge is intended for flat work, the depth of the slot depends on the nature of the work.

Snap Guages for Cylindrical Work. As previously stated when snap gauges are to be used for gauging cylindrical pieces it is necessary to make the opening a trifle deeper than one-half the diameter of the piece to be measured, as shown in Fig. 304, in which A represents the cylindrical piece to be gauged.

When making a snap gauge of this form the stock should be blocked out somewhere near to shape and annealed; after annealing the sides may be made flat and parallel, and the size and any distinguishing marks stamped as shown, after which the gauge part may be worked to a size .008 to .010 inch smaller than finish to allow for grinding. The outer edges should be rounded somewhat to prevent cutting the hands of the operator.

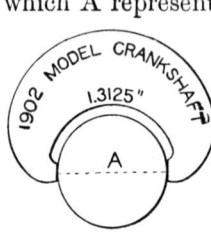

Fig. 304.

When hardening gauges of this type, some tool makers harden only the prongs that come in contact with the work, while others harden the entire gauge. If the contact points alone are to be hardened, the heating can best be done in a crucible of red-hot

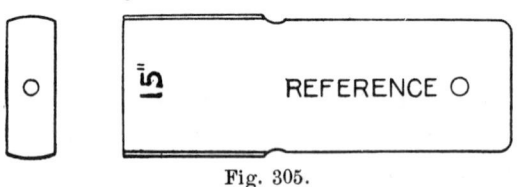

Fig. 305.

lead, but if this is not at hand a piece of flat-iron may be placed each side of the gauge, allowing the ends to be hardened to project beyond the pieces; the whole may now be grasped in a pair of tongs, and placed in the fire. The points will reach a hardening heat before the portion between the flat pieces is very much heated. It may be plunged in water or brine to harden.

If it is considered advisable to harden the gauge all over, it should be heated very carefully in the fire, making sure that the blast does not strike it; turn it frequently to insure a uniform heat. When it reaches a low red heat remove from the fire and plunge in the bath; if the gauge is quite thin a bath of oil will harden sufficiently; if it is dipped in water or brine the bath should be warmed somewhat in order to avoid as much as possible any tendency to spring.

After hardening, the gauge is ground to a size .0005 inch smaller than finish and lapped to size; the method used in grinding gauges of this character will be described later.

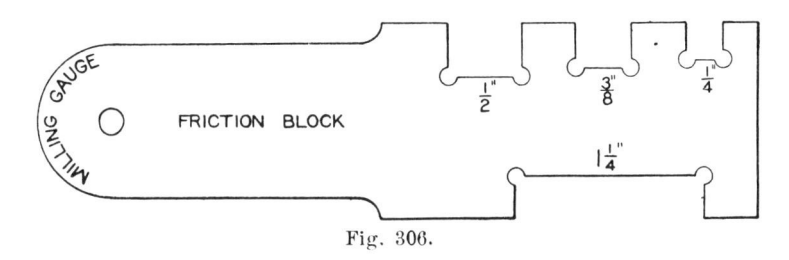

Fig. 306.

In order to be able to give gauges the correct size, it is often necessary to make male gauges. The simplest form of male gauge is shown in Fig. 305; it is a flat piece of tool steel, made slightly small on one end to avoid grinding to size the entire length. After hardening the large end, it is ground to size; it is then ready for use in testing the size of the female snap gauges while the latter are being lapped to size; or when grinding if lapping is not considered necessary. When it is necessary to make a snap gauge for gauging two or more dimensions on a piece of work, the gauge may be made as shown in Fig. 306, while Fig. 307 represents the piece to be gauged.

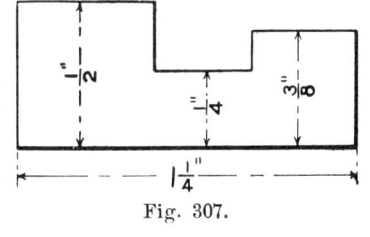

Fig. 307.

After cutting off the steel for the gauge, the sides may be planed to remove the "skin." One of the flat surfaces may be colored with blue vitriol, or it may be colored by holding over a fire until the surface becomes blue. The handle and the openings that constitute the gauges may be laid off on the surface. After milling the handle to shape the holes shown at the corners of the openings may be drilled; these holes facilitate the operations of filing and grinding, particularly the latter. The openings may be milled or planed to a size somewhat ($\frac{1}{32}$ inch) smaller than finish and the gauge is ready for annealing. After it is annealed the two flat surfaces may be planed or filed until flat and parallel. The name of the piece to be gauged and the size of the openings may be stamped as shown. If the gauge is intended for gauging work where a few thousandths of an inch either way would make

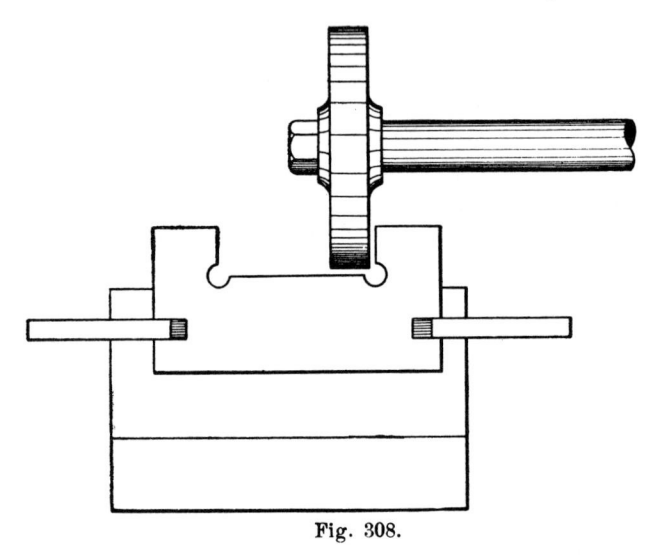

Fig. 308.

no particular difference, it is customary to make the openings to the given sizes before the gauge is hardened. However, if the gauge must be exact to size, it is necessary to leave from .003 to .005 inch on each measuring surface to allow for grinding, and if it is desirable to have the gauge retain its exact size for any considerable length of time, it will be found necessary to finish the gauge to size by lapping *after* it is ground.

Grinding Snap Gauges. Snap gauges may be held in a vise on the universal grinder when grinding the openings to size provided the gauge is held in such a manner that it cannot spring. If it were sprung in any manner while being held, it would assume its normal shape when taken from the vise, and consequently the measuring surfaces would not be parallel. This would destroy the accuracy of the gauge, as it is highly important that the measuring surface of the opening be parallel.

A snap gauge may be clamped to an angle iron which may be held, while grinding, in the vise as shown in Fig. 308, or it may be clamped to a piece of machinery steel or cast iron which is centered as shown in Fig. 309. This holder should be placed between the centers of the grinding machine.

If the opening whose gauging surfaces are to be ground is of sufficient width, an emery wheel of the form shown in Fig. 310 may be used, or a wheel may be recessed on its sides as shown in Fig. 311. If a wheel of the form shown in Fig. 310 is used it

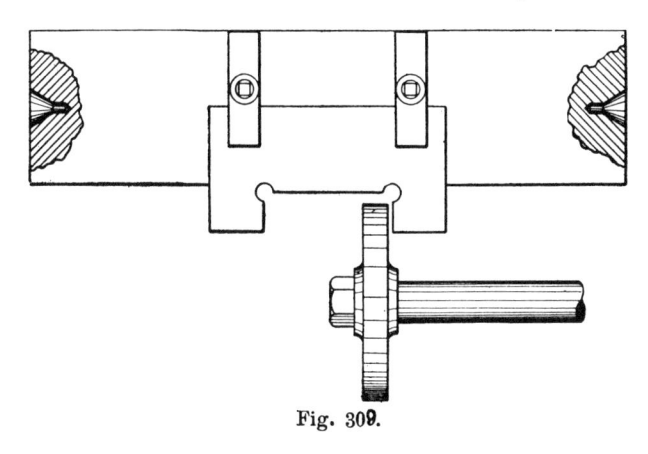

Fig. 309.

will be necessary to remove the wheel after grinding one wall of the opening and reverse it to grind the other. If, however, the opening is too narrow to allow a wheel of the form shown above to be used, a very thin wheel may be made to answer the purpose, but it will be necessary to swivel the head of the grinder a little in order that the wheel may touch the surface to be ground only at the corner of the wheel.

If a grinding machine is not available, an engine lathe or a bench lathe can be used. If the lathe is provided with a grinding attachment, the holder to which the gauge is attached may be placed between the centers of the lathe, and the grinding attachment used in the ordinary manner. If the lathe is not provided with a grinding attachment the emery wheel may be mounted on an arbor between the centers of the lathe. The arbor may be driven from any accessible pulley either on some overhead countershaft or some machine having a pulley in line with a small pulley on the arbor, on which the driving belt is supposed to run. If this method is used it will be necessary to have hardened centers in both head and tail spindles. If a *thin* wheel is used in grinding the surfaces of a narrow opening, the tail center of the lathe may be set over each way to give the desired amount of clearance to the side of the emery wheel. The holder mentioned may be fastened to the tool rest, or the gauge may be fastened to the rest as shown in Fig. 312. At the right is shown a side view of one of the clamps used in holding the work to the rest while grinding; the center is represented as being cut away in order that it may bear at its ends thus removing any chance of its tipping the work being ground.

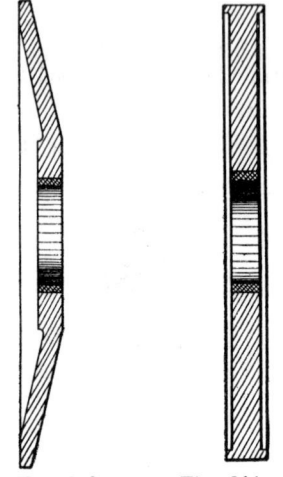

Fig. 310.   Fig. 311.

Lapping a Gauge to Size. Where it is essential that gauges retain their exact size for a considerable length of time, the gauging surfaces must be lapped to size after grinding. The surface left by the emery wheel, even when the utmost care is used, consists of a series of small ridges or irregularities which wear away as the gauge is used and leave the opening too large; lapping the gauging surfaces with oil and emery grinds these minute particles away, leaving a perfectly flat surface, thereby increasing the durability of the gauge.

A convenient form of lap for use in lapping the gauging surfaces of snap gauges is shown in Fig. 313. It consists of a piece of copper or brass wire, bent as shown; the surface A is filed or hammered flat and charged with some abrasive material, as emery; extreme care must be used in lapping the surfaces that they remain perfectly flat and parallel. Unless the operator has had considerable experience in this particular branch of the business, he will be likely to cut the edges away more than the center. To avoid doing this, pieces of hardened steel may be clamped to each side of the gauge before grinding, as shown in Fig. 314. As the tendency when lapping is to make the outer edges round, the portions rounded will be the edges of the pieces clamped to the gauge. After the gauge has been lapped to size these pieces may be removed.

Adjustable Snap Gauge. Snap gauges that are in *constant* use soon wear to an extent that renders them useless, making it

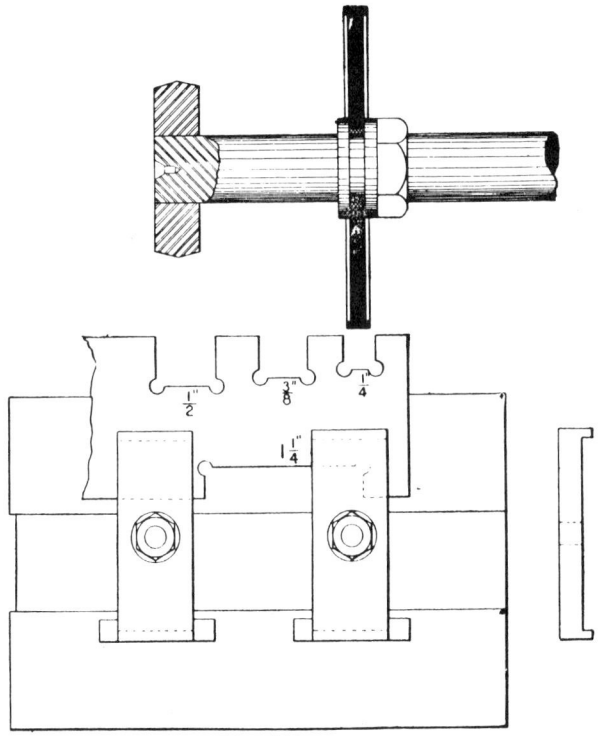

Fig. 312.

necessary to close them in and grind and lap them to size again, or else replace them with new gauges. This tendency to wear and the consequent labor and cost of resizing or replacing has caused the adoption of a style of snap gauge whose size could be altered when necessary; this form of gauge is styled an adjustable snap gauge.

The method of adjustment differs in different shops. Fig.

194   TOOL MAKING.

315 represents a form of adjustable snap gauge which is not expensive and gives excellent results in that its size may be readily adjusted. After blocking out the gauge somewhere near to shape, the screw hole for the adjusting screw C should be drilled and tapped, and the slot milled for the adjustable jaw. The jaw should be made as shown having a slot through which the binding screw D may pass. The jaw should fit snugly in the slot in the frame and placed in position after stamping the name and any distinguishing marks. The aperture E should be worked to a size .010 or .015 inch smaller than finish. The adjustable jaw B may now be removed and the gauging (or contact) surface hardened, being careful not to harden the entire length of the large portion or a crack may appear in the sharp

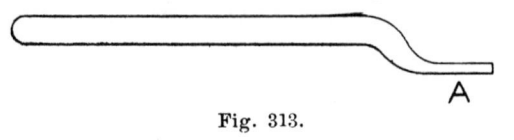

Fig. 313.

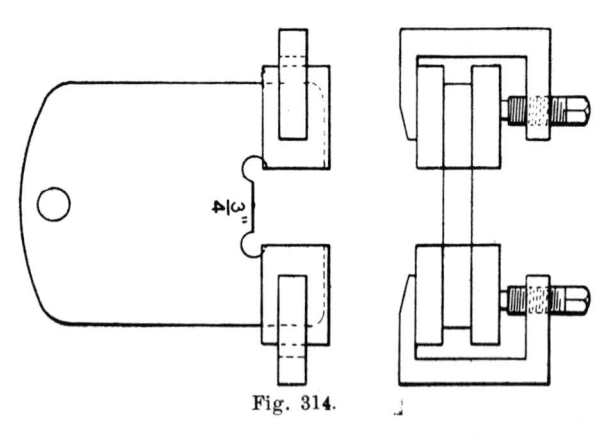

Fig. 314.

corners on account of the unequal size of the two portions. In order to heat the contact surface and not heat back into the sharp corners, the face may be immersed in red-hot lead, leaving just long enough to sufficiently heat the face; or the smaller portion may be held in a pair of tongs letting the end of the jaws come against the shoulders of the piece. It may then be heated in a gas jet or ordinary fire. For most purposes it will not be necessary to harden the gauge all over; if the gauging portion A is hard ened it will be found sufficient. After hardening, the gauge may be assembled and ground and lapped as already explained.

LIMIT GAUGE.

Where it is not necessary that work be of exact size, and a small limit of variation is permissible, limit gauges are used. They prevent a waste of time in attempting excessive accuracy, yet leave the work so that the corresponding parts when brought together will fit well enough to meet requirements.

These gauges are also valuable in roughing work for finishing.

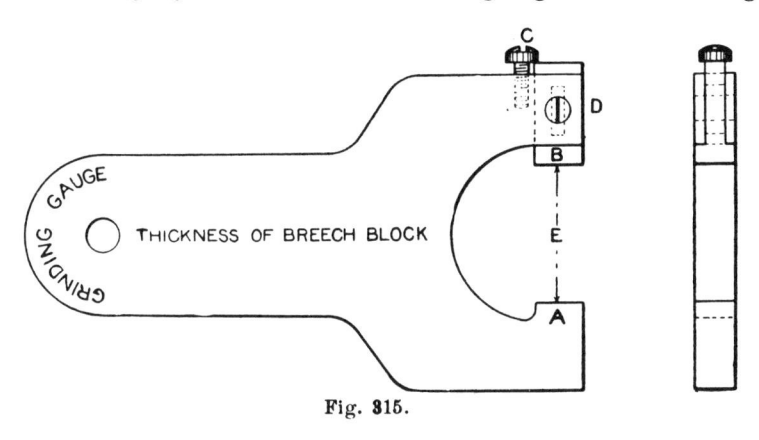

Fig. 315.

When so used practically the same amount of stock is left on each piece, thus facilitating the finishing process.

If a cylindrical piece is to go in a reamed hole, and the piece fits well enough for all requirements when .003 inch smaller than size of hole, it is folly to spend the time necessary to get a more accurate fit.

The amount of variation allowable must be decided in each case; on one job a limit of variation of .001 inch might be all that could be allowed, while on another piece of work .010 inch might be allowable.

In deciding the allowable limit of variation it is advisable, where it is possible, to take into consideration the natural changes that take place in a gauge from wear. For instance, suppose a piece of work .250 inch in diameter just fills the hole it is to go in, and a limit of .0015 inch is allowable; that is, if the piece is

.2485 inch to .250 inch diameter, it would be folly to make the large end of limit gauge for this work .250 inch as there would be no allowance for wear of either the external or internal gauge.

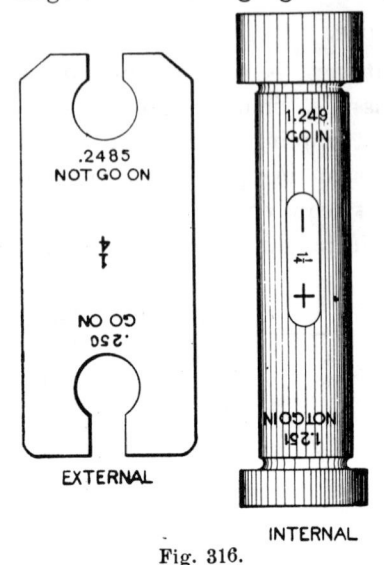

Fig. 316 gives an idea of one form of a snap gauge used for external measurements.; however, it is not necessary to make them of the styles shown. The plug gauge may be made as shown in Fig. 317; while the snap gauge may be made as shown in Fig. 318. The same general instructions given for making plug gauges and snap gauges apply to limit gauges of the same character.

Fig. 316.

RECEIVING GAUGE.

When it is essential that the various working points of a tool, part of a machine or apparatus should be in exact relation to one or more given points, a receiving gauge is used. This gauge as the name implies is made to *receive*, or take in, the work; that is, the piece of work is *placed in* the gauge, and the exact location of the different points is determined by the eye.

Fig. 319 shows a gun-hammer, while Fig. 320 represents a receiving gauge for *accurately* gauging the points C, D, E, F, G and H in relation to the fulcrum screw hole A and the face B. These points must also be in exact relation to each other; hence the necessity of a gauge, of this character. When making a gauge of this type, it is customary in most shops to gauge only those parts that must be located in exact relation to some other point or points.

In the case of the gun hammer under consideration the fulcrum-screw hole A must be the main working point because when it is operated it is pivoted at this point, consequently every point must be in exact relation to this hole. The point of next importance is the face B which strikes the firing pin; in order that the face of the hammer may be the proper distance from the firing pin when half cocked, or full cocked, it is necessary that the half cock notch D, and the full cock notch E be properly located as regards the face of the hammer. They must also be in exact location as regards the fulcrum-screw hole A. In order that the main spring may exert the proper amount of force on the hammer, it is necessary that the spring seat G be exactly located. As the portions marked C and H are intended to just fill the opening in the gun frame when the hammer is in any position, it is necessary that they be located the proper distance from the center of the fulcrum-screw hole A; hence the need of a gauge that will determine the exact location of all points as related to A and B and to each other. As the por-

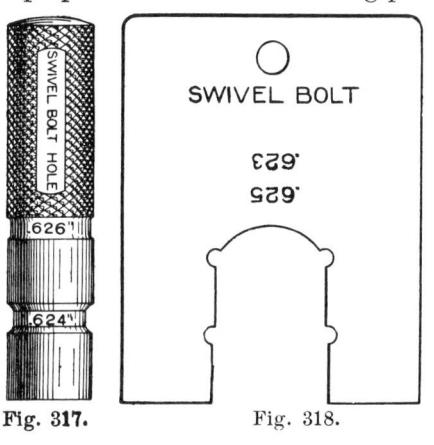

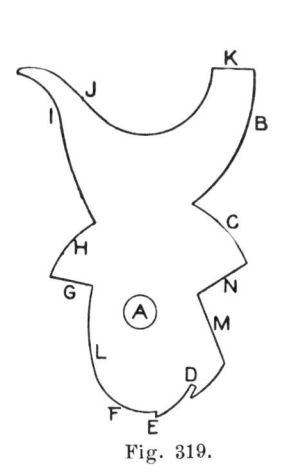

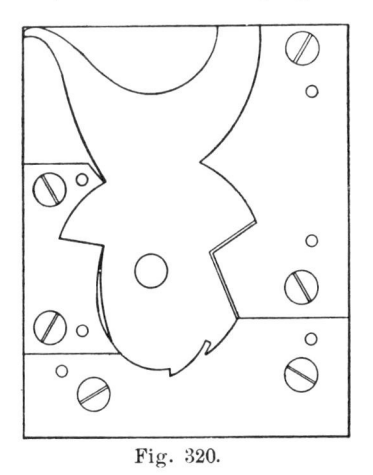

tions marked I, J, K, L, M, and N must be in *exact* location to the other points or to each other they are gauged with a *separate* gauge because each additional gauging point on a gauge of this description complicates matters.

When making gauges of this character a piece of machinery steel is usually taken for the base; this is planed to size and ground or filed for finish; a hole is drilled and reamed to receive a pin the size of the fulcrum screw hole. This pin is made of a piece of drill rod a few thousandths inch larger than the desired pin. The piece of drill rod should be long enough to be held in the chuck of the grinding machine, and should be cut of the proper length as shown in Fig. 321. The short end should be hardened and the temper drawn to a straw color; after which the

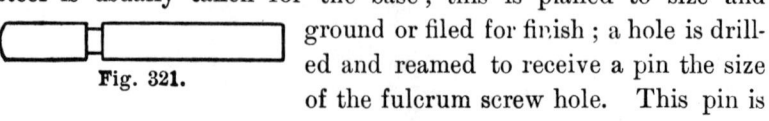

Fig. 321.

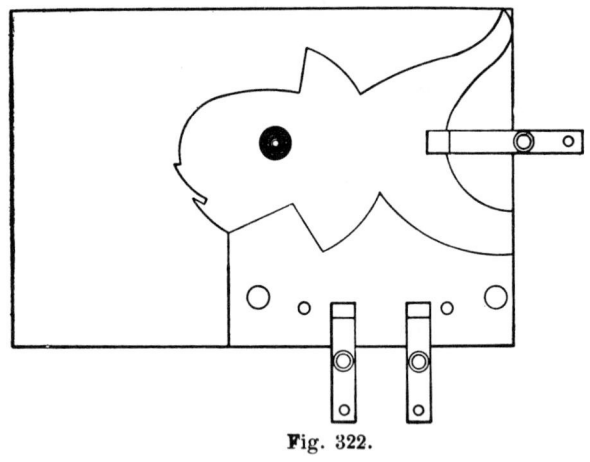

Fig. 322.

wire may be placed in the chuck on the grinding machine and the pin ground to the desired size. After grinding to size it may be broken off and the end ground; this can be done by holding the pin in the chuck, leaving the broken end out in order that it may be ground square, the pin should now be forced to place in the hole in the base.

The gauge proper may be made of one plate worked to the proper shape, but better results will follow if it is made in three pieces as shown in Fig. 320 on account of the tendency of the plate to spring when hardened.

TOOL MAKING.

These plates may be made either of tool steel or machinery steel, if made of tool steel the pieces should be machined all over and thoroughly annealed, after which they may be planed or milled to thickness.

One surface should be colored by the blue vitriol solution, or the pieces may be heated until a distinct blue color appears; the desired shape should be marked on the colored surface and the pieces machined and filed until they fit the model, the necessary degree of accuracy must be determined by the nature of the work.

After the pieces are properly fitted to the model, they may be attached to the base by means of the fillister head cap screws shown. The model should be laid on the base having the fulcrum screw hole on the pin. After arranging the model in its proper location it may be clamped as shown in Fig. 322. The sections of the gauge which should have been previously drilled for the screw and dowel pins, may now be clamped to the base in their proper positions. After drilling, the holes in the base may be tapped, and the screws put in place. If it is found necessary to make slight alterations in any of the shapes, they may be readily made as the plates can be moved a trifle because the bodies of the screws need not fit tightly in the holes in the plates. The dowel pin holes should not be transferred into the base until after the plates are hardened.

The plates may now be removed and hardened. If of machinery steel they may be case-hardened, dipping them in oil rather than water. If made of tool steel best results will follow if the plates are pack-hardened, running them 1 to $1\frac{1}{2}$ hours after red hot and then dipping in raw linseed oil.

If the process of pack-hardening cannot be used, satisfactory results may be obtained if they are carefully heated in a tube in an open fire, or placed in the muffler of a muffler furnace. When red hot, sprinkle a small quantity of finely powdered cyanide of potassium, or a little yellow prussiate of potash on the contact surfaces, place in the fire again, bring to a low red heat and plunge in a bath of oil.

After hardening, the plates may be attached to the base by means of the screws; if any of the gauging points have become distorted by hardening, they may be brought to the proper shape by oil-stoning.

When the plates are properly fitted and located in their exact positions, the dowel pin holes may be transferred into the base and the dowel pins put in place.

LOCATING GAUGE.

This form of gauge is used for determining the location of one or more holes in relation to another hole, a shoulder, or working surface, or any similar measurement.

Fig. 323 shows a gauge for showing the proper location of the hole from the edges A and B, Fig. 324. This gauge consists

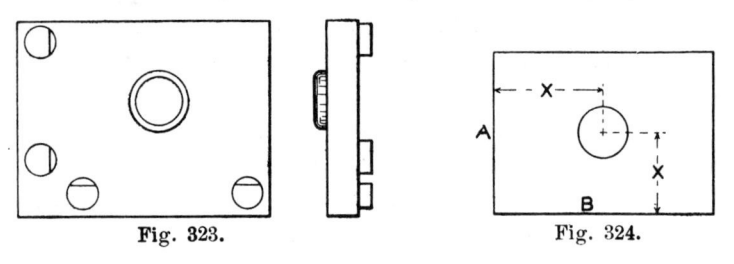

Fig. 323.   Fig. 324.

of a base having four pins for the edges A and B, to rest against. These pins are flatted on the contact edges to prevent wearing. The piece of work to be gauged is placed in position and clamped to the gauge with machinists clamps as shown in Fig. 325. The gauge is fastened to the face plate of the lathe in such a manner that the piece of work can be removed without disturbing the location of the gauge.

A short plug is now inserted in the hole in the model. It is necessary that the plug should fit very accurately. By means of a lathe indicator the gauge can be located so that the plug runs perfectly true. When this has been accomplished the model may be removed and the bushing hole drilled and bored to size ; after which the bushing may be made, hardened, ground to size, and forced to place.

The location of the drilled hold may be tested by placing the piece of work on the gauge against the pins, and entering the gauge pin in the hole in the work and bushing, as shown in Fig. 326. If the pin is a close fit in the holes a very slight error in

TOOL MAKING. 201

location may be detected. When a slight error in location is allowable, and it is not considered advisable to hold the location too close, the pin may be made a trifle small, thus transforming the gauge into a limit gauge.

When it is necessary to make a locating gauge for testing the center distance of two holes, one pin may be made removable, while the other is rigidly fixed as shown at C Fig. 327.

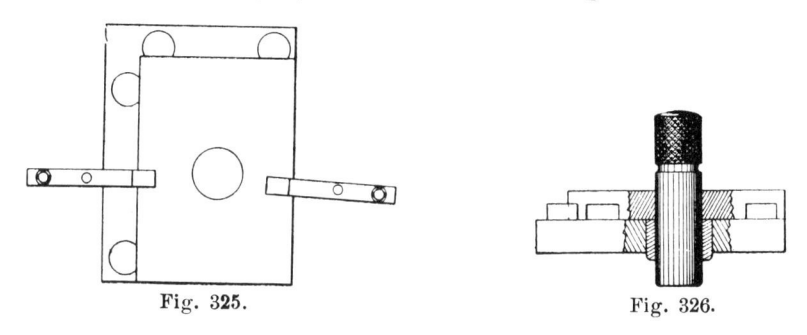

Fig. 325.

Fig. 326.

If the gauge is made with both pins fixed it is a difficult operation to remove the piece of work, provided the pins are a good fit in the holes. Withdrawing one pin allows the piece of work to be readily taken from the fixed pin.

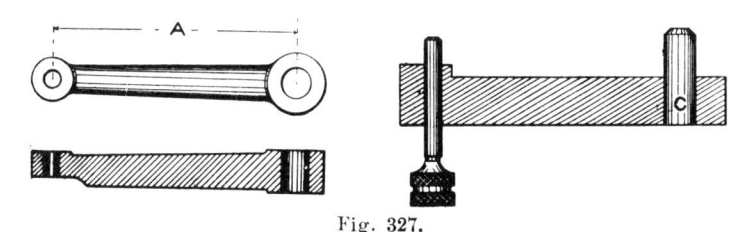

Fig. 327.

When making a gauge of the form shown in Fig. 327, the fixed pin C may be located by approximate measurements; but the hole should be drilled by some method that insures the pin standing perfectly square with the base of the gauge. If a small limit of variation is permissible in the center to center measurement A, the model may be placed on the gauge with the large hole on the fixed pin C, and the location of the hole for the movable pin may be transferred from the model by drilling and reaming. If extreme accuracy is essential, it will be advisable to place the model on the gauge as described, clamp the model to the gauge, then fasten the gauge to the face plate of lathe, place an accurately fitting pin in the small hole in the model, and by means of a lathe indicator locate the gauge so that the pin runs perfectly true. The model may now be removed and the hole drilled and bored to size.